M000105459

Higher Education in Prison
A Contradiction in Terms?

Higher Education in Prison
A Contradiction in Terms?

Edited by Miriam Williford

National University Continuing Education Association

AMERICAN COUNCIL
ON EDUCATION
Series on Higher Education
ORYX PRESS
1994

Copyright © 1994 by American Council on Education and The Oryx Press

Published by The Oryx Press
4041 North Central at Indian School road
Phoenix, AZ 85012-3397

Published simultaneously in Canada

All rights reserved
No part of this publication may be reproduced or transmitted in any form or by
any means, electronic or mechanical, including photocopying, recording, or
by any information storage and retrieval system, without permission in writing
from Oryx Press.

Printed and bound in the United States of America

∞ The paper used in this publication meets the minimum requirements of
the American National Standard for Information Science—Permanence of
Paper for Printed Library Materials, ANSI Z39.48, 1984.

Library of Congress Cataloging-in-Publication Data
Higher education in prison: a contradiction in terms? / edited by Miriam
Williford
        p. cm. -- (American Council on Education/Oryx series on higher
education)
"National University Continuing Education Association."
Includes bibliographical references and index.
    ISBN 0-89774-861-1
    1. Prisoners—Education (Higher)—United States. 2. Education,
Higher—United States. 3. Prison administration—United States. I.
Williford, Miriam, 1926–. II. National University Continuing Education
Association (U.S.) III. Series.
HV8883.3. U5H54 1994   94-2250
365'.66—dc20   CIP

Contents

· · · · · · · · ·

Preface

· · · · · · · · ·

In 1987, my colleague Kevin Aiken, administrator of the Division of Continuing Education at the University of Massachusetts at Amherst, approached me about the possibility of our offering a degree program at several of our state's prisons. My reaction was not positive; despite my many years of experience as a faculty member, adviser, program director, and higher education administrator, I knew little about higher education in prison but recognized the enormous political risk of such a program. I met with Kevin and the man who was to coordinate the program, Walter Silva, a retired faculty member, known personality within the corrections system, and dedicated proponent of prison higher education. I told Walt that as associate provost, I would not approve the program until he had letters of support from the deans of the Arts and Sciences colleges that would offer the courses. I was somewhat taken aback by the quick, positive response from the deans. The program began offering courses at the Massachusetts medium and minimum correctional institutions at Gardner, Lancaster, and Shirley.

In the meantime, I searched and searched but could find no single volume that identified the problems, opportunities, and difficulties in offering prison higher education programs. During this time, I sought to learn from my colleagues across the country whose continuing education operations sponsored programs in prison. Not knowing who they were, I organized a breakfast meeting at the 1990 annual conference of the National University Continuing Education Association (NUCEA), which was meeting in New Orleans. Thirty-six persons attended—their institutions covered a full range from small to large, public and private: University of Pittsburgh, Mary Arundel Community College, Utah State University, Boston University, Ball State University, Mary Baldwin College, UCLA Extension, Southern Baptist Seminaries, University of Wisconsin at Stevens Point, to name a few. Together we organized within NUCEA a Prison Higher Education Caucus—a consortium of people willing to share knowledge and information about prison higher education. At this initial meeting, I asked the attendees to identify a book that I could read as an administrator of a prison higher education program. They all said, "There isn't one. Write one." Thus was born the idea of this book.

Prison higher education is a growing area of adult and continuing education practice. From its beginning more than 30 years ago in the form of a few scattered programs, it has blossomed into a movement involving the continuing education departments of more than 300 colleges and universities which now offer courses to more than 50,000 prisoners each year. Despite the scope and diversity of continuing education programs in American prisons, there are few resources practitioners can draw upon as they grapple with day-to-day problems or begin the process of implementing new programs. After more than three decades, it is notable that not a single higher education-based journal devoted to prison higher education has emerged.

This book is an effort to address the manifest problem posed by a scarcity of useful information about an inherently specialized practice. In this one volume are 16 essays about diverse aspects of continuing higher education practice in prison. It is intended, on the one hand, to be descriptive and serve as a reference for current continuing education practice in adult prisons. On the other hand, it is intended as a resource capable of providing insight into the challenges and rewards prison higher education holds for those who are or wish to be involved in it.

The focus of this volume is on building programs that facilitate personal growth and self-actualization. Education has played a role in prison for more than 200 years, but that role has almost exclusively been legitimated as a vehicle for the rehabilitation or reformation of criminal offenders. Accordingly, in recent years, education in the prison has been based on a medical model, which sees education as instrumental in curing the offender, and a cognitive deficiency model, which seeks to correct deficiencies in problem-solving, interpersonal, and social skills. Clearly, both of these models regard prisoners as deficient individuals and see the goal of education as one of "correction."

Discussions with educators, prison officials, and prisoners convinced me that these models may do more harm than good. One thing is certain: Despite unsubstantiated claims to the contrary, education based on these models has never achieved its goal of reducing the likelihood that prisoners would commit fresh offenses once released from prison. Education need not be focused on corrections to be of value. This book emphasizes that what education is capable of doing, for prisoners as for others in the larger society, is to provide opportunities to improve one's self, to accomplish personal goals, to learn and grow, and to acquire the credentials and skills that are increasingly needed for participation in even the lower realms of the occupational structure.

Like other historic attempts to include new groups within higher education, prison higher education is marked by controversy. The earliest higher education programs for prisoners were able to develop largely outside of public scrutiny because of their small number and size, but the proliferation of programs combined with new public attitudes toward criminal offenders and a pessimistic economic outlook have resulted in claims that prisoners are receiving a privilege they do not deserve at the expense of taxpayers. Educational practice is a social matter, and it is always shaped by debates in the larger society about the wisdom and necessity of educating members of a given social category, the type of education that might be appropriate for those members, and its potential impact on society. In short, we cannot pretend that a clear line divides educational philosophy and practice.

For this reason, this volume is an edited collection of essays that focus on the organization and experience of continuing education practice, but also reflect the wider social contexts in which the possibilities of practice are shaped. Accordingly, its initial chapters examine the current socioeconomic climate and the implications it holds for higher education in American prisons. This is followed by a review of the historic relationship between education and incarceration, which uncovers the roots of many systemic aspects of our practice in this unique environment, and a survey of the scope and diversity of current efforts to deliver postsecondary education in the prison.

Subsequent chapters examine the development of programs focused on human renewal and self-actualization, reveal the unique patterns of conflict and accommodation necessitated by the circumstances of confinement, share the experiences of those who teach and learn within the prisons, review the difficulties that have hindered the delivery of higher education to women prisoners, and demonstrate how relatively basic assessment and evaluation tools can focus and improve efforts to deliver educational opportunities to those in confinement.

This volume is based on experience. Its chapters have been written by practitioners who know firsthand the problems and rewards of delivering prison higher education programs. It is written for all who are interested in the practice and specifically for those who find themselves involved in prison education. It goes without saying that it is hoped that others who may question the practice might read this book and perhaps reconsider their own views on the subject.

More, however, is at stake. Prison higher education comes into being and is limited by our vision of what is appropriate for prisoners to learn. In this it is not unique. If we truly understand how the education of prisoners is the product of contradictory beliefs and opposing aims, we may be better able to grasp how these same contradictions and tensions play themselves out in our efforts to extend opportunity in the larger society. Prison education compels any educator to do some deep thinking about educational programs grounded in the very cultural designations he or she wishes to see transcended.

Acknowledgments

· · · · · · · · ·

W ithout the support and guidance of Kay J. Kohl, executive director of the National University Continuing Education Association (NUCEA), this book would never have been published, nor would the NUCEA Caucus on Prison Higher Education have come into existence.

I am indebted for my own understanding of prison education to Raymond Jones, whose stimulating debates from a social science perspective challenged and broadened my own humanistic (and academic) views of prison education; to Walter Silva, whose persistence led to our offering such a program; and to all of my colleagues in the Prison Higher Education Caucus. Dean James Danglade of Ball State University, current chair of the caucus, was unstinting in his support of the book.

Gratitude is owed to all those who gave of their expertise and time to make this book a reality—the authors.

I acknowledge with appreciation the counsel, wisdom, and time that Milton Stern, our editor, has given to this work. His dedication and vision strengthened and enhanced the final product.

Finally, I recognize with much thanks the support and assistance of my staff here at the University of Massachusetts at Amherst, particularly Kevin Aiken; Gloria Fisher, who proofread every word of the manuscript; Linda Eldred, my secretary, who has done yeoman's work since the book's inception; Mary Slonka, who prepared the text for submission; and Debra Davidson, for her dedication to the caucus, her help in identifying authors, and whose skill with Word 5.0 brought all the pieces together.

To all these, my respect and esteem.

The Paradox of Higher Education in Prisons

by Raymond L. Jones and Peter d'Errico

· · · · · · · · · · ·

EDITOR'S INTRODUCTION

Prison higher education embraces a diverse blend of postsecondary educational programs delivered within an equally diverse range of prisons from minimum to maximum security. This may explain why higher education faculty and staff who become involved in the education of prisoners speak not only of feeling overwhelmed by a seemingly unending stream of issues and problems, but also of a belief that most of them are, to a great extent, unique to their programs. Since the founding of the NUCEA Caucus on Prison Higher Education, I have had the opportunity to talk with many people involved in the education of prisoners. From these discussions, I have become increasingly aware that the issues and problems confronting prison higher education programs across the nation appear to be more common than unique.

Jones and d'Errico, in their examination of the issues confronting prison higher education, offer critical insight into the basis for the common experience of diverse programs. They argue that the issues confronting prison higher education are ideological and moral, arising in the tension between competing visions of what prisoners themselves *are* and, accordingly, what prisons *should* or *ought* to be. They are aware that beneath competing visions there nevertheless exists a general consensus about the moral legitimacy of incarceration and a shared social belief that prisoners are both different and lower in any "scheme of social types."

Raymond L. Jones is visiting assistant professor in the Legal Studies Department at the University of Massachusetts, Amherst.

Peter d'Errico is associate professor in the Legal Studies Department at the University of Massachusetts, Amherst.

Their attempt to illuminate the paradoxes that shape higher education in prisons is grounded in a rejection of the assumption that prisoners are inherently different from others who pursue postsecondary education. This position may appear fanciful to many, but it is an analytical device that brings to light variations in beliefs about what it means to be incarcerated, the nature of prisoners, and, accordingly, expectations about what the education of prisoners ought to be. Their approach underscores the reality that what prison higher education is, and has the potential to be, is largely shaped by these expectations; but it argues also that some disagreement with these expectations (and, therefore, with the general public; prison officials; prisoners; and even some, if not many, higher education faculty and staff) may at times be necessary if prison higher education is to prove an effective vehicle for promoting the growth and renewal requisite to the individual change that most educators in the prison hope to foster.

· · · · · · · · ·

INTRODUCTION

P rison: a remote and forbidding place that, for most people, exists somewhere, perhaps anywhere, else. The image is not accidental. Prison both symbolizes and brings about the removal of criminal offenders from the legitimate order of society. Sykes (1958) describes the prison as a complex of deprivations deliberately imposed upon offenders. He is careful to emphasize that such deprivation, not in its material but rather in its nonmaterial or symbolic form, is what distinguishes imprisonment from simple punishment. He paraphrases Walter Reckless' observation that "it is the moral condemnation of the criminal—however it may be symbolized—that converts hurt into punishment, i.e., the just consequence of committing an offense, and it is this condemnation that confronts the inmate by the fact of his seclusion."

Sykes posits that the denial of liberty and autonomy, and the deprivation of goods and services, heterosexual relations, and personal security represent the loss of "that basic acceptance of the individual as a functioning member of the society in which he lives." The prison symbolizes the offender's removal from the legitimate order. It is a "shaming" that annihilates the individual's relationship with the social world and reduces his or her identity to nothing more than the meaning of an act of deviance.

Higher education dared to enter this real and symbolic place of deprivation in the last three decades. While prison teaches offenders that they are incompetent, irresponsible, and without moral or social worth, higher education in the outer society "symbolically redefines graduates as possessing special qualities and skills gained through attendance" (Kamens 1977). One might well imagine that the combination of two such contradictory social meanings would produce special tensions within prison and higher education alike.

Prison higher education at present is the product of scattered attempts to offer prisoners an opportunity to construct meaningful lives both in prison and following release. Programs initially sought to offer prisoners a chance to remake themselves in their own eyes and in the eyes of others, without regard to the fact that they were imprisoned. In 1967, at the height of the rehabilitative era, only about 3,000 prisoners—less than one percent of the total—participated in some form of postsecondary education, and most of these were involved with correspondence courses (Adams 1968).

We have witnessed since 1967 a remarkable growth in both the number of educational programs offered and the number of prisoners participating. In 1977, 66 percent of the 327 reporting federal and state prisons offered some postsecondary educational opportunities (Bell 1977). A survey of American prisons conducted in 1981 revealed that at least 28,000 prisoners were participating in higher education (*Sourcebook of Criminal Justice Statistics* 1982). Although current national figures are difficult to obtain, colleges and universities active in the education of prisoners number in the hundreds, and, if prisoner participation rates are stable, more than 60,000 prisoners would appear to be involved in college-level course work. Indeed, prison higher education programs are rapidly becoming commonplace.

The best approach to understanding the issues that confront prison higher education may be to view it as a recent and special case in the more general pattern of inclusions that characterize the historic expansion of American higher education. By "inclusion" we mean nothing more complex than an attempt to extend access to higher education to previously excluded groups. We need only think of the historic debates surrounding each stage in the gradual inclusion of African Americans, women, and other social categories in order to grasp that the inclusion of new social groups within higher education has seldom failed to generate controversy about whether a given group should be educated, the type of education that ought to be offered, the proper aims and goals of that education, and the potential impact of the inclusion of the new group on the larger society.

SHOULD PRISONERS BE EDUCATED?

Those involved in the education of prisoners assume both that their work has value and that its value will be readily appreciated by others. Perhaps it could not and should not be otherwise, but this assumption tends to manifest itself in the inclination to view favorable responses to the education of prisoners as evidence of "right thinking," while unfavorable responses are regarded as the product of the uninformed or irrational opinion of presumably reactionary individuals. The extension of educational access to nontraditional groups, however, is seldom without legitimate controversy, and prisoners may be an exemplar of this principle. Whether a college education is appropriate for prisoners is largely an ideological or moral question, and the answer to this question depends on one's expectation of what it means to be a prisoner. The answer, in short, depends on how different people believe a prisoner ought to be treated during his or her incarceration.

Favorable and unfavorable attitudes toward prison higher education mirror long-standing and idealized views about the meaning of prison. On one hand, there are those who believe imprisonment consists precisely of the deprivation of those things that have real and symbolic value in the outer society. On the other hand, there are those who believe that such deprivation is only the precondition for the reintroduction of the prisoner into the outer society and that, therefore, prisoners should enjoy access to a range of resources that serve to promote this goal.

No debate in recent years has reflected the polarization between these two positions as well as that regarding whether prisoners ought to retain access to the benefits and entitlements of the Higher Education Act (*see* Appendix 2). Prisoners, whose ties to the occupational structure have been destroyed by the fact of incarceration, seldom receive more than a token income from prison work and lack the means to pay for a college education. Pell Grants, which are among the entitlements available through the Higher Education Act, are the principal means by which prisoners are able to pay for the courses and materials that colleges and universities make available within the prisons. Without access to these funds, most prison education programs in the nation would be unlikely to survive. Opposition to prisoner eligibility for Pell Grants was in evidence at every stage in the legislative process leading to the successive reauthorizations of the Higher Education Act in 1992 and 1993. A task force formed by the National Association of Financial Aid Administrators concluded that that organization should recommend that Congress eliminate prisoner eligibility. Although that recommendation was ultimately not made, several amendments seeking the same exclusion were independently offered in both the U.S. Senate and the House of Representatives.

This debate may have been partially fueled by a faltering national economy and apprehensions about the level of federal spending, but it also revealed, in perhaps its starkest form, the fundamental tension between those who would simply punish and those who would improve the lives of prisoners. There was no real debate about the efficacy of educating prisoners. Those who advocated that prisoners enjoy continued access to this vital source of funding pointed out that prison higher education should be supported because it fostered rehabilitation and, ultimately, made it less likely that individual offenders, once released, would commit fresh offenses and return to prison. The opposing side did not argue that prison higher education did not work. They opposed the funding because, in their view, prisoners do not deserve access to higher education, regardless of whether it reduces the likelihood of recidivism. One side favored prison higher education because it rehabilitates; the other opposed it, whether or not it rehabilitates. (Ultimately, Pell eligibility was retained by most prisoners. It was lost however, for those inmates serving life sentences that preclude parole and by those prisoners awaiting execution.)

Ambivalence about whether prisoners ought to receive access to higher education is reflected in the marginal status of prison education programs, both in the prisons and within the colleges and universities that sponsor such programs. The problems of meeting program costs in the face of uncertain funding, recruiting competent faculty, securing access to academic resources, and overcoming ideological resistance to the education of prisoners preoccupy program directors. Few programs receive funding from their parent organizations. Most are parts of self-supporting continuing education departments, but they depend on shrinking state and federal entitlement programs to meet program costs. The politically aware administrator will be cautious about appearing to divert funding that might otherwise be used by on-campus students. College-in-prison offers none of the "frills" and denies many of the "necessities" that seem basic to higher education in the larger society. Prisons lack the comprehensive libraries and other educational resources presumed to be essential to higher learning. The recruitment of competent faculty is hindered by a general lack of awareness about prison higher education, geographical obstacles, and departmental lack of interest or outright opposition, and this compels reliance on part-time instructors who are often inexperienced.

Within prison, higher education faculty and staff are often perceived as intruders; many report the necessity of circumnavigating the hostile attitudes of regular correctional staff. Conflict arises when it appears that prisoners are receiving a benefit that is beyond the reach of many correctional personnel and their families. Significant conflict also arises when correctional personnel

perceive that representatives of higher education may not share their assumptions about prison or their view of the appropriate role of staff in the
deprivation process (Tiller 1974).

The social world is organized in ways that affirm for each of us that we really
are who and what we think we are. Prisoners confront a social world that
affirms at every opportunity their rightful place at the very bottom of the
social ladder. In the simple act of striving to learn and, in the process,
acquiring formal educational credentials, people who are confined for past
deviance essentially become deviant once again: Their inclusion within
higher education is seen by many as a case of deviants improperly located
within the social world that dictates their confinement. The issues of prison
higher education take shape in the attempt to make the education of prisoners
appear rational within a social world that can't shake the feeling that they
shouldn't be educated at all and may, in fact, be getting away with something
they don't deserve.

TO CORRECT OR EDUCATE

This ambivalence about what it means to be a prisoner and whether and how
prisoners should be educated shapes prison higher education. It became
possible to include prisoners in higher education, in part, because higher
education explains its practice in the prisons as a specialized context, one in
which (1) educational aims and (2) educational practice make sense in
relation to (3) a specific category of persons. Thus, it is not surprising that
higher education has for more than three decades legitimized itself as a vehicle
for the reform of criminal offenders in the prisons. As one writer notes:

> The theoretical assumption behind all the education programs devel-
> oped, however, is that if becoming a criminal is a learning process, the
> remaking of useful citizens is more the task of education than it is the
> outcome of custody or punishment (Corcoran 1985).

Perhaps it could not be otherwise, for reformation remains a powerful social
legitimation of contemporary prisons. A survey conducted by the U.S. Department of Justice (1989) reported that 84.5 percent of the American public
considers offender reformation among the purposes of incarceration. Offender
reformation was regarded as "very important" by 71.5 percent and as "somewhat important" by another 13 percent. As offenders are sentenced to finite
terms of incarceration, many who stress the prison's punitive aspect may
simply view punishment itself in corrective or reformative terms.

Prison, however, has never proven an effective vehicle for the reformation of offenders. Historically, a majority of prisoners released from custody have ultimately committed fresh offenses and returned to prison. There is significant research suggesting that incarceration encourages rather than discourages criminal activity (Fyfe 1991). In the face of this historic failure it is ironic that the United States has come to rely even more upon incarceration as a solution for crime. A 1989 article by *U.S. News and World Report* criticized a Bush administration anticrime plan that assumed it was possible to "incarcerate our way out of the crime problem." Despite such criticisms, the United States incarcerates more people (approximately one million at the time of this writing), at a higher rate among the whole population, and for longer periods of time than does any other nation.

The earliest prison higher education programs in the country emerged between 1950 and 1970, an era in which rehabilitation based on a medical model comprised the principal rationale for incarceration. That model assumed criminal behavior to be the product of antecedent causes traceable to various aspects of the offender's social and psychological history. The offender was regarded as a diseased person who needed to be "cured" and, as such, became an object, a thing to be examined, studied, and acted upon. The collapse of this model may have been inevitable. In regarding human behavior as the product of deterministic forces, it posed a fundamental conflict with the notions of individual responsibility that lie at the heart of American criminal justice.

Although higher education has yet to articulate a coherent philosophy for its practice in prisons, a new model now dominates secondary education in correctional settings. The cognitive deficiency model assumes that prisoners are responsible human beings who do not differ from humankind in general but "are simply deficient in certain analytic problem-solving skills, interpersonal and social skills and in ethical/moral development" (Duguid 1981). The task confronting correctional education is to provide the offender with opportunities for cognitive and moral development. Duguid, for example, suggests that the liberal arts can alter prisoners' perceptions of others while also promoting moral development that alters the way in which they interpret their perceptions and, ultimately, how they behave.

Clearly, both of these models regard prisoners as deficient individuals and see the goal of education as one of correction. Those who support prison higher education almost intuitively speak of it as a rehabilitative necessity. Higher education, faced with a world that demands to know why it should support the education of prisoners, explains education as something capable of doing what prisons themselves were supposed to be doing all along. Yet the more compelling questions raised by this explanation for what higher education hopes to do in the prisons do not concern its effectiveness at reforming or rehabilitating prisoners. The more compelling questions are: What sort of education is it that is based on the implicit or explicit recognition of individual failings? and What sort of education is it that is based on the need to correct?

These are not benign questions. Education that presumes the deficiencies of those it serves may do more good than harm, but it clearly is not education based on respect for the individual learner. Nor is it an education that admits the same social meaning and value as that received by others in different social contexts. Because higher education in prison has no coherent philosophy to which programs and educators must conform, every higher education practitioner in the prisons must grapple afresh with what the education they offer will claim to be and, therefore, will come to mean for both participants and members of the wider society. Every prison higher education program has the opportunity to promote another model. That model is one in which prisoners who pursue a college education are treated like students who are not prisoners; in which prisoners are recognized to be very much like other human beings; in which the education offered mirrors as closely as possible that which is offered in the larger society; in which education offers itself as a tool for human renewal by promoting awareness and self-esteem. At the same time that we need to think of prison higher education as an inherently specialized practice, the challenge is to develop a specialized practice that takes into account the unique circumstances in which teaching and learning occur without constraining possibilities for growth in conformity with social expectations about prisoners.

WHO SHOULD EDUCATE?

The first prison higher education programs in the United States were founded by individuals, both in and out of higher education, who made it their business to include prisoners in higher education. It is only a slight overgeneralization to say that the early programs were typically offered by four-year colleges and universities. The early prison education programs cited by Roberts (1971), for example, are the University of Maryland at Maryland Penitentiary, 1953; the University of Kansas and St. Mary's College at Leavenworth, 1957; the University of Southern Illinois at the state prison in Menard in 1957. This picture has rapidly changed during the past decade, however, as two-year community colleges have entered the prisons in force. In Massachusetts, for example, two community colleges account for more than 80 percent of all enrollments in prison higher education in that state. The importance of the issue of whether community colleges or four-year institutions ought to provide the backbone of prison higher education cannot be overstated. It speaks to a whole set of interrelated issues about the meaning and value of educational participation in the prisons.

One reason for concern has been addressed at the national level. Most university-based prison programs account for an infinitesimal percentage of total university enrollments, but a growing number of two-year institutions actually have more prisoner students than on-campus students. Although community colleges are often well positioned to deliver educational programs in the prisons and many provide programs of quality, we have witnessed an alarming trend in which involvement in prison higher education appears to be principally motivated by the need for new or increased revenues. This problematic situation, and the abuses associated with it, has led to the enactment of federal guidelines that strictly limit the percentage of a student body that can comprise prisoners.

Higher education is not a system of institutions that have equal meaning and value. Higher education is "an objective classifier" (Bourdieu 1984) and one of the most important bases for classification is the status of the institution in which learning has taken place. Although four-year institutions offer an educational credential with greater value, their programs are becoming fewer in number than two-year programs in the prisons, and when community colleges and four-year institutions offer complementary programs of study in the same prisons, there is a tendency for the community college to absorb a vast majority of enrollments.

The question may well be asked whether the trend toward community college predominance in prison education reflects an attempt to reduce institutional tension within prison higher education by incorporating a model of education less antagonistic to the deprivation model of prison. If the answer is yes, prison higher education may be confronted with an alarming trend. Community colleges not only absorb most entering students, but have a strong appeal to individuals who perceive all college participation as equal. In addition, less rigorous academic standards allow the community colleges far greater leeway in responding to the expressed interests of students. In many states, prison officials have demonstrated a preference for the community college's involvement in prison higher education. We need to consider what this preference may suggest. Correctional administrators, sensitive to public criticism that offenders might "benefit from their crimes," have historically refrained (Reagan and Stoughton 1976) from offering programs that have significant value beyond the prison. Support for the community colleges may well be the continuation of an historic pattern of offering an education that does not conflict with what it means to be a prisoner.

WHAT SHOULD PRISONERS LEARN?

What curriculum is best for prison education? One of the most striking features of prison education programs is their emphasis upon the liberal arts and the humanities. (The exception to this rule is, of course, community college programs that offer specialized vocational training tied to the lower realms of the occupational hierarchy.) This emphasis has been rationalized in relation to higher education's reformative mission within the prisons. If the goal is to make moral reasoning an asset of a person once deficient in this area, the liberal arts make the goal reachable by presenting compelling circumstances that transcend the spatial and temporal boundaries of personal existence and focus upon the resolution of complex issues and problems. It furnishes opportunities to develop critical thinking skills instead of rigid, personal dogma. Cognitive development is accomplished by enabling the student to perceive in ways that credit multiple perspectives; moral development is accomplished by enabling the student to interpret alternatives in ways that reflect mature consideration of competing consequences; and reformation is achieved when higher cognitive and moral functioning lead to the acquisition of new values that will guide the actual behavior of the offender (Barker 1984; Duguid 1981, 1987).

On the other hand, the emphasis on the liberal arts and humanities has the quality of a practice desperately seeking a theory. As the founder of Boston University's prison program noted, this emphasis on liberal education was not deliberate. It actually evolved, without prior theory, to create a program that is both particular to the prison in its cognitive-moral emphasis and standard to the university in its academic requirements and criteria (Barker 1984).

The simple truth appears to require little theory. The liberal arts and general studies curricula dominate because of the difficulties of funding and delivering a sufficiently broad spectrum of courses to make pursuit of specialized degrees a viable possibility. Many programs are able to offer only a handful of courses each semester and, in such cases, a liberal arts concentration offers considerably more flexibility for both the programs and for students focused on obtaining a degree. Additionally, prison security militates against some types of courses—especially those in the sciences and others requiring access to specialized equipment—in prison settings.

The practical reasons that make the liberal arts curricula the mainstay of most programs do not necessarily address which curricula are best suited for prison education. Put another way, it does not follow that the best curriculum for a prison education program is also the best for each participant in the program. The ideal circumstance would be to possess sufficient resources to deliver an array of courses that would enable each individual to pursue chosen areas of interest. That circumstance is unlikely to come about for most programs, and the result may be a decreasing responsiveness to variations in student interests and motives for participation.

To the extent that increased employability after release is among the most frequently expressed motivations for participation, it is not surprising that prisoners seek out vocational courses. This accounts, in part, for the appeal of the community colleges. They have the ability to deliver a broad array of technical and vocational offerings that suggest more concrete possibilities for employment subsequent to release. But even here, we must be cautious. The technical and vocational programs offered by the community colleges may not be an equal alternative to the liberal arts curricula offered by four-year colleges and universities. There is a real need for program administrators from four-year colleges to develop the possibilities of more skill-based curricula. Except in those rare cases in which the size of the college-eligible population of a prison is sufficient to support both academic and vocational alternatives, prison higher education will constantly find itself in the position of limiting the possibilities of learning for either the vocationally or academically inclined.

It may be true that, as Cosman (1981) has noted, "the actual curriculum may be less important than might be supposed." Yet the actual curriculum is less important only in relation to a particular goal—rehabilitation or reformation of the prisoner—to which educators have chosen to tie it. We would assert that the actual curriculum is vitally important because it crystallizes the most fundamental issue about learning in the prisons. Will prison higher education be shaped by the social world according to its expectations about what prisoners as a social group can and ought to be, or will it be responsive to what each prisoner has the potential to be? In determining whether we ought to respond to the expressed educational desires of prisoners, we are deciding nothing less than whether education will be a thing that acts upon them or a thing through which they choose to act upon and improve themselves. Perhaps the most important curricular decision a prison education program can make is to resist the temptation to devise an education appropriate to prisoners. Such an education would be a reflection of, and likely reproduce, the cultural meaning of incarceration.

THE QUESTION OF DELIVERY

The emergence of innovative new technologies and their application to education forces us to consider how higher education should be brought into the prison. What should constitute the classroom of a higher education program in the prison? Should prison education programs favor traditional classroom approaches to learning? Should they instead be inclined toward the use of new technologies that replace the traditional classroom while overcoming many of the obstacles inherent in delivering education to prisoners? Should we combine traditional and innovative technological approaches, and in what balance? By what standards do we choose from among the varied modes of teaching and learning?

Traditional classrooms offer the advantage of the warm body in front of the room. Those with considerable experience in prison education programs frequently note as important that teacher-student contact in traditional classroom settings is heightened in the prison. The instructor is typically the prisoners' exclusive contact with the academic side of higher education. Technologies that enable *distance education*, on the other hand, offer decided advantages in institutional settings. They allow learning to occur at times and places that do not disrupt the daily life of the institution, offer a cost-effective way to deliver educational programming to remote areas, make available a wider array of courses, and facilitate communication between faculty and students by providing a *virtual access* into the prison. Specialists in independent (distance) study frequently observe that, if undertaken in a nonexploitative framework, interaction between teacher and student is frequently superior to the traditional classroom.

Although it seems clear that technology can play a vital support role in all educational enterprises, the decision concerning whether to employ traditional classroom instruction, distance education, or a combination in prison is likely both to reflect local considerations as well as the broader implications. No issue better reflects the impact of the varied circumstances in which hundreds of prison education programs operate. In some states, colleges and universities involved in prison higher education are numerous and the geographical distance between the prison and the school is insignificant. In these circumstances, it may be reasonable to have the traditional classroom as the norm. In other states, a single college may provide postsecondary education to a large number of remote prison sites. In these circumstances, distance education has enormous appeal and may even be the only mechanism that enables courses to be offered.

Despite the practical issues that govern the choice made by various programs, there are important implications to the use of distance technologies as the mainstay of an education program. Our sense is that the practical decision to use distance technology ought to be significantly influenced by its general social meaning. Proximity to faculty—the business of studying under the authoritative gaze of a faculty member—is one of the ritual structures through which the meaning and value of education is regulated. Concepts such as "University without Walls" and "Open University," for example (Robinson 1977), bespeak the desire to decentralize learning in order to reach special populations and emphasize self-directed and prior learning at the expense of traditional instruction. The invisible student is often the by-product of both low and high technology distance education programs, including correspondence courses and computer-based instruction, in which faculty-student contact hours are minimal or nonexistent. Education received outside the direct supervision of faculty is always suspect on the grounds of rigor and quality.

INTERSYSTEM RELATIONS

The director of one prison higher education program is fond of saying, "They don't tell us how to teach, and we don't tell them how to lock people up." If the divide between higher education and corrections were just that starkly drawn in practice, there would seldom be controversy between representatives of the two institutions. The literature of prison higher education is replete with references to the inherent conflict and tension between educators and correctional officials, but it is important to recognize that these programs could not exist without the cooperation of these same officials. That higher education's presence in the prison involves both conflict and accommodation with correctional staff seems obvious. The principal question that those who conduct prison higher education programs must ask themselves is whether, in conforming to or contesting one or another dictate of a prison administration, the program is likely to compromise fatally its own goals and objectives. And this is a question that must not be asked only once, but constantly.

The grounds for potential conflict appear most acute between instructors in prison education programs and lower-level correctional staff, who may be most likely to oppose prison higher education. Prisons are indeed about the business of "locking people up" and that business will often dictate such matters as instructor access to the prison facility, the time when classes will be held, their duration, whether they may be held at all on a given day, and prisoner access to whatever supplies, libraries, or study resources may be available. Lower-level correctional staff are the most visible representatives of correctional authority and become the focus of the frustrations of educators even as they do no more than respond to the directives of their superiors.

But it is also true that the *systemic* features of incarceration are maintained through the routine behavior of lower-level correctional staff. The good prisoners, in the ideology of line staff, "know their place." They do not seek meaningful change in their lives. They work at menial jobs, pass their time watching television, and "talk sports." The good prisoners have accepted their fundamental lack of worth and are resigned to a life without social or economic status, during and after incarceration. Prisoners who strive to better themselves through higher learning are viewed as "problematic" and "arrogant," or are accused of "conning the system" by pretending to be something they are not. They are subjected to increased personal harassment and other forms of interpersonal terrorism (Jones 1982). Educators are an alien presence in the prison. They become, to some extent, powerless in a constant struggle between captors and captives. Educators are often seen by correctional staff as wrongheaded individuals who are naive about the nature of those they are dealing with. They are perceived as taking the side of prisoners against correctional officers and making the job of maintaining order significantly more difficult.

In our anxiety to overcome these routine conflicts, there is a danger that we will forget the price of accommodation. There is no doubt that accommodation has its rewards. Yet one point should not be overlooked. The prison has failed for two centuries to achieve the vision of the reforming jurists to be a place where the process of reformation requalified offenders as useful citizens. The prison has succeeded for two centuries as an institution that creates a class of outcasts who are unlikely to be anything but criminal. For all the professionalism of contemporary corrections, it cannot claim to have found a way to alter this tragic, historical outcome of incarceration. We would have to look long and hard to discover a reputable publication that claimed that incarceration improved offenders or led to reductions in criminality. Indeed, the failure of the prison is almost axiomatic in the literatures of penology and corrections itself.

This is the light in which higher education must view the possibilities of accommodation. Higher education has the opportunity to achieve something in the prisons. It can be a vehicle through which incarcerated men and women might be able to transform their lives. Its ability to do this well may be almost wholly dependent on its willingness to maintain a healthy distance from, and with it, a measure of sustained conflict, with corrections. Higher education could easily do the things that might placate correctional staff members and lessen their antagonism toward prison higher education programs, students, and faculty. The real question, however, is whether in the process of placating corrections, higher education is advancing or surrendering its principal ideals. Put bluntly, to the extent that higher education shapes itself according to the needs of the prison, it may well be surrendering its own goals and objectives in favor of the organizing principles of an institution that has produced decidedly different results since it came into being.

CONCLUSIONS

We have attempted to present here a rather general discussion of the forces that have and are currently shaping prison higher education in the United

States. We elected not to linger on the details of specific issues, but rather placed emphasis on the fact that while the education of prisoners can take many forms, the form it does take will be shaped by our attitudes about crime, criminals, and the purposes of punishment. Prison higher education is indeed a specialized area of continuing education practice, but it is critical that we remain cognizant of the fact that it is a specialized area precisely because we believe that those confined in our nation's jails and prisons are, in some fundamental way, unlike others in society. What we believe them to be has shaped our expectations about whether, what, and how they should learn. The practitioner in prison education would do well to realize that there is no area of practice in the prison that is not affected by the social meaning of incarceration and perceptions of the social value of prisoners.

It is essential that we pay significant attention to the distinction between learning and education and its implications for educational practice in the prison. Learning—facilitated by the provision of materials and instruction—has always been a possibility within the prison, and it is that possibility that historically has provided the substance for claims about the role of education in the prison. What was seldom provided, however, was a role for the formal apparatus of education. To be granted access to that apparatus is to realize the possibility of a learning whose social and symbolic meaning can be located within the system of regulated values—the legitimate uses to which learning may be put—in the larger society. The historic role of education in the prison has been limited to programs of learning devoid of social and symbolic value in the larger society, while opportunities for inclusion in the system of learning that possesses social currency have been resisted and thwarted.

More important, the learning available to prisoners has tended to be in the service of the panoptic regime of discipline, surveillance, and control. Learning was tolerated within the prisons only to the extent that it participated in the reformative project that emerged from the birth of the prison. Foucault has noted that education, like other elements of the panoptic regime, limited its deployment and social meaning to treatment of the attributes of delinquency and came to affirm delinquency as an objective attribute of offenders precisely by claiming its centrality to their reformation. Such an education regards its students as essentially diseased people who need to be cured and, as such, ought to be treated as objects, things to be examined, treated, and cured. It was and continues to be learning termed "correctional," bespeaking its compatibility with the "unmaking" of human beings, denial or limitation of human potential, and ease with participation in the historic failure of the prison's reformative project.

Given the historic failure of the prison to affect the reformation of offenders, the notions of human renewal and reformation that comprise the ideal of higher education may require a practice and theory that sustains the fundamental conflicts between higher education and corrections. If higher education grapples effectively with the meaning of its own success within the prisons, it will come to recognize that increasing levels of integration with corrections threaten its ideals, goals, and objectives. Higher education seeks to transform the social status of prisoners in ways that fundamentally contradict the degraded and delinquent status that prisons reinforce. Yet this goal is illusory within the limits of established educational theory and practice that are symbolically linked to the assumptions of other institutional realms.

There is a need to redefine professional roles within prison higher education. Those who brought higher education into the lives of prisoners may not have been aware of the structural conditions that shape the social value and symbolic meaning of specific educational enterprises. A new professional role will recognize at the outset that the meaning and value of the education offered to prisoners, if it equals its counterparts by level and type within the larger society, will already be limited within the hierarchy of institutional types within higher education. It will recognize, in short, the external limits to the possibility of shaping social meaning within the site where learning occurs. It will also recognize that for much of its history, higher education has not participated in the debate about its own meaning.

There is no doubt that if we shape our professional roles in ways that challenge existing social expectations about prisoners, we will provoke conflict both within education and between education and other social institutions. The professional voice that challenges the taken-for-granted attitudes of the social world also challenges the legitimacy of other institutional realms. Conflict within the institutional realm, however, is a fundamental aspect of meaningful social change. To avoid that conflict allows the meaning and value of educational participation to be dictated by other social institutions. But its greatest danger is in perpetuating the farcical notion that the highest ideals of education—democracy and equality in learning—can be achieved without some measure of conflict with those institutions that seek their antithesis.

A Brief History of Prison Higher Education in the United States

by *Walter Silva*

· · · · · · · · · · ·

EDITOR'S INTRODUCTION

If prison higher education is in fact shaped in the tension between competing visions of what prison and prisoners can and should be, this is hardly a recent development. The issues that influence prison higher education have an all-too-familiar feel to those who possess knowledge of the history of the American prison. Walter Silva, in "A Brief History of Prison Higher Education in the United States," argues that, although education has played a role in the social mission of the prison throughout its history, that role has been shaped in the systemic conflict between security (the whole set of arrangements necessitated by captivity) and treatment (the practices that seek to decrease the necessity of captivity by promoting changes in the behaviors of individuals).

Silva appears to concur with Jones and d'Errico's assumption that both treatment and security are shaped by our notion of what prisoners are and what, therefore, should be done about and for them, but he calls attention to the fact that the meaning of incarceration and the characteristics ascribed to prisoners are not historical constants. He traces the transformations in both the meaning of incarceration and notions of the criminal and relates each to varying approaches to education.

It is noteworthy that Silva, who has been involved in prison higher education for more than two decades and currently directs one of the oldest and most successful prison education programs in Massachusetts, does not view questions of conflict and accommodation between higher education and corrections in simplistic terms. Rather, he reminds us that despite myriad

Walter Silva is director of the Prison Education Program at Boston University, Boston, Massachusetts.

examples of opposition to prison higher education, colleges and universities
are able to deliver education to prisoners precisely because prison administrators allow it and are generally supportive. This calls our attention to the
possibility of cooperation between higher education and the prisons.

On the other hand, Silva is not unaware that, however desirable we might
find support and cooperation, prisons and higher education do not share the
same mission. His suggestion that prisons might, in the future, be placed on
university campuses does appear radical, but I agree wholeheartedly with its
spirit: the certainty that public beliefs and attitudes about prisons and prisoners will change, and that we in higher education need to anticipate these
changes and begin to formulate responses that will heighten the scope and
effectiveness of the role of education in reducing the necessity of confinement.

· · · · · · · · ·

In the 200-year history of prisons in America, there has never been a time
when some type of education did not exist in these institutions. Although
higher education is a relative newcomer, the earliest concept of the prison, as
an alternative to the then prevailing norms of criminal sanctions in this
country, and, in fact, throughout the western world, embodied in its philosophy the redemption of the errant, a novel and radical thought for the last
decade of the eighteenth century.

The very first keepers of the prisons, the Quakers of post-Revolutionary
Philadelphia, could not have foreseen the results of their efforts two centuries
later, but certainly they believed that the Bible and repentant solitude would
better serve to return the offender to the fold than would the then current
sanctions of public humiliation, several forms of corporal punishment (including branding and maiming), and the gallows. As part of that thinking,
education in its varied forms was always regarded as the torch by which to
show the way.

In considering the possibilities of prison higher education, we must realize
that the vacillating attitudes concerning restorative as opposed to punitive
programs for convicted criminals over a period of even two decades is not
unusual. The massive support to alleviate the condition of prisoners in the late
1960s and 1970s, for example, with legislation allowing for previously un-
heard-of liberties—furloughs, prerelease work opportunities, extensive edu-

cation programs behind the walls—is simply one swing of the perpetual criminal justice pendulum. The swing in the opposite direction taking place in the early 1990s—the prevalent attitude to incapacitate and incarcerate more citizens for less serious crimes, the increase in prison construction, mandatory sentencing, the move to exclude inmates from entitlement educa- tion programs—are not unlike other swings in public persuasion since the 1790s.

The ongoing conflict between prison administrators and educators, be- tween the need to exercise absolute control over prisoners for "security reasons" and the desire to bring into the prison programs which would promote meaningful growth and change, occurred as early as 1787. Consider how the very first prison educators, if we may call them that, were greeted when, at the direction of the Philadelphia Prison Society and with the permission of the Board of Governors of Pennsylvania, Bishop William White and Dr. William Rogers arrived at the gates of the Old Stone Prison to offer religious sermons and lectures. The warder, one John Reynolds, who had amassed a considerable fortune in the sale of inmate labor to the public and the sale of liquor to the inmates, initially refused to allow the preachers entrance and only complied at the direct order of the sheriff. In his attempt to prevent these outsiders from breaching his institutional security, he lectured them at length on the probability of bodily harm that would come to them if they ventured within the walls and urged them to at least leave their valuables and watches on the outside. In a final, desperate act of intimidation, Reynolds had a cannon placed on the platform next to the clergymen and a guard standing by with a lighted wick, ready to fire into the assembled crowd should the occasion demand (Teeters 1955). The inmates, of course, displayed only courtesy and appreciation. Although those of us engaged in prison education today may not be subjected to quite the same degree of intimidation, it is not uncommon to experience an uncomfortable word of warning as we pass through the security checks on the way to the classroom.

EARLY PRISONS AND EDUCATION

The inspectors of the Walnut Street Jail, the first true American prison, an institution where confinement itself was the punishment rather than a way station to being punished, stated in their first report (1791) that they held three main objectives in their responsibilities: "(1) The public security . . . (2) The reformation of the prisoners . . ." "(3) Humanity toward these unhappy members of society." In keeping especially with the latter two objectives, the inspectors provided that "edifying persons have at all times access to the prisoners." By 1798, a school was introduced to the prison as "the most beneficial employment . . . for learning for some and improving others in the first Principles of reading, writing, and arithmetic." A library of 110 books, not all religious in nature, was provided at a cost of $55.17 (Teeters 1955).

Beginning in the 1820s at the Eastern Pennsylvania Penitentiary, the Quaker reformers practiced a prison policy of total separation, a policy that would become internationally known as "The Pennsylvania System." At the same time, a competing system was developing in neighboring New York State and would become known equally famously as "The Auburn System" for the prison where it was born. Because the prisoners were totally separated, day and night, the administrators of the Pennsylvania System were able to offer only the most rudimentary moral education in the form of a chaplain who would visit from cell to cell during the evening to discuss readings from the Bible and, occasionally, more contemporary matters of interest. The chaplain, by necessity, was the very first prison teacher. Obviously, if a prisoner could not read the Bible, he could neither contemplate its teachings nor, with that benefit, reflect upon his own errant life, which was the ultimate goal of the penitentiary. It was therefore incumbent upon the chaplain to provide lessons in reading for the illiterate in order to offer the appropriate avenue for salvation.

By the 1840s, the Pennsylvania System began to fall into disfavor, largely because state legislatures, in comparing it with the Auburn System, quickly determined that the solitary cottage industries of the Pennsylvania System could not compete economically with the mass production industries of the Auburn System, where men worked congregately by day, although in total silence. The founders of the Auburn System disagreed with three basic principles of the earlier Pennsylvania System: They believed that convicts had not been treated with sufficient severity, that too much faith had been placed in their reformability, and that drastic changes would have to be made if the penitentiary idea was to succeed (Lewis 1965). The monotonous routine of the Auburn System allowed little time for formal education, and the warders were largely unsupportive of such efforts. If the Pennsylvania System of reformation by contemplation, embraced by the peaceful, brotherly loving Quakers of Philadelphia, was considerably to the left of contemporary thinking, the Auburn System of lockstep, piece work, pay-your-way-for-incarceration, endorsed by the Tammany-connected, Jacksonian politicians of New York, can certainly be considered as something to the right, and politically very popular.

Stephen Allen, one of the founders of the Auburn System and later the mayor of New York City, held that educational efforts in prisons were unwise because they took time away from the inmate's labor, that criminals "had not the same claim upon our commiseration that the honest and unfortunate part of our species have," and that "the reformatory plan, or the system of attention, kindness, and forbearance, has failed, and will fail, wherever, or whenever it is put into operation." Reflecting that popular sentiment, Samuel M. Hopkins, a member of the New York State legislature during the 1820s, contended that inmate life had not been sufficiently severe and should produce more terror and suffering (Hardie 1824). These thoughts have a remarkably contemporary ring.

Gustave de Beaumont and Alexis de Tocqueville (1833), reporting their interview with Elam Lynds, the first superintendent charged with implementing the new policies at Auburn, indicate well how severe they were and how far departed was the thinking of the new breed of prison administrators from the Pennsylvania Quakers. Rather than being seen as fellow beings capable of the entire range of human intelligence and emotion, convicts were now thought to be something between man and beast who needed first to be broken and trained. When questioned by the young French researchers, "Do you believe that bodily chastisement might be dispensed with?" Lynds replied, "I consider chastisement by the whip the most efficient, and, at the same time, the most humane . . . I consider it impossible to govern a large prison without a whip. Those who know human nature from books only, may say the contrary." It is of no surprise, then, that when questioned about the ability of convicts to benefit from education, Lynds stated that prisons "are filled with coarse beings, who have no education, and who perceive with great difficulty ideas, and often even sensations" (1833).

The last half of the nineteenth century witnessed a new, more complex notion of the criminal. Zebulon Brockway, the first warden of the Elmira (New York) Reformatory, was convinced that even the most fractured soul could be remolded into a productive and useful being. He suggested that not all criminal behavior could be laid at the feet of the individual offender, that society bore at least some of the burden for the miscreant's behavior. Criminals, he argued, were a product of their environment and economic status, determined by an accident of birth. Therefore, the prisoner should be allowed at least the opportunity for regeneration, and that regeneration could most effectively be offered through education and individually assisted reintegration into the community. With Brockway's penal philosophy implemented at Elmira came the beginnings of the Reformatory era—the introduction of the indeterminate sentence, parole, job specific education, and the first explorations of postsecondary education (Brockway 1912).

NEW CENTURY—NEW APPROACHES

At the turn of the century, as urban industrialization gave rise to the need for universal secondary education, prisons began to recognize the utility of vocational education. As usual, education programs were introduced into the prisons only after they were accepted and well established and commonplace in the community (Jones 1992b; Seashore et al. 1976). The earliest outside correspondence courses came from Columbia University, soon followed in the early 1920s by other, primarily land grant, colleges. Other programs were developed by the individual prisons. Thomas Mott Osborne, serving as chairman of the National Society of Penal Information, led a team of researchers that evaluated state and federal prisons across the country on a number of criteria, including education. In the earliest study (Osborne 1925), the Society reported that "as the function of the prison is primarily, if not exclusively punitive, it is not surprising that little or no attention is paid to the education of the inmates. In most of the state prisons, there are elementary classes in which illiterates are instructed in the rudiments of English and arithmetic, but rarely do we find anything more . . . . There is a total lack of intellectual stimulus in the American prison." However, in this 1923 survey, covering "only 11 states of the North and East, via: Maine, New Hampshire, Vermont, Massachusetts, Rhode Island, Connecticut, New York, New Jersey, Pennsylvania, Delaware, and Maryland" and two federal prisons, there is mention of inmates taking correspondence courses in all but Rhode Island and Vermont prisons.

The correspondence courses included studies in agriculture, real estate, salesmanship, and a number of remedial-level "academic" courses in English grammar, mathematics, and foreign languages. The first mention of "college-level" studies in prison came through a correspondence course program offered to inmates at Sing Sing Prison by Columbia University in 1923. Levring Tyson, the director of that program, reported that "these courses are of college grade level and for those sufficiently prepared for such work can be of real advantage in giving mental relaxation and an incentive to work out a worthwhile future for themselves after leaving prison." He pointed out, too, that the courses were unlike the usual vocational education then available in prisons. "These courses are not valuable as purely vocational subjects as they are of college grade . . . These courses are worthwhile alone for their effect on the men's futures and their molding influence may easily become very valuable" (Smith 1930).

Interestingly, Tyson noted a factor about which prison educators still complain 70 years later, that "the chief objection is that of interruptions due to transfers or discharge." Also at that time, in the Massachusetts State Prison in Charlestown, 40 prisoners were taking university extension courses from the Massachusetts Department of Education. At the Rockview Prison in Pennsylvania in 1924, there is evidence of what was probably the first personal contact between inmates and college faculty. At this prison, "the educational work is supervised by professors from State College. The classes offered cover from the first to the eighth grade," and "some special courses are offered by the faculty members of State College." Because there is no indication that these special courses were accredited college courses and because the archives at Pennsylvania State University (formerly State College) do not record these endeavors, the evidence is that this early articulation between college and prison was ad hoc, at best. At the Ohio Penitentiary in 1924, 200 prisoners were enrolled in correspondence courses on everything from poultry raising to advertising and commercial art. It is here, in that year, that we may have for the first time a linkage between postsecondary education and recidivism, for it was reported that "a survey of convicts completing these courses indicated them as successful after release from prison" (Smith 1930).

The 1929 Garrett and MacCormick edition of *The Handbook*, as it soon became known in prison and academic/criminal justice circles, provided, for the first time, comparative and extensive national statistics. Through surveying all 48 states and the Federal Bureau of Prisons (including military prisons), *The Handbook* was able to amass inmate interviews and record checks listing information by state or jurisdiction of the inmate's age, nationality, race, previous incarcerations, and educational level at time of incarceration. *The Handbook* also provides sketchy, but interesting, information about the level and intensity of prison education programs by state. We know, for example, from analysis of the raw data of these studies that, of those inmates under custody of the Federal Bureau of Prisons, 14 percent had entered high school prior to their incarceration while about 2 percent had had some college education. In the state prisons, the level of inmate education nationally was about 17 percent for those who had attended high school and about the same, 2 percent, for those who had college experience.

There were, of course, significant differences between southern and northern states, as well as eastern and western states. California continued to lead the way with the most extensive prison education programs in the country. In 1928, San Quentin Prison reported that, in addition to those inmates enrolled in basic literacy, grade school, and high school studies, there were 438 prisoners enrolled in University of California Extension Division courses. It was further revealed that the inmate students had "averaged a higher grade than outside students" who were taking the same courses (Garrett and MacCormick 1929). In Illinois, Iowa, Kansas, Massachusetts, Minnesota, New Jersey, New York, Pennsylvania, and Wisconsin, inmates were enrolled in extension courses, primarily from their land-grant colleges and state education agencies. In New York, at Clinton Prison, inmate teachers participated in weekly Normal School training sessions offered by the civilian head teacher so they could be certified by the state Board of Regents as elementary school teachers. In 1927, a large percentage passed successfully the certification test.

At the New York State Reformatory at Elmira, in keeping with Brockway's tradition of linking education with parole, compulsory education up to the eighth-grade level was required and both academic and trade classes were held in 30 classrooms throughout the day. In Pennsylvania, five professors from State College taught vocational courses to some 50 inmates at Bellefonte Prison, while at the Eastern State Prison, 50 inmates participating in a correspondence course on poultry raising met with agriculture professors from State College twice a week. The University of Wisconsin, at that time, offered free extension courses in mathematics, English, bookkeeping, accounting, languages, and engineering to inmates at Waupun Prison. Faculty from the university met with students twice weekly, while the director of university extension programs visited with the inmates in order to solicit their advice on further courses and to attend to administrative matters twice a month (Garrett and MacCormick 1929). Although inmate students could have profited from postsecondary education at this time, and several colleges, particularly land grant colleges, were prepared to offer more than correspondence and cell study courses, the time was not yet ripe. It is clear, though, that the mid- to late 1920s witnessed the first articulation between prisons and colleges, although systematic college course offerings and degrees would not come for several more decades.

Not surprisingly, the 1938 edition of *The Handbook* (Cox and Bixby), reporting prison conditions during the Great Depression, indicated only modest advancement in the development of prison education in association with state and private colleges. The level of previous education attained by prisoners rose only slightly, to about 19 percent who had experienced some high school and only 4 percent who had been in a postsecondary program. For the most part, programs that existed 10 years earlier maintained their viability, while a few more land-grant colleges, notably in the Plains states, began to serve inmates with extension courses. The southern states continued to offer little to no education programs with the exception of a few, isolated literacy programs. An interesting program at the St. Cloud Reformatory in Minnesota brought 16 college students to the prison for practice teaching under the guidance of their professors from the State Teachers College. At the same time, the faculty supervised a small group of "inmate teachers in preparing suitable lesson material" for elementary education (Cox 1938).

Echoing the sentiments of Warden Elam Lynds of Auburn Prison 100 years earlier that prisoners "perceive with great difficulty ideas" (de Beaumont and de Tocqueville 1833), the New York Commission to Study Education in Prisons, appointed by Governor Lehman in 1933 and chaired by Dr. N. L. Englehardt of Teachers College, Columbia University, and the "Annual Report of the Commissioner of Corrections of the Commonwealth of Massachusetts, 1936," questioned the educability of most prisoners. The Massachusetts report listed the IQs of inmates at Concord Reformatory as: "Above average - 3.4%; Average - 7.2%; Low average - 8.4%; Inferior - 31.3%; Borderline defective - 28.2%; High moron - 17.2%; Low moron - 4.0%; Imbecile - .3%" (Lerer 1939). With almost 50 percent of the prison population's intelligence reported between "Borderline defective" and "Imbecile," it is little wonder that college education was not high on the list of priorities for prison officials.

During World War II, little attention was paid to prison education. However, by the conclusion of the war, and with the subsequent benefits of the G.I. Bill, higher education in America took an unprecedented turn. Thousands of veterans began to appear on campuses, and universities were forced to examine adult education as a new and distinct phenomenon. Raymond Jones (1991) argues persuasively that higher education for prisoners became acceptable only as higher education for the masses became the norm. The college degree, reserved for the elite from colonial times to the 1940s, would, in postwar years, rapidly become the equivalent of the high school diploma of only a few years previous, especially because of the state college and university continuing education divisions and the developing community college systems. Within this context, prison higher education would be allowed to take root.

Although there are anecdotal reports of professors offering courses in a number of prisons in the late 1940s, the first degree program was initiated by Southern Illinois University at Carbondale at the Menard State Prison when, in 1953, 25 inmates registered for classes. Shortly after initiating this pioneer program, Southern Illinois began similar programs at the Vienna State Prison and Graham Correctional Center. Part of the University Studies degree program, inmate-students were funded by state aid and university grants. These initial efforts in prison higher education lasted until the early 1980s when the prison administration insisted that outside volunteers, including university faculty, must submit to drug check urinalysis tests. The dean refused to subject the faculty to this indignity. Thus, ignobly, ended the nation's first college prison program (Silva 1993).

With lack of funding a persistent problem, the 1950s witnessed slow and sporadic development of prison college programs. In 1954, for example, only one other college was involved in prison education, and only marginally. In that year, the University of Maryland offered one course per semester at the Maryland State Penitentiary. By 1965, more than 10 years after the initiation of the first college program, only a dozen postsecondary college programs were operating on a regular basis in the nation's state and federal prisons (Taylor 1992).

PELL GRANTS—AND OTHER SUPPORT PROGRAMS

The single most important event in the development of higher education for prisoners (and other low-income students, for that matter) occurred in 1965. In that year, Congress passed Title IV of the Higher Education Act, a major part of which was the Basic Education Opportunity Grants (later to be named the Pell Grant[1] in honor of Senator Claiborne Pell, the bill's sponsor). Grants became available to inmate-students, who could usually qualify for the maximum funding possible because of their minimum income. The Pell Grant program, legislated to be used to supplement other funding sources for low-income students, was frequently abused, becoming the easy target of quasi-legitimate postsecondary prison education providers in a number of states. Although the vast majority of colleges receiving this federal support used the funds legitimately and productively, a few illegitimate programs brought federal support of prison college programs into question in congressional circles. With the reauthorization of the Higher Education Act in 1992, new guidelines, effective July 1, 1993, were established with which the states must comply, including assurances that the Pell Grant is used to supplement rather than supplant state funding.

Perhaps the most ambitious of the early college prison programs was "Project Newgate," named for the seventeenth-century British jail (Seashore et al. 1976). In 1967 and 1968, the Office of Economic Opportunity funded five college programs. The five programs were at prisons in Rockview, Pennsylvania; Saint Cloud, Minnesota; Ashland, Kentucky; Sante Fe, New Mexico; and Englewood, Colorado. Three other non-Project Newgate sites—Lompoc, California; Manard, Illinois; and Eastham, Texas—were included in the final, 1972 study. Most of the participating colleges had had cursory contact with the prisons as early as the 1920s and 1930s through correspondence courses. The initial concept of Project Newgate was to establish, as nearly as possible, a campus experience within the prison walls. Inmate students were relieved of other job assignments and, in some cases, provided special living quarters and library facilities. Also included in the Project

---

[1] See both Appendixes One and Two for more on the Pell Grant Program.

Newgate mission was a postrelease component. Inmates who had begun their degree programs in prison would be encouraged and financially supported to continue their studies on the campuses of the cooperating colleges.

Three primary measures of success were included in the final Project Newgate report. They were (1) lessened recidivism, (2) achievement of stability, and (3) realization of life goals. The first measure, "lessened recidivism," was the murkiest for this study and has remained so for the countless college prison program evaluations since. It has, of course, no equivalent in measuring the success of college graduates who are not ex-offenders. Although the easiest variable to measure (whether the subject has been returned to custody), the reasons for failing this test are inconsistent and pernicious. Counted as a failure by this standard would be an ex-offender who had violated the conditions of parole by, for example, "association with ex-prisoners, drinking, co-habituating, borrowing money . . . leaving the county without permission, not attending school, etc." (Seashore, et al. 1976, 73). However, if parolees were to be murdered, or commit suicide, or leave the country never to be heard of again, they would pass this test. The other two measurements, although not quite as subjective, are questionable as well.

"Achieving stability" included certain measurements of time employed or in school, success in maintaining a residence and paying bills, lack of involvement with drugs and alcohol, and abstention from criminal activity. The third measure, realizing life goals, attempts to assess the degree to which the subject has established a relatively secure and satisfying life-style. In spite of the nebulous quantifications, Project Newgate was deemed a success and worthy of replication. The Seashore/Haberfeld study includes suggested guidelines to ensure initiators of prison college programs the potential for optimum success.

The late 1960s was a time like no other in the history of the prison. It marked the beginning of the medical model in prison treatment programs. Criminals could be "rehabilitated" or, as some preferred, "habilitated." Reminiscent of Brockway's model, over a period of time convicts would go through a program of self-discovery through group and individual therapy and education, then be reintegrated into the community. Coincidentally, this was also the era of the first major civil rights movements and heightened equal opportunity consciousness. Funds were available from a number of government and private agencies, including the Law Enforcement Assistance Administration, the Ford Foundation, and the Lilly Foundation, to experiment with prisoner rehabilitation. Prisons were renamed "correctional institutions" and inmates became "residents" or, in some institutions, "clients."

With the 1965 implementation of the Pell Grants, prison college programs entered a stage of rapid expansion. In 1967, Marin Junior College was offering an associate's degree to inmates at San Quentin, Kentucky Wesleyan University was at the Kentucky State Prison, and Ashland University was actively involved in the Mansfield (Ohio) Correctional Institution. In 1968, there were college programs in 13 states, the District of Columbia, and in the Federal Bureau of Prisons (Roberts 1971; Silva 1993). By 1970, 33 states offered college programs in their prisons (Reagan and Stoughton 1976). In 1973, there were 182 programs; by 1976, 237 programs; and by 1982, 350 programs (See Appendix Two).

As of this writing, 43 states and the Federal Bureau of Prisons are providing associate's degrees for qualified inmates, while in 31 of those states the bachelor's degree is also offered. Nine states and the Federal Bureau of Prisons offer master's degrees; in Indiana, Maryland, Massachusetts (on prerelease status), and the Federal Bureau of Prisons, it is possible to earn a doctorate degree (Maguire 1992; Silva 1993).

Higher education in prisons has been most successful when it has met the needs of the correctional institution as well as the incarcerated students. The point of friction between the goals and purposes of the prison and those of the university has been the least grating when the university is in the position of offering something to corrections that the prison cannot supply. Such an offering might take several forms, but it is a reality about which prison educators must be constantly reminded. This is not to say that all prison administrators oppose all higher education programs in their institutions all of the time. Nothing could be further from the truth. In fact, many, if not most, prison wardens/superintendents are supportive of the college programs. This support frequently comes because the chief administrator knows full well that the program is of significant value in giving the inmate-student a sense of self-worth, perhaps for the first time, and a real chance of staying out of prison once released. But often, too, support is proffered for other than altruistic reasons—when institutional jobs and other programs are in short supply, the college program keeps a number of inmates busy; that makes an institution look good when the American Correctional Association is determining if it should be accredited, etc. Certainly, the fact that inmate college students cause far fewer problems than others is well documented. Also, a small number of colleges offer institutional staff courses leading to degrees at greatly reduced or no cost at all. These efforts go far in buying the participating college considerable goodwill. They also lead to a sense of permanence and partnership with the hosting prison.

CONCLUSION

What we have witnessed in the course of 200 years of American prisons has been a systematic swinging from left to right and back again of a prison philosophy into which prison education has been intricately woven. These swings have been tied to political and economic factors, of course. But it is of more than passing interest to compare the remarkable similarities in attitudes and actions of the controllers of the prisons when these swings are at their zenith. The most liberal moment in prison reformation was the very founding of the prison by the antiwar, anti-death penalty, brotherly loving, humanitarian Quakers during the last decade of the eighteenth century. These very same humanitarian concerns are evident in Zebulon Brockway's pro-education, pro-reclamation philosophy 100 years later. And it would be impossible not to find the same thread in the thinking and action of prison reformers and antiwar activists (often the same people) in the late 1960s and early 1970s.

Conversely, we find the "lock them up and throw away the key" attitude, so prevalent in the Auburn System years of the mid-nineteenth century, reflected in the Depression years between the World Wars and in the "get tough on crime" politicians of the past decade. How contemporary, for example, is a remark made by one of the founders of the Auburn System that criminals have "not the same claim on our commiseration, that the honest and unfortunate part of our species have" when we hear in a May 1991 CBS News "60 Minutes" television program incumbent Massachusetts governor William Weld suggest that he could not support a Boston University program that offered higher education opportunities to inmates in three Massachusetts prisons. He suggested instead that the university offer its free program "to poor, law-abiding citizens who have committed no crime" and reintroduce to the inmates "the joys of making small rocks from big rocks." One can only wonder where the governor believes the vast majority of incarcerated men and women resided prior to their arrest. Sadly, the most recent research indicates that this governor's attitudes are pervasive.

> Only eleven states and the Federal Bureau of Prisons reported that academic education is a top or high priority in their departments. Twenty-six states indicated that education programs enjoy about the same level of priority as industry, vocational, and other treatment programs. Ten respondents reported that academic programs are a low or very low priority in their departments. . . . While the intrinsic value of learning seems nakedly apparent, and the benefits of releasing into society a more educated individual ought to be self-evident, it is difficult to convince legislators facing billion dollar deficits and prison administrators facing overcrowded facilities . . . that inmate education ought to be given a high priority . . . [probably] the best we can hope for is to maintain the current level of educational programming and search for ways to encourage inmate motivation while we hope for an improvement in the fiscal climate that might allow prisoner education to become a national priority. (Maguire 1992)

The reality of the prison and its conjunction with higher education is that the two institutions are charged with antithetical missions. It is common to hear corrections administrators refer to inmate-students as prisoners who are also, incidentally, students. Conversely, college faculty and administrators usually regard the same population as students who also happen to be prisoners.

Perhaps the most interesting concept regarding inmate higher education is one that has been bandied about for at least 20 years. That is to simply acknowledge the differences that will inevitably make less effective a prison higher education program in the traditional context and separate those inmates who would clearly benefit from a college program from those who would not, either by personality or eligibility. It has been suggested by a number of educators and at least one ranking corrections administrator, Frank Hall, that future prison development might logically be in conjunction with colleges (Hall, personal conversations, 1972-74). According to Hall, a highly regarded corrections consultant, this could be particularly successful with state land-grant universities, where a "White Paper" transfer might easily transpire, as is currently the case when a corrections department is given the use of state-owned facilities formerly used by another agency, notably deinstitutionalized mental health hospitals and juvenile detention facilities. Underutilization of dormitory space on state college and university campuses for the past few years is well known, as is the overcrowding in the nation's prisons. This nationwide financial crisis might be the catalyst to implement the obvious. Barr and Zunig have stated that notion more specifically:

> The building of prisons on university campuses is the third evolutionary direction for corrections to assume. American universities, as the centers of knowledge, have helped solve problems ranging from the development of the atomic bomb to landing a man on the moon. Corrections and academia have always maintained a cool relationship with each other, though some of the largest American universities, like California, Illinois, Michigan, and Ohio State, are in the same states as the largest prisons. We suggest that the next fifty prisons constructed in the United States be built on college campuses, one in each state. Not off campus, or just beyond the city limits, but right smack in between the law school, the medical school and the social science building, near the campus chapel. It would help educate the public to the fact that resolution of correctional problems is in its own best interest, with particular regard to eventual success in improving law enforcement, crime control techniques, and understanding of the relationship between criminal behavior and social policy. (1970)

Although this position may seem radical, in comparison to the first prison experiment 200 years ago, it is not. What would make more sense in a time when there are too few prison beds and too many empty dormitory beds on the campuses of our major state universities? With a new administration in Washington touting advantages for the disadvantaged and the inevitable swing of the pendulum, we would be well advised to begin now to explore these initiatives in hopes that the next chapter written on the history of prison higher education will include the turn of the twentieth century as at least as significant to inmate education as was the Walnut Street Jail to criminal sanctions at the turn of the eighteenth century.

The Scope and Diversity of Prison Higher Education

by Daniel W. Lawrence
· · · · · · · · · · ·

Editor's Introduction

Much of what passes for knowledge about prison higher education programs—the rationales and objectives of specific courses and general curricula, the abilities, interests, and motivations of students, indeed, virtually every general claim made about any facet of programming—may be reviewed with some skepticism for two reasons. First, though we can generalize about prison higher education, there are significant discontinuities in the level, structure, and quality of higher education programs available to prisoners. Second, we cannot at present do more than guess about the scope and diversity of prison higher education in the United States because there is a critical lack of the descriptive and exploratory research that would enable us to state anything with relative authority.

With this caveat, Daniel Lawrence puts forth a number of generalizations regarding the scope and diversity of prison higher education in the United States. First, the prevalent approach to delivering postsecondary education in the prison is through on-site courses, though correspondence and technology-based distance education are employed in some circumstances. It is relatively rare that programs operate by bringing prisoner-students to on-campus classes. Second, despite some variations in the way programs are funded, they have in common the experience of inadequate and uncertain funding. Third, curricu-

Daniel W. Lawrence is the executive assistant to the chief of operations at the Oklahoma Department of Corrections, as well as adjunct professor at the University of Oklahoma and Oklahoma City University.

lar decisions have tended to be circumstantial, based mainly on the availability of courses and instructors at nearby colleges. A clear implication of this fact is that curricular rationales tend to be de facto. Lastly, programs have tended to develop without benefit of planning, and therefore prisoners who participate often lack adequate resources and support services.

· · · · · · · · ·

It is difficult to determine how many postsecondary education programs in prisons are operational at any given time. Most recent surveys indicate that virtually all of the 50 states offer some form of postsecondary education to those incarcerated. That postsecondary programs exist in most states does not, however, mean that they have proliferated. In some instances, South Dakota, Montana, and Louisiana, for example, as few as 10 to 20 students are served at any given time by a single institution of higher education. States such as California, Georgia, Illinois, Minnesota, Michigan, and Ohio, on the other hand, typically serve the postsecondary education needs of many inmates (Littlefield 1989; Ryan and Woodard 1987; Wolford and Littlefield 1985).

How accurate those figures might have been at the time they were gathered, much less now, is difficult to evaluate. Surveys of this type usually involve sampling *known* programs, but many of those programs contacted often do not respond. Not much of a network has developed among postsecondary prison educators, leaving most programs to operate in semi-anonymity. There is also no clearinghouse for prison higher education programs and practitioners.[1] The Correctional Education Association (headquartered in Washington, D.C.) maintains a directory of members, which gives some insight into locations where programs might be found, but not all educators involved in prison higher education belong to the association. Still, the association's *Journal of Correctional Education* may come as close as there is to a journal that represents correctional postsecondary education.

---

[1]In 1990, the National University Continuing Education Association organized a Prison Higher Education Caucus whose purpose is to develop a network and a means of communication for those involved in prison higher education. This book is a result of the first Caucus meeting. A number of states, including Indiana, Massachusetts, and others, have state organizations or councils that meet regularly to discuss problems and progress in delivering higher education to prisons.

There are two major problems confronting anyone attempting to survey the scope of prison postsecondary education in North America: the paucity of current data and the transitory nature of some of the programs. Programs that are here today may be gone tomorrow due to changes in educational or correctional philosophy, budget cuts at parent institutions, or lack of grants and scholarships to fund individual inmates' courses of studies.

In many postsecondary programs, inmate-students have been expected to generate their own funds to pay for tuition and materials. Most inmates have little, if any, money to apply toward expenses that most "free world" students would have taken as a matter of course. In Oklahoma, for example, inmates in the state corrections system are paid between $9.00 and $37.50 per month for their labors, which could include an assignment as a full-time student. Actually, the *average* pay for Oklahoma inmates was $15 per month, of which 20 percent was to be saved for release, leaving most inmates with a total of $12 per month net pay. Unless a prisoner-student had a patron or benefactor, or secured a student loan, scholarship, or grant, there was little hope of progression beyond the high school level of education. Remedial elementary and secondary education are usually provided by most correctional settings as part of their standard program.

Camp and Camp (1991) estimate that there were more than 800,000 inmates incarcerated in America's prisons and jails on January 1, 1991:

- State and District of Columbia prisons   671, 502
- Federal prisons   60,734
- Jails   28,615
- Other facilities   <u>41,577</u>
- TOTAL   802,428

In 1975, more than 300 colleges and universities offered courses to more than 50,000 prisoners annually (Bell 1977). This would imply that somewhere in the range of six to seven percent of all prisoners in America were involved in higher education at some level and time during the year. If one factored out jail prisoners, who are unlikely to be involved in postsecondary education due to the short-term nature of their incarceration, then the figure climbs about one percentage point. Five percent of the U.S. population was in college at the time of this survey (*Chronicle of Higher Education Almanac* 1992). Thus, the percentage of higher education inmate-students compared more than favorably with the general population of the United States.

It has been generally accepted in modern American society that continuing lifelong education is the way to get ahead and stay ahead. Education is, in addition, perceived as a motivating factor by those who simply wish to experience learning. It is not surprising, then, that prison inmates have become involved in that process as well. Prisons and prisoners tend to reflect the attitudes, trends, fads, fashions, and desires of the general population. If there is a fad or fashion moving through the free-world population, it can also be found in U.S. prisons. If that free-world trend takes the form of a desire to learn and improve oneself, the same motivation will likely be found within prison populations as well.

Education has long been held as a positive value by American society. It has been the pathway by which recent immigrants could share the American dream, for example. Many immigrants to America sacrificed much so that their children could go to school and, as a result, have a better life than did their parents. It should not be surprising that educators and inmates alike see education in general, and higher education in particular, as a means of helping inmates fashion a more productive, meaningful, and exemplary life, preparatory to an inmate's release back into society. Numerous studies have been conducted in an attempt to determine whether or not educating inmates has the desired effect. The author's own investigations reveal that for every study indicating that education is a factor positively affecting a prisoner's ability to stay out of prison, there is another that concludes that education makes no difference whatsoever (Lawrence 1991). Many arguments in favor of higher education for inmates also beg the question of why individuals who already possess college degrees go to prison.

Apologists for prison higher education have never completely defused the argument, held by correctional personnel and many members of society at large, that inmates are lawbreakers and do not deserve what is perceived not only as a benefit, but a benefit that many members of society themselves cannot afford for their children or themselves. This leaves the prison educator maintaining the more esoteric stance that inmates should be afforded educational opportunities, regardless of the fact that they are criminals, because it is the "right thing to do." The New York Department of Correctional Services has come to much the same conclusion, not only because they believe that it lowers recidivism but also because educated inmates can assist other inmates during the course of their incarceration (Morrison 1984). Fortunately for prison higher education, more citizens seem to believe that it is the right thing to do than do not. Otherwise there would be no higher education programs found anywhere in U.S. correctional systems, given the economic realities of the shrinking state and local governmental budgets of the 1980s and early 1990s.

The 1970s were the heyday of the 13-year span of the federal Law Enforcement Assistance Administration (LEAA). Billions of dollars were channeled to law enforcement, corrections, and jail agencies and facilities. Funds were readily available for law enforcement and correctional equipment, staff education, criminal justice research, and a wide variety of demonstration projects. Some $260 million was allocated to as many as 3,000 incarcerated students between 1968 and 1981 (Allen and Simonsen 1992). Prior to LEAA, criminal justice was rarely thought of as a system, much less an academic curriculum. As much as anything, LEAA gave rise to prison higher education on a large scale, making available sufficient funds to transcend arguments that inmates were undeserving of higher education. Colleges, universities, and private contractors received sufficient funds to offer educational opportunities to law enforcement personnel, correctional staff, and inmates alike. This federal largesse almost guaranteed that higher education could be made available to inmates for the first time on a substantial, systematic scale.

PROJECT NEWGATE

One of the best known of the federal demonstration projects of the 1970s was Project NewGate (or Newgate). Project Newgate was originally funded by the Office of Economic Opportunity (OEO). It was an outgrowth of the Upward Bound concept pioneered at the Oregon State Prison in the late 1960s by sociologist Tom Gaddis (of *The Birdman of Alcatraz* fame). The Newgate concept was more ambitious and comprehensive than any other prison college education program of the time. The purpose of the program was to begin to prepare inmates for college while they were still incarcerated. Newgate was intended to be a self-contained program within the host prison which incorporated quality college courses, academic and therapeutic counseling, and individual attention in an enriched atmosphere. A corollary benefit, it was hoped, would be that the program would also improve the general atmosphere of the prison. To accomplish the goals set forth by Project Newgate, the program was designed to function as a separate entity within the host prison—a well-intentioned concept but a source of some conflict due to a perception on the part of the regular institutional staff that the Newgate staff and inmates considered themselves elitist (Seashore, et al. 1976).

The obstacles faced by the Newgate programs were formidable indeed. Prisons were at that time not generally considered viable places for college-level learning to take place. In that respect, the original Newgates faced many of the same problems that confront college prison programs today. Prisons were and are by definition places where security reigns supreme. Educators then and now are expected to follow the rules of the facility closely or suffer covert and overt repercussions from security staff and, perhaps, administration. Prisons operate on strict schedules that affect every facet of institutional daily life. Interruptions in the institution's daily routine, such as a lock-down for a recount of prisoners or an institutional shakedown, can entirely cancel one or more days of classroom schedules. Although such interruptions are often unavoidable, they create severe problems for educators and students alike.

Inmates usually come from disadvantaged socioeconomic backgrounds and have typically not fared well in traditional academic settings prior to their incarceration (Lawrence 1991). Minorities are overrepresented in U.S. prison and jail populations, thus tending to reinforce subtle discrimination and institutional racism in some instances. Moreover, it is difficult for many long-term prison staff to believe that inmates are quite human, much less candidates for education at a higher level than many have achieved themselves. In 1966 in Oklahoma, for example, correctional officers were only required to have a sixth-grade education (National Council on Crime and Deliquency 1966). One improvement is that today correctional officers in most states (even Oklahoma) are required to have a minimum of a high school education to qualify for the job, and many now have some college education if not a degree. This fact alone considerably improves the level of acceptance of college-level educational programs for inmates among correctional staff in general and correctional officers in particular.

The five original Newgate programs, their associated colleges and universities, and the degrees available were:

- Federal Youth Center, Ashland, Kentucky: Ashland Community College (AA) and Morehead State University (BA), administration of the program later shifted from Morehead to the University of Kentucky (BA).
- Minnesota State Reformatory, St. Cloud, Minnesota: St. Cloud State College (BA); and the University of Minnesota (BA).
- New Mexico State Prison, Santa Fe, New Mexico: College of Santa Fe (AA).
- Oregon State Prison, Salem, Oregon: University of Oregon, Eugene (provided administrative services as well as course work); and Portland State University (BA).
- Rockview State Correctional Institution, Bellefonte, Pennsylvania: Pennsylvania State University (BA).

Each of the programs offered a traditional liberal arts curriculum, which included English, history, economics, and psychology. All were accredited courses taught by certified instructors from neighboring colleges or universities. Each Newgate also offered varying levels of support services for inmate-students. Students who successfully completed their inside programs and participated in a positive and productive manner were eligible for release to the street phase of the program. There, students were eligible for admission to the college or university with a fuller range of curricular studies, as well as financial aid, job placement, and in some instances, housing. The following is a list of the courses and major fields of study offered by the Newgate programs, as well as courses offered at three non-Newgate programs that were used as controls for purposes of comparison (Menard, Illinois; Lompoc, California; and the Eastham Unit, Texas Department of Corrections): English, history, economics, political science, art, psychology, sociology, mathematics, biology, general business, education, social welfare, liberal arts, medical technology, business statistics, western-tradition history, conservation, physiology, and geology (Seashore et al. 1976).

Newgate was an extremely ambitious program. In addition to its academic agenda, Newgate offered the following programmatic components:

- Transition from institution to the street;
- Academic counseling in both the institutional and street phases of the program;
- Housing, in some cases;
- Therapeutic counseling in a community or milieu atmosphere inn some programs, such as Minnesota's;
- More overt structure than most college students have;
- Some form of ongoing correctional supervision.

Newgate participants were not the "cream of the crop." Few had previous college experience and participants' tested grade levels were comparable with those of the general prison population from which they were drawn (Seashore et al. 1976).

Seashore et al. found that the Newgate program participants consistently performed better academically and personally than did the control group participants. Gains recorded by the control group participants could have as easily been attributable to other factors such as the college program in which they participated, according to the authors. As a result of their study, the Newgate investigators recommended four features as being necessary to ensure the success of a prison higher education program:

1. Active outreach and remedial components, which may attract and hold inmate-students who would otherwise not attend college;
2. Availability of activities and services outside of the classroom offered as a part of the overall program;
3. Sequencing support and transitional services, including financial, to students after release from prison;
4. Integral involvement in program activities of a strongly committed college or university, preferably one with a congenial campus atmosphere.

Once government funding lapsed around 1982, most of the programs either faded or changed their program structure and dropped the Newgate name. Several of them were incorporated into existing prison higher education programs at their host facility, without the therapy and support services component, as was Minnesota's when administrative and instructional services reverted from the University of Minnesota to St. Cloud State University.

Newgate was in its way a grand experiment. Program moneys were available then that may never be duplicated. The mood of the times was right. Perhaps the single lesson to be learned is that support services for the inmate-student are important and go a long way toward ensuring success for students who, for the most part, had consistently failed in traditional educational endeavors. In spite of the end of Newgate, however, once postsecondary programs had begun in prisons, they continued.

PRISON HIGHER EDUCATION INSTRUCTIONAL SYSTEM

Colleges and universities employ one or more of the following delivery methods for their prison programs:

- Distance education, including both televised instructional services (TIS) and correspondence courses;
- On-site education, in which the course of instruction is provided at the facility;
- On-campus education, in which the student is allowed released time (such as work release) from his or her facility to attend specific classes or make supervised trips to the college or university to take regularly scheduled classes.

The first two delivery methods are by far the most popular and widely used for prison education. The third poses a number of difficulties, especially for inmates who are not housed in community security housing or halfway houses, or who are assigned to some form of house arrest. Supervised trips to campus are frequently at the inmate's expense, if they are allowed at all, and are obviously not within the financial means of most inmates.

The Oklahoma Department of Corrections (ODOC) experimented with supervised trips to campus in a few selected cases, but abandoned the effort due to the difficulty of supervising inmates while on campus and the apparent conflict of interest generated by having an inmate pay an off-duty correctional officer to supervise him or her. However, no problems ever came to light as a result of the experiment, and inmates still occasionally pay off-duty officers to escort them to funerals of family members. The concern was that one unfortunate incident could lead to the cancellation of the arrangement, thus jeopardizing the Department of Correction's entire prison higher education program. For better or worse, most correctional administrators and programs operate on a belief that a low-profile approach is best and that publicity is almost always negative.

There is, in addition, a fine line between what the public may consider a sound program and what the public may perceive to be an "exotic" program. For instance, I found while working in one northern state that cross-country skiing is considered an acceptable activity for inmates to engage in, while downhill skiing is not. Both involved skis and snow; however, the public's perception of the two activities was vastly different. Downhill skiing was considered to be a luxury not everyone could afford to engage in, much less inmates, while cross-country skiing was considered to be a healthy exercise—work, in other words. Likewise, attending college in prison by means of on-site classes or distance education will generally be considered acceptable by the public. It is highly likely, however, that the majority of the public will consider released time from a correctional facility to attend on-campus classes as exotic.

DISTANCE EDUCATION

Distance education is least likely to disturb current social attitudes about what prisoners are supposed to be and do. Distance education is a family of instructional methods in which the teaching behaviors are executed apart from—at a distance from—the learning behaviors, leaving communication between teacher and learner to be facilitated by means of mechanical, print, electronic, or other devices (Garrison 1989).

Distance education perhaps originated as early as the 1720s, as noted in references to correspondence education. Certainly by the 1830s, correspondence education existed as simple correspondence between teacher and pupil. The term *distance education* came into popular usage in the 1970s and is international in its use and appeal. Distance education has long been a vital part of the educational scene in the Australian Outback, for example. A second definition of distance education suggests that it is a form of study at all levels not under continuous, immediate supervision of tutors present with their pupils, but that nevertheless benefits from planning, guidance, and teaching from a supporting organization (Holmberg 1990).

In many prison higher education programs, students' only educational opportunity is via distance education. For example, the Oklahoma Department of Corrections (ODOC) has relied almost entirely on distance education, specifically televised instructional service (TIS), from the inception of its postsecondary educational programs.

Oklahoma TIS began as a result of Senate Bill 452 of the 1970 Oklahoma legislature. The bill authorized the Oklahoma State Regents to establish and maintain a system of televised instruction as an integral part of the Oklahoma State System of Higher Education. In 1975, TIS classes began at the Oklahoma State Reformatory (OSR) at Granite. From there the program spread.

The Oklahoma State Regents for Higher Education Televised Instructional Services provides TIS classes to 10 ODOC facilities around the state. A courier service for the exchange of homework, examinations, and other course materials was originally established to complement class instruction, a service now handled through the mails. Off-campus extension (correspondence) courses are offered at six ODOC facilities. Correspondence courses can be taken at any facility within the ODOC if the education staff is willing to ensure and monitor test security. Staff members, in addition to inmate-students, are eligible and frequently participate in courses alongside inmates. Higher education enrollment for the fall 1992 semester within the Oklahoma Corrections System was approximately 300. Twenty staff members also enrolled. Twelve institutions—one private, six state universities, three state colleges, and two junior/community colleges—offer TIS courses that include the humanities, social sciences, business, education, criminal justice, and vocational education.

The ODOC had put 103 computers in service throughout its educational program by the fall of 1992. The computers were purchased with funding resulting from direct legislation approved by the Oklahoma legislature. All of the computers are used for adult basic education and GED courses. None of the computers are used by or programmed for higher education purposes. A review of the available prison higher education literature seems to confirm that computers, while in use in a number of prison education programs, are not in widespread use as dedicated tools for postsecondary education.

The American Association of Community and Junior Colleges forecasts increased cooperation among colleges to enlarge the educational experience of those currently not well served by institutions of higher learning, including ethnic groups, minorities, and prisoners (Rossman 1992). Early on, as prison higher education expanded, it appeared that community and junior colleges were more aggressive and flexible in working with correctional departments to develop postsecondary educational programs. Four-year colleges and universities seem to have become much more involved during the 1980s and early 1990s, however. Distance learning makes it relatively easy for all types of institutions of higher education to share their curriculums with inmate-students. From a review of the sparse literature available, it appears to me that it would be fair to say that two-year colleges are more flexible about providing on-site correctional facility instruction to inmate-students. For whatever reason, more on-site instructors seem to have come from two-year institutions, while more distance learning courses seem to be generated by four-year institutions. With the expansion and proliferation of computer-assisted instruction, satellites, and CD-ROM informational sets (Rossman 1992), the early trend may yet even itself out.

The limitations of TIS and correspondence instruction, particularly in pursuit of a technical four-year degree, could be summed up by the experiences of an Oklahoma inmate who for several years had assiduously pursued a degree in mathematics. Mark R., as he shall be called, had taken every TIS and correspondence basic preparatory and mathematics course offered by one Oklahoma university. He had completed all of the courses the university would allow by TIS or correspondence—algebra, business calculus, and some trigonometry—but was unable to progress further. Mark had even written the Mathematical Association of America for assistance and suggestions as to how he might proceed. He had not at this writing received a response. Mark was listed as a senior, but one with no hope of completing his curriculum under the present circumstances.

Mark R.'s conundrum is not an uncommon one for inmate-students pursuing instruction and degrees in technical and scientific fields. Much of the problem is due to the difficulty of offering courses that require laboratory work where expertise with highly technical equipment is required. While it is commonly accepted that Americans in general lack education and training in science, mathematics, and highly technical fields, those academic areas have for the most part been denied de facto to the majority of correctional students. Unfortunately for inmate-students, those areas also may have offered some of the better opportunities for employment once they are released from incarceration. Mark continues to borrow and buy mathematics books and study them in his off-hours in the hope that his situation will change. Further exacerbating his problem is the fact that the ODOC property matrix only allows three cubic feet of personal property at a time. As Mark said at the time of the interview, math books tend to take up a lot of space.

Not all of the postsecondary education programs in Oklahoma serve ODOC inmates. Redlands Community College in El Reno serves the Federal Correctional Institution at El Reno (FCI-EL Reno, a level-four federal prison; Leavenworth Federal Penitentiary, by comparison, is designated a level-five institution). For the fall 1992 semester, Redlands counted 85 inmate-students as having been enrolled and taking classes, eight courses offered on-site and eight courses via telecourses. Courses are selected using inmate surveys. Associate degrees are offered in business administration and psychology. Approximately 12 students graduate per year.

Donna Diaz is the college coordinator at the Lexington Assessment and Reception Center (LARC), Lexington, ODOC. She exemplifies concerned, aggressive correctional higher education involvement. From 1989 through the spring semester of 1992, the LARC college program graduated 50 students, including 31 Associate of Arts, 17 Bachelor of Arts, and two Master of Arts. A few of the graduates were staff members from LARC and a neighboring ODOC facility. All of these degrees were earned via TIS and correspondence. None of the inmates had the opportunity to attend a regular college classroom during their matriculation. This might have been seen by some as evidencing a flawed and incomplete educational process, and so it might have been. It is likely, however, that whatever the students lost in quantity and quality of information, they compensated for in determination and tenacity, also useful qualities in college graduates. It is not an easy task to earn a degree of any kind in this manner as the inmate-students themselves will likely be the first to so attest. They all undoubtedly would have preferred to attend regular classes during the quest for their degrees, but they did the best they could with what was available to them.

ON-SITE EDUCATION

Wolford and Littlefield (1985) reported that the majority of postsecondary educational programs studied were conducted on-site at the correctional facility. Only 3 percent of higher education programs for inmates reported that classes were held on campus; 13.5 percent of the programs surveyed indicated that the courses were provided by means of correspondence, tele-courses, and other electronic means. That left on-site instruction as the most widespread method of delivering higher education programs to recipients. One of the less publicized aspects and advantages of prison higher education is that of acculturation. As Cioffi (1981) pointed out, inmates are simply unaware of many social, cultural, and intellectual events that much of American society takes for granted. Inmates do not need to be patronized by avant-garde pedagogues, but they do need to develop awareness of a wider world and its expectations and realities if they are to succeed after release. One of the strengths of an on-site program, whether staffed by full- or part-time instructors, is that inmate-students have the opportunity to experience didactic materials firsthand, rather than through the electronic media or print. Secondarily, but perhaps as important, the students share to a full degree the college experience described by Cioffi. Throughout all of the on-site college experiences, teachers have the opportunity to role-model as well as to teach. As important as knowledge is in this context, the milieu surrounding the educational experience is of almost equal importance.

Schell (1981) comments on the sense of fraternity that he found to be important in his prison college courses. He believes that this feeling made in-class work more successful than in conventional campus teaching situations. Whetstone (1981), who was an inmate-student at the time he wrote, substantiates the sense of campus fraternity to which Cioffi referred. My own research likewise confirms the sense of campus camaraderie within the LARC educational program (Lawrence 1991). This perhaps unexpected finding seems to have been one of the more important by-products of an on-site prison educational program, be it remedial, secondary, or postsecondary. This is especially true when one considers the atmosphere of mistrust and outright paranoia that permeates virtually all prisons. To engender a positive milieu such as that within a prison program of any type is indeed a remarkable achievement.

Groucho Marx once commented that he did not wish to belong to a club whose standards were low enough to admit him. Prospective inmate-students frequently feel the same way about a college program that would admit them (Pittman and Whipple 1982). Inmates have notoriously low self-esteem, so it is a task of the first magnitude for an instructor to convince them they can succeed at college-level work. It is a nurturing process in the beginning, reemphasizing the importance of the student-teacher relationship in the first few semesters of postsecondary study.

Potential instructors are often intimidated or just plain turned off by the prospect of teaching inmates in a prison. The realities of doors and gates clanging shut behind one on entering a prison are often more than some can tolerate. Others simply believe that inmates are undeserving of higher education. One TIS instructor stated at the beginning of a course offered to the inmate-students at LARC that he did not believe that inmates ought to have the advantages of his services and that if he had his choice they would not. He was only teaching them, he stated in no uncertain terms, because it was his job to do so and because he had no choice in the matter. As destructive as the beginning was, the inmate-students proceeded through the course. The difficulty was that the instructor would not interact with any of them. He simply ignored their requests for clarification and assistance throughout the semester while interacting with those students he knew were not inmates. As a result, the inmate-students simply had non-inmate members of the class ask their questions, a deplorable but necessary subterfuge. As unconscionable as this attitude may seem to some, it is not as atypical as one may suspect. Fortunately, such attitudes are in the minority and most prison higher education teachers provide positive role models and useful instruction.

ON-CAMPUS EDUCATION

Like Project Newgate, the Hagerstown (Maryland) Junior College Prison Program (HJC) attempted to make a transition between prison and the streets, using the college education program as the bridge. The program, which began in 1969, has been suspended. Nevertheless, the formula is worth repeating. The program was authorized by the Maryland Correctional Training Center (MCTC) to offer programs in accounting, business, and administration of justice. An HJC prison liaison coordinator worked with the MCTC to screen inmate students for the privilege of attending on-campus classes. Released students were selected using guidelines established by correctional classification personnel, correctional education personnel, and the college. The college MCTC release guidelines are typical of most programs of this type:

- Travel to and from campus is to be as quick and by as direct a route as possible;
- All activities and classes are to be held on campus;
- Inmate-students are not allowed to receive visits or conduct personal business while on campus;
- Illegal chemicals cannot be possessed or consumed while on college release;
- Students are to attend all scheduled and approved classes, to contact the facility if classes or activities are canceled, and to conduct themselves in a courteous and responsible manner at all times;
- Students are to follow all other institutional and college rules and regulations (Parsons 1982).

The HJC program, like the ODOC experiment recounted earlier, operated on relatively simple ground rules, but with a tremendous leap of faith. Correctional officials were required to trust that inmates would honor their agreement to attend classes and not embarrass themselves or the administration in the process. The HJC was asked to trust that inmates would not take advantage of an open setting with more freedom than they were used to, and that the public and other students would at least tolerate free-world students and inmates attending class together. The inmate-students were asked to demonstrate that, when given the opportunity, they could function as they would be expected to once they were finally released from incarceration.

What caused the HJC program to be suspended by the Maryland Department of Corrections is not known and is perhaps no longer important. What is important is the realization that this type of program had proven itself to be especially susceptible to even minor turbulence in the winds of politics, the so-called Willie Horton effect. Willie Horton murdered someone in Maryland while on furlough from a Massachusetts prison. The case gained national attention in 1988 when the Bush campaign successfully used it as an example of Michael Dukakis' stand on criminal justice. Such anecdotal cases are often pivotal to the success or failure of correctional policy. Future on-campus programs, therefore, continue to require patience, attention to detail, commitment on the part of all parties, and the understanding that nothing is forever.

DEGREE OF SUPPORT FOR PRISON HIGHER EDUCATION

The ODOC operational budget for fiscal year 1992 was approximately $189 million. Its educational budget for salaries, equipment, and supplies was more than $3.8 million. Add to that figure another $193,000 from federal funds for chapter I and adult basic education and the total amount available to the ODOC education program for instructional purposes was just under $4 million. This represented approximately two percent of the total operating budget, even though not all of the funds came directly from the state. Unfortunately for the college-run programs, virtually all of these funds were earmarked for secondary or remedial purposes. The only monies that could be said to have been devoted to higher education were the salaries of the ODOC college program coordinators and the supplies they were allocated. In spite of this, the ODOC Board of Corrections Report for September 1992 counted 316 inmates as having participated in postsecondary TIS and on-site educational offerings (Oklahoma Department of Corrections 1992).

The only state that can claim to earmark more than five percent of its correctional budget to education is Texas (11.4 percent); the national average reported by Ryan and Woodard (1987) was approximately three percent. The average expenditure reported by the respondent states was $4.4 million, and the mean representation of the respondent's inmate population participating in postsecondary education was 4.8 percent. This figure was boosted, however, by small states with high percentages of involvement (Wyoming with 21 percent and Nebraska with 30 percent). Following were: Kentucky, 11 percent; Kansas, 10 percent; and Texas, Illinois, and South Dakota, with about 9 percent each. Most of the rest of the respondents clustered close to or below the 4.8 percent mean.

Lack of financial support is not an uncommon problem for prison higher education programs. Correctional departments tend to funnel their personnel efforts and relatively meager correctional financial support into secondary and remedial education with the expectation that higher education can for the most part fend for itself. This attitude on the part of correctional administrations is not as unfeeling as it might seem at first glance. Literacy tends to be the first priority of correctional education programs. Chronic prison overcrowding also tends to soak up any additional funds that facilities and departments might have. The reality is that prison higher education programs are required to depend heavily on grants (particularly Pell Grants), scholarships, and the good offices of institutions of higher education to survive. The New York Department of Correctional Services, for example, has made it clear that while it supports prison higher education programs, it will not finance them. New York inmates are expected to pay tuition costs themselves or arrange for financial aid through routine state and federal tuition aid programs (Morrison 1984). That expectation seems to be fairly universal among prison systems.

To help compensate for the lack of higher education resources, especially for those students confined to receiving instruction at their assigned institutions, the use of inmate and volunteer tutors was developed by a number of programs. The Hagerstown (Maryland) Junior College (HJC) Prison Program, for instance, formalized use of inmate-tutors for those students needing assistance by involving those students who were proficient in particular subjects. Three criteria were used to determine assignment of inmate-tutors: student request, instructor's recommendation, and monitoring of grades by program staff (Parsons 1982). The ODOC has likewise made use of student and volunteer tutors over the years. By October 1992, the ODOC had trained 600 inmate-tutors, of whom 195 were active. Although few of the tutors assisted in the higher education program as tutors, many of them, who were postsecondary students themselves, assisted with GED and adult basic education programs at their respective facilities (ODOC 1992).

Montgomery College (Maryland) and the Montgomery County Detention Center's Model Learning Center have been involved with one another since 1975. Courses offered in 1983 included: English grammar, techniques of reading and writing, algebra, psychology, sociology, criminology, speech, anthropology, economics, business law, American history, and computer science. Perhaps more important was the volunteer program. Volunteers were active in the areas of one-to-one tutoring, group lectures and instruction, pre- and post-GED instruction, and street law. The latter course was presented in conjunction with the Montgomery County Bar Association and included lectures on patent and family law, as well as other related legal subjects (Baughman 1983).

It has been suggested that over time selected long-term inmates—especially those who might be incarcerated for life with no possibility of parole—might be educated and certified as teachers. They could then assist other inmate-students, as would a staff teacher, and make their own lives more productive and meaningful. A special inmate pay plan for such inmate-teachers would provide added incentive and might help fill the need for qualified instructors at all levels (Unger and Buchanan 1985).

SUMMARY

A summary of the scope and diversity of prison higher education programs shows that three major educational approaches have been used throughout the 20- to 25-year history of these programs. They are on-site education, on-campus education, and distance education.

On-site instructional programs, whether provided by full-time or part-time instructors, seem to be most widespread and regarded most favorably. This is for good reason. On-site classes offer a greater opportunity for instructional interaction between students and teachers. They enhance opportunities for role-modeling on the part of instructional staff, as well as providing an opportunity for students to develop a sense of campus fraternity and camaraderie. On-site programs prove to be more diverse because they also have the option to offer distance education where and when appropriate. That combination, in effect, potentially provides the student with the best of both educational approaches. On-site programs, while often lacking the benefits of technical equipment and laboratory facilities, still deliver a wider range of subjects and approaches than do most distance education courses. Colleges and universities appear to be more likely to honor the integrity of courses required for major fields of concentration leading to the granting of a bachelor's degree when they are taught in person, especially in technical fields. It seems more likely that instructors who teach on-site classes do so because they want to, not a small consideration in reaching what had been a previously unreachable population.

Distance education is often used to supplement on-site and on-campus programs. In the case of Oklahoma, however, it was until recently the sole means of instruction. Distance education has been a viable method of overcoming geographical barriers for both the general educational and prison populations. Without it many students both in and out of prison would have been left out of the higher education process. With the addition of electronic aids such as satellites and CD-ROM, both TIS and computer-assisted education have been enhanced and will be more so in the future. Distance education has suffered from its limited ability to exchange communication and ideas. Large classes, broadcast to multiple sites, further reduce this communication. Distance can also amplify prejudices and allow instructors the opportunity to disregard unwanted students.No matter how interested and involved distance educators are, it can also be more difficult for them to apply the personal touch that may make the course more meaningful to the student.

On-campus educational opportunities are the least used of the three major programmatic approaches in correctional higher education. The ability of an inmate-student to participate in on-campus instruction and have access to all of the facilities and support services available to other students undoubtedly is the zenith of prison higher education. The difficulties associated with implementing an on-campus program are daunting for those who undertake the task. Gaining permission and acceptance of all of the necessary parties, as demonstrated in the case of the HJC program, was a complicated and tenuous process at best. Supervision of on-campus inmates, where required, is difficult and not likely to be very effective. The specter of a correctional officer waiting for his or her charge outside of a classroom door, for example, can be unnerving to students and instructors alike. Temptations presented to the inmate in such a scenario are considerable. Those dangers, perceived or real, tend to place the burden of program integrity on inmate-student selection and classification processes. The dangers that such a program appear to pose to correctional and educational administrations are great. Typically it is believed that more is at risk than the fate of an inmate-student. Whole educational programs are felt to be in jeopardy should even one unfortunate incident occur, with accompanying media coverage.

Certain problems plague most prison higher education programs. Prison programs at any level frequently suffer from a high turnover of students. Some of the turnover is due to inmates losing interest in the program, some is due to disciplinary actions, and some is due to the high rate of institutional transfer endemic to most correctional systems.

A second difficulty plaguing most prison higher education programs lies in curricula. Programs seem to form around the availability of courses nearby colleges or universities are willing to offer. Like "Topsy," curricula and major concentrations are not so much born as they "just grew up." Because of that dynamic, most prison education programs have a decidedly liberal arts flavor with few science, mathematics, or technical courses offered.

Criminal justice concentrations abound. Whether or not that is due to the simple availability of these courses or some more deep-seated belief that inmates ought to be interested in a system that, for the most part, controls their lives is unknown. Following release from prison, what jobs are available to those former prisoners in the field of criminal justice? Police agencies tend to have outright prohibitions against hiring convicted felons, not to mention the fact that the 1968 federal gun control act prohibits felons from possessing a firearm—which by federal definition could include even being in the vicinity of one. There are few jobs within law enforcement that ex-offenders can perform without the need to handle firearms, and the resistance from regular law enforcement personnel to hiring ex-offenders is overwhelming.

An opinion seems to be growing on the part of some prison higher education theorists that there may be a philosophy developing that holds that inmates require a specialized curriculum for them to succeed. Certain groups, women for instance, have experienced periods in their educational history where others believed that they were not quite capable of mastering a standard curriculum. Hence the feeling that a modified course of study was more appropriate for a given group developed. This may in part explain the abundance of criminal justice curricula found throughout prison higher education programs. Unfortunately for prisoners with degrees in criminal justice, once free their only viable outlets are in the areas of higher education, research, and writing. Consequently, institutions offering prison education programs need to give greater consideration and planning to course and degree offerings for this population. Inmate-students frequently have to deal with limitations placed on them in the form of a lack of availability of certain types of classes, but much of the curriculum limitation inmates face is probably situational and not the result of a minimalist design. Motivated inmates, like motivated free-worlders, can successfully negotiate any curriculum made available to them if given the opportunity, encouragement, and means to do so.

Wolford and Littlefield (1985) report that approximately 93 percent of respondent colleges and universities offering postsecondary instruction to inmates have been doing so for less than 15 years. Prison higher education is a relatively recent enterprise in the overall American educational scheme. There are hundreds of colleges and universities providing course work and thousands of inmate-students participating in those courses. Arguments justifying postsecondary education for inmates on the basis of reduced recidivism—not returning to prison once released—continue to be made. Taylor (1992), for instance, is of the opinion that paying for education is cheaper in the long run than incarceration, along with all of the measures that it takes to catch and keep individuals against their will. He reviews studies that found that inmates who had earned an associate degree prior to release from prison were, one year after release, employed at almost double the rate of those inmates who had been high school dropouts. Although studies such as these may or may not prove anything substantial about the true worth of correctional higher education, they are nevertheless encouraging.

As a former correctional administrator, I believe that not enough emphasis has been placed on the positive aspects of prison higher education, regardless of whether an inmate ever earns release from prison. Taylor (1992) comments that studies of the impact of prison higher education also indicate that racial and ethnic divisions, a primary cause of tension in prisons, are reduced among prison college populations. The advantages of inmate-tutors, and perhaps even inmate-instructors, has been chronicled earlier in this chapter. The benefits of higher education for those staying within prison populations may in the long run be easier for investigators to demonstrate than the benefits for those inmates who have been released. Langenbach, North, Aagaard, and Chown (1990), for example, show that disciplinary actions are reduced for those inmates actively engaged in educational programs. Data for studies involving incarcerated populations generally provide for easier access and are less problematic than those requiring long-term tracking of released offenders. For those who may be in search of fruitful arguments in defense of postsecondary prison educational programs, data on incarerated students may prove helpful to offset recidivist-based arguments.

Part of this chapter has been devoted to the dangers and stresses placed on facilities and staff involved in prison higher education. Inmates also are often placed in stressful situations as a result of involvement in higher education programs. Programs of this type do not reflect the values of the larger inmate population, and in fact are often in conflict with them. As a result, those inmates involved in such programs need to be nurtured and protected to a certain extent. Inmates have to learn to tread the narrow path between education goals and ideals and the mine field of prison life. Inmates, for the most part, will be more aware of this reality than will staff, but inmates can occasionally forget, too. It is incumbent on the education staff to remember the reality in which their students live and to protect them from themselves when necessary, especially in the early stages of the process when the inmate-student is particularly vulnerable.

Historically, correctional administrations on the whole have shown themselves to be very conservative, so it should not be surprising that a conservative approach would be applied to higher education programs as well. Of all of the correctional educational focuses—remedial, Chapter I, adult basic education, GED preparation, secondary, and postsecondary—postsecondary has been the most controversial and has appeared to many to have the least amount of justification attached to it. A cautious, slow-going approach may not have not been as unfeeling, poorly thought out, or unrealistic as it may have seemed to some. In many instances it may have protected inmates by not placing them in situations with which they could not cope, or worse, situations that might be taken away just as they are on the verge of an educational renaissance. However, that caution should not become atrophy.

Three Programs for
Human Renewal
· · · · · · · · ·

EDITOR'S INTRODUCTION

Prison higher education has, in many respects, been the product of a narrow, albeit important, focus: Provide this group of nontraditional students the opportunity to take college-level courses for which they might earn credits and, eventually, college degrees. Opportunities for learning and growth, however, need not be limited to this form. At one prison in Massachusetts, for example, Boston University organizes a regular Poetry Reading at which outside poets and prisoners—without regard to educational background—share in the reading of original works. At another facility, prisoners come together with the support of independent academics to publish a journal on alternatives to current criminal justice policy. The writers who have contributed articles to this chapter offer glimpses of a few of the many possible approaches to fostering growth and renewal among those in confinement.

Art and the creative impulse, like learning, have always played a role in prison life. William Cleveland writes about a unique effort to heighten that role: California's Arts-in-Corrections program. This program, initiated in 1977 as a pilot project called the Prison Arts Program, sought to bring together working artists and prisoners in order that the latter might "gain the satisfaction of creation rather than destruction . . . ." The fact that the program has come to be thoroughly integrated within the prison system and now operates in every one of California's 23 adult correctional facilities is indeed a remarkable accomplishment, offering strong support for those who believe that programs of human renewal need not be structured in opposition to the correctional policies that structure confinement. During a single year, 700 faculty artists and 8,000 prisoners participated in the program.

Two other articles are included in this chapter. Nancy Johnson describes a project that grew out of a master's degree program in American Studies. *Concrete Garden* is a publication that began as a yearbook and continues to be published annually. It includes poetry, fiction, drama, essays, and monochrome artwork by inmates in the New York Correctional Facilities. Second, Sheila Stevens' straightforward account of the Library program at the Massachusetts Correctional Institution at Norfolk includes the statement that "reading is probably the most popular recreation in this prison—perhaps in all prisons." Stevens writes of one library program located in a single facility; what she reports coincides with the observations of many higher education faculty and staff who work within the prisons. In an age in which only one out of every 20 adult Americans read a complete book each year, what she reports about library usage and the role of literature in the lives of prisoners is remarkable.

When men and women are confined for periods of 10, 20, or more years, they do their best to create as rich a life as possible within the structure of confinement. Indeed, incarceration is survivable only to the extent that prisoners can find ways in which to thwart the deprivations it exacts. The prison offers few outlets for the talents and creativity of those held captive there. It may be easy for prison higher education programs, preoccupied with the difficult task of delivering course work in a hostile environment, to overlook the myriad possibilities for offering opportunities for prisoners to use what they have learned within the prison. Higher education has typically judged the success of its efforts in terms of lessened recidivism or what the prisoner does once released from confinement. However, given the average length of time of incarceration in this nation, we may do well to focus on outcomes that can be realized in the structure of confinement.

· · · · · · · · · · ·

California's Arts-In-Corrections: Discipline, Imagination, and Opportunity

by William Cleveland

. . . .

Arts-In-Corrections (A-I-C) makes use of the creative processes to raise inmate self-esteem and lower institutional tensions. Participation in A-I-C fine arts activities allows inmates to acquire skills that are socially acceptable expressions of individuality and that demand self-discipline and long-term commitment.

California Department of Corrections administrative manual, 1987

I wrote myself out of prison, silence, and heroin addiction. Creativity has the power to rearrange lives. Writing has transformed me. I am not the "wimp" that used to whine at every little obstacle in my path. I am a proud, productive black woman striving to become an artist.

A-I-C "Graduate" Linda Harvey, from testimony presented to the California Task Force to Promote Self-esteem and Personal and Social Responsibility

INTRODUCTION

In the early 1970s, opportunities for arts education and appreciation were beginning to diminish throughout the United States. In response, many professional artists began to look to society's forgotten members for a new constituency. Working with patients and prisoners through institutional programs offered an alternative opportunity for artists to contribute to a

William Cleveland is an author, arts administrator, and musician. He directed California's Arts-In-Corrections program from 1981 to 1989. He is currently the director of the Center for the Study of Art and Community in Sacramento, California. His book, *Art in Other Places: Artists at Work in America's Community and Social Institutions*, was published by Praeger in 1992.

society that many felt was turning its back on its arts community. The emergence of these programs provided a challenge to society's preconceptions about the power of the creative processes—a challenge that was as related to the issue of survival as that of aesthetics.

As part of the institutional art movement, many artists and arts organizations succeeded in developing programs in state and federal prisons. In California, the pioneering work of Eloise Smith and the William James Association proved the value of the creative process to inmates and prison administrators alike. This effort eventually led to the creation of the largest residential arts program in the country, the California Department of Corrections Arts-In-Corrections program (A-I-C).

THE PRISON ARTS PROJECT

In 1977, the nonprofit William James Association initiated a pilot arts program at the California Medical Facility at Vacaville. The project was funded by the California Arts Council and the National Endowment for the Arts, the San Francisco Foundation, and the Law Enforcement Assistance Administration (LEAA). Dubbed the Prison Arts Project (PAP), the project provided a faculty of professional artists, supplies, and equipment to more than 250 inmates at the institution who became regular participants during the two and one half years of program activity. Program offerings included music, ceramics, creative writing, jewelry making, and leather work.

The PAP approach was as simple as it was revolutionary. The program's originators began by acknowledging that whether or not it has been encouraged, art has always been part of prison life. Their idea was to meld this historic creative presence with the fine arts model of excellence, risk taking, and discipline. The resulting hybrid would provide a safe and supportive environment for the outlaw to learn from the creator to "gain the satisfaction of creation rather than destruction, earn the respect of his fellows, and gain recognition and appreciation from family and outsiders" (William James Association 1977).

The professional artist was seen not only as a source of expertise and information, but as an example of achievement. The professional faculty members were consciously presented to inmate art students as models of self-discipline and independence. The Prison Arts Program offered participants an opportunity to exert a degree of control over a small corner of their lives in exchange for commitment and hard work. These activities were available to all mainline inmates as a leisure time activity on a first come, first served basis. Also, because of the recent passage of determinant sentence statutes, PAP participation would have no bearing on release dates or sentencing.

The program's rigorous work ethic was as alien to prison life as were the artists who instituted it. Teaching artists were told to demand the kind of persistence and adherence to standards that characterized their own work. This was done primarily through the introduction of short-term, hands-on projects that were often collaborative. Verne Stanford, the PAP Vacaville coordinator, felt participants would have to learn to associate work with something positive before they acquired the confidence they would need to accept the risks inherent in creative exploration. Because this was the way they approached their own work, the project-based approach was very comfortable for the faculty.

Many corrections veterans saw this approach as naive, even dangerous. The program's early history proved them wrong as inmates responded enthusiastically to both the program's subject matter and its inherent demands. After early wrangling over space and scheduling, institutional officials grudgingly acknowledged that something different was going on with the inmates involved with the program. It was clear that a high percentage of participants were sticking with the program and that many of the inmate art students were spending increasing amounts of personal time studying, practicing, and rehearsing. From the administration's point of view, this meant PAP students were less likely to become involved in illegal and/or disruptive behavior.

For PAP faculty and administrators, the intense commitment exhibited by many of the program's students confirmed their belief that the study and practice of art could insinuate a "positive addiction" into the prison environment. The arts faculty were seeing some of the most disruptive and least motivated inmates at Vacaville commit to a new kind of work. The more they worked, the more they learned. The more they learned, the more they invested in the success or failure of their efforts. For most of the PAP students this was a new experience. For some, the exercise of creativity opened a door to the development of a personal sense of self-worth quite different from that normally available in California prisons.

ARTS-IN-CORRECTIONS

The Vacaville pilot sought to prove not only that the introduction of fine arts into the correctional environment could improve the quality of the prison experience, but that it was in the best interest of the Department of Corrections to supports its expansion. The first step in that direction occurred in 1979 when the California Arts Council and the Department of Corrections jointly funded an interagency liaison to explore the development of additional arts programming. Then in July of 1980, the state legislature, through an augmentation of the Department's budget, appropriated $400,000 for a departmentwide Arts-In-Corrections program.

With the establishment of the Arts-In-Correction program, a unique public/private partnership had borne fruit. The initial funds provided the country's first civil service prison arts faculty chairs, called artist/facilitators, for six of the state's 12 prisons and a program manager position to coordinate the statewide program. Also included were monies for bringing in a multidisciplinary arts faculty and contracting with community arts organizations for performances and workshops, as well as funds for supplies and equipment.

CURRICULUM

The program's expanded curricular design evolved from the unique pedagogy that drove the original pilot project. Both Eloise Smith and Verne Stanford believed that artist-centered teaching provided the best opportunity for engaging inmates in the creative processes. This approach focused on artist-driven projects that emphasized process and collaboration. Although structured and sequential lessons did find their way into the curriculum, they functioned more as a support mechanism for the widely varied projects artists brought with them from their own studios and stages.

Given this fairly unorthodox educational approach, the larger program was purposely organized outside the purview of the Department of Corrections' Education Department. This was done, in part, to ensure that the state's credential requirements would not get in the way of A-I-C's hiring the state's most accomplished fine artists. It was also done to protect the program from the territorial wars that are typical of the correctional milieu.

As with the original Vacaville Prison Arts Project, the departmentwide effort needed time and experience to establish itself as a responsible and creative part of the correctional environment. After three years of operation, inmates and staff responded to the program's quality with increased confidence and cooperation. This growing acceptance gave the program's management and faculty the confidence to begin gradually introducing an organizational model that was a radical departure from the Department's traditional top-down hierarchy. Rather than mandate a statewide programmatic formula, the institutional artist/facilitators were encouraged to operate as directors of California's twelve prison arts schools. This decentralization of authority dramatically expanded each program's potential for diversity and innovation.

This orientation allowed the lead faculty to take maximum advantage of local arts resources and develop curricula and programs that responded to the needs and capacities of their particular institutions and inmate populations. As a result, different sites developed unique curricular strengths and programmatic orientations. The California Training Facility, for example, became a "music joint," at times supporting more than 30 different ensembles. Under the influence of choreographers Sara Elgart and Myrna Garwyn, modern dance became a fixture at the California Rehabilitation Center, where the first ever men's correctional modern dance company was established. The influence of the visual arts could be found throughout the state but was particularly strong at northern California institutions such as San Quentin, Folsom, and the California Medical Facility at Vacaville. San Quentin's lineup of classes for the third quarter of 1989 is shown in Table 1; it offers a good example of the curricular variety available (Arts-In-Corrections Quarterly Report, Third Quarter 1989).

TABLE 1.

SAN QUENTIN'S CLASS LINEUP, THIRD QUARTER 1989

Class	Instructor
Animation	Peter Crosman
Drawing	Lorraine Garcia
Visual Arts Criticism	Lorriane Garcia
Painting	Lorraine Garcia
Visual Arts on Condemned Row/cell study	Patrick Maloney/Joan Thornton
Jazz Workshop	Aida de Arteaga
Music Theory	Aida de Arteaga
Nigerian Drumming	Malonga Casquelord
Rhythm and Blues Workshop	Stephen Herrick
Creative Writing (Prose)	Judith Tannenbaum
Creative Writing (Poetry)	Floyd Salas
Drama	George Burrows
New Vaudeville Circus Arts	Sara Felder

The program also sponsored several special projects: The Oakland Interfaith Choir performed for 500 inmates in the dining hall. The concert was documented and broadcast by CBS (Charles Kuralt) and SQTV. Inmates participated in a mainline visiting room mural project, in which four four-by-eight-foot portable mural panels were completed and installed. Finally, artist Lorraine Garcia worked with the condemned row mural team to complete three murals for the Marin County Abused Children's Center.

FACULTY

The artists, musicians, dancers, writers, actors, directors, and craftspersons that made up the faculty of the Arts-In-Corrections program were highly regarded practicing professionals. Many were considered stars on the outside. Visual artist Jonathan Borofsky, writer Carlos Fuentes, concert pianist and lecturer Lorrin Hollander, actress Ruby Dee, video artist Gary Glassman, and choreographer Sarah Elgart were typical of the caliber of the more than 150 artists involved in the program.

Involvement with A-I-C brought such artists face to face with a raw and sometimes unsettling culture—a culture that only respected outsiders for their abilities and had no cognizance of current trends and forces at work in the art world. Artists working in the program had never confronted clients who asked them for proof of their technical ability before they would accept them in the role of teacher.

For professionals engaged in the highly competitive and often unrewarding struggle for artistic survival, this highly unusual standard of value was both threatening and refreshing. Many who accepted the challenge relished the chance to establish respect on the basis of their skill and knowledge—a respect, that for those who persevered, clearly ran both ways. These artists came to know that they would be taking out as much as they brought in. They recognized that rather than introducing a cultural community in prison, they were joining one.

For some artists, the A-I-C experience also offered a creative rebirth. Teaching in prison gave them a place to reconnect with what one artist called his "original passion for communication and service." After the initial shock, gaining respect in prison proved to be a uniquely valuable and empowering experience for a majority of the faculty, so much so that the supply of quality artists vying for A-I-C positions far outstripped the demand.

RESEARCH

It is difficult to measure the impact that arts programs have on social institutions. However, for the A-I-C program to survive and grow during the politically conservative 1980s, it was absolutely necessary to document the program's impact in terms of the Department's overall mission. The A-I-C research effort began with an analysis of the program's comparative costs and benefits.

Cost/Benefit Analysis

In 1983, a cost/benefit analysis of the program was conducted by San Jose State University sociologist Dr. Lawrence Brewster. In it he concluded that in the four institutions studied, the program produced 68 percent more in measurable benefits than costs. Specific evidence of reduced incident rates by art program participants was also cited. The evaluation stated that 75 percent of the participants at the California Medical Facility and 81 percent of those at the Correctional Training Facility demonstrated improved behavior through fewer disciplinary actions (Brewster 1983).

Recidivism Study

Responding to legislative inquiries, A-I-C engaged the Department's research division in 1988 to conduct a study of the program's impact on the recidivism rates of a sampling of its graduates. Parole outcomes were studied for 177 randomly selected inmates who had participated in at least one A-I-C class per week for a minimum of six months. Outcomes were studied for periods of six months, one year, and two years after release. These data were then compared to statistics compiled on the parole outcomes for all California Department of Corrections parolees for the same time periods.

The results showed that the A-I-C participants had a significantly higher percentage of favorable outcomes than did the overall release population studied. Specifically, six months after parole, A-I-C participants showed an 88 percent rate of favorable outcome as compared to a 72.25 percent rate for all department releases. For the one-year period, the A-I-C favorable rate was 74.2 percent while that for the total California parole population was 49.6 percent. Two years after release, 69.2 percent of the A-I-C parolees retained their favorable status in contrast to a 42 percent level for all releases (California Department of Corrections n.d.).

The research also showed that, as time-since-release increased, the difference between the percentage of favorable outcomes for A-I-C and all California releases became greater. The data indicated that after six months the A-I-C favorable rate was 15.75 percentage points higher than the overall rate. Two years after release that difference increased by 27.2 percentage points (California Department of Corrections n.d.).

COMMUNITY SERVICE

While Arts-In-Corrections was using the arts resources available in surrounding communities for institutional programming, many artist/facilitators were recognizing the value of giving back to the community. In the middle 1980s, various institutions began making the artistic skills acquired by inmates available to local communities. These individual projects led to the establishment of an innovative statewide prison-based public art program. This unique program, called ArtsWork, used A-I-C visual and performing arts faculty members and the program's best students as a positive resource for both prison facilities and the communities that surround them. As a result, members of more than 100 communities throughout the state have experienced prisons and the people who live and work in them as highly visible community contributors. The following are examples of ArtsWork projects.

- Inmate artists, organized as a permanent mural crew at the California Institution for Women, prepared backdrop scenery for a theatrical production by the Exceptional Children's Foundation, a Los Angeles-based program for children with developmental disabilities.
- An inmate production of Samuel Beckett's *Waiting for Godot*, was presented to an audience of more than 600 non-inmate persons at San Quentin Prison. Donated proceeds benefited Bay area victims' rights organizations.
- The combined efforts of muralists from the California Institution for Men and the California Institution for Women produced a series of permanent murals for the senior citizen center at Angeles Plaza in downtown Los Angeles.
- A joint community murals project instituted at the California Training Facility at Soledad produced 10 outdoor murals for the cities of Oceanside, Monterey, and Gonzales.

THE CURRENT PROGRAM

During the 12 years since A-I-C's establishment, the California Department of Corrections has undertaken one of the largest public works facilities expansions in U.S. history. The Department has grown from six institutions housing 24,000 inmates in 1980 to 23 institutions housing 108,000 in the fall of 1992. The true integration of Arts-In-Corrections into the Department's infrastructure is evidenced by the fact that all 23 California prisons operate a fully functioning arts program complete with a full-time artist/facilitator, permanent classroom and studio facilities, and a multidisciplinary faculty. The Department's prison construction standards also mandate an arts facility and appropriate program resources for each of the seven new prisons slated to be built during the next five years.

During the 1991-92 program year, over 700 Arts-In-Corrections faculty artists provided more than 100,000 hours of instruction to 8,000 inmate participants. Through these classes, inmates received instruction in painting, dance, ensemble jazz, graphic design, video arts, computer animation, paper-making, improvisational theater, poetry, clay sculpture, and 136 other creative disciplines. During the same period, 361 performances by inmates and outside professional music, dance, and theater groups were provided to an audience of more than 20,000 inmates and staff. The year also produced 22 publications of poetry and prose and 43 public art projects created by ArtsWork crews for California State Correctional Institutions and surrounding communities (California Department of Corrections 1992).

After 12 years of growth and increasing stability, the program's mission remains basically the same as it was when it began. The program's role as a provider of arts programs in California prisons has been to make available a place where possibility and choice and skill are rewards for those who accept a personal responsibility for their own success or failure. The program's goal has been to improve the prison experience by providing participants with an opportunity to affect their own environment and begin changing their attitudes about themselves and others.

Current Arts-In-Corrections manager Jim Carlson believes that the program's goals must be tempered by the realities of prison life. Writing in a recent A-I-C exhibition catalogue he reiterates the program's mission with this firmly in mind:

> It would be naive to believe that the creation of one or two pieces of art is going to markedly alter one's value system overnight. It has been our experience, though, that over time each step forward in the personal struggle for mastery and completion in the artistic process is a small down payment on a new and solid sense of respect for one's self and one's fellows. The vast majority of our participants will not become "artists," but many will retain the capacity for self-discipline and self-sufficiency. For some, these modest steps are a life changing experience (Carlson 1989).

Concrete Garden

by Nancy Johnson

· · · · · · · · · · ·

Concrete Garden came into being as a vehicle to publish the work that was being produced by the participants of the American Studies master's degree program. The first issue was designated as a yearbook for the first graduating class of the program. It featured academic work, research papers on which the students had worked. Because the first issue of *Concrete Garden* was considered a yearbook for the graduating class, it carried only their work. The students really enjoyed seeing their work in print; it was a tangible object that was readily available for public consumption.

Concrete Garden was so successful with both the students and the community of people interested in the criminal justice system that we decided to continue the project. As editor, I decided to refocus the next publication's forum as a creative outlet for original fiction, prose, and/or poetry. The submission response we received from the students was overwhelming. The work we reviewed was professional and very creative.

The extent of the students' desire to be published in *Concrete Garden* was not evident until I turned down a submission I felt was not suitable for publication. The story lacked the quality of writing manifest in the rest of submissions that I had accepted. I notified the student that his writing had not been selected for publication, and he in turn wrote back the following impassioned letter:

> Simple messages and yet they are profound messages because they were
> sent from this dark hole of pain and anguish where character is more often

Nancy Johnson, a Native American, edits the *Concrete Garden* at the State University of New York at Buffalo.

destroyed rather than made; where adulthood is forged in the crucible of mental/emotional pain; where screams are often muted by concrete walls and stereotypical thinking. Think again of the story and messages.

From despair, I direct attention to hope. From indifference, I direct attention to concern. From loneliness I direct attention to love. From this hell, I direct attention to dreams. Without dreams, we are nothing!

This story was designed to become a beacon of light to push back the darkness of fear, despair, loneliness, bigotry, sexism and self-loathing.

I thought the letter was an excellent piece of writing. I met with the student and negotiated. I would include his piece if he would agree to work on it further. We worked together on rewrites, and while it was not as good a piece as I would have liked, his willingness to work on it and his desire to be included in the publication became more important than the end product.

A Prison Library

by Sheila Stevens

· · · · · · · · · · ·

The Massachusetts Correctional Institution (MCI) at Norfolk is a medium-security prison for men located about 30 miles southwest of Boston that houses approximately 1,300 inmates. Built in 1931 as the Norfolk Prison Colony, it was an experimental prison for convicted felons who had shown by their behavior in other Massachusetts prisons that they were capable of functioning well in a community setting. Security was achieved by enclosing 35 acres of land within a concrete wall 5,000 feet in perimeter and 19 feet high. Eighteen housing units, an administration building, and a school building were built by inmates under staff supervision. The housing units featured rooms instead of cells, with each unit accommodating up to 35 inmates. Two wings were added to the administration building: One was a hospital where inmates' illnesses were addressed and the other was a disciplinary unit where those found guilty of rule infractions were sent for varying lengths of time. The disciplinary unit did have cells, and those remanded there lost privileges until their release.

The school building housed the libraries, which were operated by inmates supervised by school staff. In 1977, two professional librarians were hired to coordinate and supervise library operations. The law library began on a modest scale in the 1940s. By 1980, under the guidance of a professional law librarian, it had become a definitive prison law library and a vital function in the prison, fulfilling a legal mandate to allow inmates access to the courts.

The general library, also headed by a professional librarian, was patterned on a small public library, with up-to-date nonfiction and fiction, a reference

Sheila Stevens is a librarian at the Massachusetts Correctional Institution at Norfolk, Norfolk, Massachusetts.

collection, and various bibliographic tools. An author-title-subject card cata-
log and a shelf list were established, and standard library operating procedures
were put into effect. Over the years, Norfolk's inner security has been
tightened, but it still retains much of its early colonial atmosphere. Now, as
then, the libraries are the only areas of the prison where inmates may go freely
without presenting a movement permission pass issued by security staff. The
general library's primary mission is to provide inmates with recreational
reading in the form of books, magazines, and newspapers.

The 6,500-book collection is added to annually, sometimes modestly,
sometimes generously, depending on fiscal considerations. LSCA grants,
awarded and dispensed by the Massachusetts Board of Library Commissioners
and totaling more than $60,000 since 1970, have allowed the library to
update the reference collection, to provide library services to the segregated
units previously without library services, and to purchase a 2,000-book
Hispanic collection.

READING

The library subscribes to 43 popular magazines, six of which are in Spanish.
We receive three daily and 17 weekly newspapers. Three are Spanish-
language weeklies, one is Asian, all are donated. Although there are always
some inmates who read only newspapers and/or magazines, most progress to
books when they see or hear about something that interests them.

Reading is probably the most popular recreation in this prison—perhaps in
all prisons. It is a very personal activity and, in an environment where there is
no privacy, a very private one. Unlike movie and TV viewers, who are mainly
observers, many readers of fiction become participants in the stories they read.
Few say that in so many words, but it's obvious when they talk enthusiastically
about the books they've read. Between the lines of their remarks they reveal
the satisfaction they find in the company of characters who, whoever they are,
are not the people they must see and mingle with every day. And the locales,
wherever they are, are not *here*. It amuses inmates to come to the library and
ask for some "escapist" literature but, in fact, that's exactly what it is.

Some inmates wrap up their sentences or go out on parole, then reappear in
this library at some later time telling me they've missed the last one or two
books by a favorite author and are anxious to catch up. Clearly, they stopped
reading as soon as they hit the street. Now that they're back, reading will again
become an important part of their lives.

STUDY AND RESEARCH

The second mission of the general library is to provide books and research materials to students of the MCI-Norfolk Adult Training Center, which offers classes in ESL, pre-GED, GED, and precollege, and works with the higher education institutions that offer college courses leading to a B.A. in liberal arts. Some graduate courses are offered. Nine inmates have received M.A. degrees since 1990.

Students receive books and handouts in class, but for research tools and supplementary reading they must rely on the general library. The nonfiction collection must be kept up-to-date, as must the Social Issues Research Series (SIRS), a series of articles on 32 subjects, reprinted annually from a large cross section of periodicals and journals. To meet the students' needs for materials not available in the general library, the librarian maintains cordial relations with staff at local public libraries, where an average of 70 books a month are allowed to be borrowed on interlibrary loan (ILL). Students fill out a specially designed ILL request form with author and title, or subject. They use a somewhat out-of-date, but still useful, set of *Books in Print* to help them with their selections. Usually twice a month but sometimes as often as once a week, depending on the number of requests, the librarian takes these requests to local public libraries and checks them on the computers and on the shelves, filling about 25 requests per trip. Five years ago, this library was invited to become a full participating member of the Eastern Massachusetts Regional Library System. As a result, titles not found at local libraries are sent on to a subregional library, Bridgewater Public, where the requests are either supplied from that library's collection or sent by computer to other subregional libraries. If a request still remains unfilled, it is sent to the Boston Public Library, the library of last recourse. The general library's fill rate for ILLs is 95 percent.

About a third of our ILL requests come from students. Another third are submitted by fiction lovers. It is not uncommon for inmates to return books they enjoyed and, at the same time, submit a sheaf of requests for titles by the same author that were copied from the panel of the book. Many carry with them their own lists of books they plan to read, crossing the titles off carefully as they finish them, adding when another book or author comes to their attention.

INDEPENDENT LEARNING

The remaining ILL requests are submitted by those pursuing independent learning. As dedicated as those enrolled in formal classes, and as determined, are the inmates who follow a personal course of study and request books on numerous subjects. In the past 10 years, we have supplied books on airplane piloting, shipbuilding, horticulture, cooking, raising pigeons, blueprint reading—and many, many more. For the past two years, two inmates have been studying yachting together, from a total of 21 books that were supplied through interlibrary loan. One inmate has been reading books on the feminist movement and just recently asked for a book on menopause so that he can understand what his wife is experiencing. I once had to explain why I was bringing into a men's prison a book on pregnancy and childbirth. It was for one of our new inmate clerks who was about to become a father. He went on to request books on infants, and then toddlers. When he was released two years ago, his daughter was five years old, and he couldn't wait to get home and put what he'd learned into practice.

The young African American men in our population are interested in reading books about African American history. The autobiography of Malcolm X has been particularly popular here at MCI-Norfolk, where Malcolm spent several years as an inmate in the 1940s and 1950s. In the book, written in collaboration with Alex Haley, Malcolm describes how he copied a dictionary from A to Z in an effort to improve both his handwriting and his vocabulary. Starting with the word *aardvark*, he worked slowly and painstakingly long into the night copying words and definitions into notebooks. After dramatically improving both his handwriting and his understanding of the words, he spent hours here in this library reading the "Harvard classics." These books, originally donated in the 1930s, have always been especially popular among members of the African American community and are more so now because of renewed interest in Malcolm and his life. Recently a young African American said to me, "What would happen if I read every one of those books?" pointing to the Harvard classics. I told him he'd be well on his way to giving himself a classical education. He looked toward the books with wonder, even awe. Then he smiled. "A classical education, huh?" he said, and went over to the shelf to select one of the books.

As part of an MCI-Norfolk rehabilitative program designed to encourage positive interests and activities as opposed to self-destructive ones, the librarian oversees a continuous reading program. The inmates sign up for eight-week segments but may sign up for succeeding segments as long as they are in the program. We average about 25 inmates per segment. They are asked to read for at least one hour a day and to keep a daily reading journal, which they bring to the librarian once a week for review. They may choose books on any subject available in the library. Because prison inmates have few options— they are told when to rise, how to dress, when to eat, and when to go to bed— this matter of choosing is particularly important, and the participants approach it carefully. Most interesting are those who say they have never read a whole book and are obviously reluctant to commit themselves now. They peruse available titles with little enthusiasm while they answer the librarian's questions about their hobbies and interests. Then they brighten and reach for a book—for one it was a biography of Sitting Bull with a picture of the chief on the cover; for another it was the mystery of the Bermuda Triangle—and, perhaps, another book lover is born. When the man who selected the book on the Bermuda Triangle expressed surprise that there was a book on the subject, he was assured that there were many books on the subject as well as on almost any subject he could think of. He left the library looking pleased and thoughtful. There's a pleasant postscript to this story: Both of these books have been in constant circulation ever since. These two men, who may not even have known each other, recommended the books to their friends, who recommended them to others. It is not surprising that this happens frequently among regular readers but when it happens among new readers, that's progress.

Those serving long prison sentences may take up reading as a way to pass the time, but as reading becomes more important to them, they can be seen to progress to more scholarly books. Eventually even those who have steadfastly ignored the offerings of the MCI-Norfolk Adult Training Center will begin to make inquiries about school courses. Fifty-three percent of the men come here with neither a high school diploma nor a GED. After interviews and tests are given by the Training Center staff, they are placed at appropriate levels.

I have seen inmates change with each educational success. Their attitudes change. Their priorities change. They even change physically, carrying themselves with more self-assurance. A 42-year-old library clerk about to receive his B.A. said to me, "You know what an education has taught me? It taught me empathy." He had dropped out of school in the ninth grade and had many brushes with the law before this incarceration. He started working on his GED and just kept going. He worked here for several years and I came to know him well. Believe me, he was totally sincere. He was released three years ago, a different person from the man who came in.

When MCI-Norfolk was built it was planned that the school and the libraries would be valuable and valued resources for inmates who hoped to go back into society better equipped to cope than they were when they came in. They *were* valuable and valued then, and they remain so.

Two Views of Conflict and Accommodation

. . . .

EDITOR'S INTRODUCTION

The initial act of accommodation between higher education and the prison occurred in their mutual willingness to create the new and perhaps ambiguous social role of prisoner-college student. In so doing, both institutions were equally in conflict with their own generally held social beliefs about what it means to be a prisoner. The relationship between higher education and the prison turns on their respective attempts to make the fact of prison higher education and prisoner-college students appear rational within their institutional realms and the larger society. Conflict and accommodation permeate the relationship between higher education and corrections. They are in conflict to the extent that higher education symbolically redefines prisoner-college students in ways that contradict the symbolic definitions that make up the goal of incarceration. Accommodation and integration take place when one institution adjusts or expands the scope and diversity of its symbolic redefinitions in order to embrace rather than contest an inherently contradictory pattern of belief.

Osa D. Coffey, a nationally recognized expert in the field of corrections, addresses prison higher education from the perspective of corrections. She acknowledges that the prison has historically failed as a means of reducing crime, reforming criminal offenders, or providing offenders with the skills requisite for a productive life after incarceration. Although higher education, in her view, has a vital role to play in helping corrections achieve the varying demands society places upon it, that role will remain unrealized without a significant increase in the level of accommodation and cooperation demonstrated by higher education faculty and staff.

Coffey argues that corrections and higher education must present a united front in supporting educational opportunities for prisoners by doing the following: (1) increasing knowledge of criminal justice and criminals, (2) learning to better deal with correctional officers, (3) developing more appropriate curricula and curricular rationales, (4) formulating standards of admission and achievement, and (5) coming to terms with the risks inherent in misuse of Pell grants.

Although it is easy to agree with the general spirit of these recommendations, they must be approached with a measure of caution. Some present significant philosophical problems, and others appear to be based on assumptions about the institutional nature of higher education. Should higher education adapt to the very philosophy and practice of corrections that is associated with the prisons' failure to rehabilitate offenders? Should curriculum rationales reflect general social beliefs about prisoner-students, or should they reflect a desire to transcend those beliefs? And, given that open admissions and remedial programs are among the hallmarks of the community college in the general society, is it really problematic that many prison education programs also have both open admissions policies and a significant commitment to remedial courses?

George Carey counters Coffey's view of prison higher education from the standpoint of corrections with a view from higher education. In "Conflict and Accommodation: A View from Higher Education," he cites many of the same tensions noted by Coffey. His reflective piece is anecdotal, moving from specific experiences to a subtle yet compelling refutation of many of the conclusions reached by Coffey. Is it possible, in fact, that higher education sees corrections more clearly than corrections sees itself? Carey, for example, does not condemn correctional officers who oppose the education of prisoners, but rather sees their opposition as the product of systemic features of the prison. If the prison has historically functioned to degrade human beings and failed to produce the "requalified citizen" that the eighteenth-century Reforming Jurists envisioned, should we accept or reject the "correctional" wisdom upon which that failure has been based?

Are prisoners less able students? Against the notion that prisoners are not quite as capable as students in outside college classrooms, this experienced senior professor speaks of the "great many very smart people who are biding their time behind all that mortar and barbed wire." He cites examples that speak not of the need for standards of scholastic achievement, but rather of the fact of achievement that rivals that of his on-campus students. Against the notion that specialized curricular rationales ought to be developed, Carey implicitly suggests that the need for such rationales does not exist within prisoners themselves, who are not different-as-students from other students. Carey sees prison higher education as providing prisoners with increased opportunities for learning and self-improvement. Therein lies the essential essence of the tension between higher education and corrections: Should higher education simply provide prisoners with an opportunity to learn, or should it shape the possibilities of learning to conform with correctional wisdom about what a prisoner ought to be?

• • • • • • • • •

A View from Corrections

by Osa D. Coffey

· · · · · · · · · · ·

Introducing a college program into a correctional facility is like bringing a new, young, sophisticated spouse home to meet your blue-collar family living in the shabby part of an old company town. You expect the old folks and other relatives to be impressed, welcoming, accommodating, proud, and grateful; instead, you end up deeply hurt and surprised when they react with fear, envy, suspicion, even hostility. "It will never work," both parties soon say. And, of course, it won't—unless both sides want it to work, give one another plenty of time to get to know and understand one another, and make the necessary efforts and compromises. And, of course, it *can* work. After awhile it might even work so well that everyone acknowledges that this new marriage led to benefits for all. Furthermore, in retrospect everyone will see that the marriage was inevitable, once the barriers between the small world and the large had been breached. But before that point has been reached, the road could have been terribly rocky and the marriage could have failed.

Higher education and corrections is a mixed marriage that needs to happen and needs to succeed. To be successful, it requires that corrections accepts that inmates have a right to educational opportunity, which can best be provided on the higher levels by a college, and that the college community accepts that correctional facilities within their geographical area are indeed part of their mission. By combining their efforts, corrections and higher

---

Osa D. Coffey is a consultant for education and criminal justice. She provides technical assistance to federal, state, and local jurisdictions; courts; and private organizations in the area of educational/correctional programming. She has been project director, Corrections Program, U.S. Department of Education, as well as superintendent, Virginia Department of Correctional Education.

education will not only humanize the prison environment and make it more conducive to positive change but will increase the likelihood that those who leave the prison will not return but will become productive citizens. The prison/college linkage is, therefore, of utmost importance not only to the parties involved but also to society.

It is well known, and need not be belabored here, that most offenders have a dismal record of school performance, work experience, and economic self-sufficiency at the time they become incarcerated. Corrections alone, and punitive correctional philosophies alone, have by now proven beyond doubt to be inadequate to the tasks of stemming crime, preventing recidivism, or returning to society in any large numbers individuals ready to go to work and take care of themselves and their families. Even correctional agencies that provide basic skills, GED, and vocational programs for their inmates are inadequate to these tasks because most of the jobs generated by today's and tomorrow's labor markets require at least another year and a half of education and training beyond the 12 of high school completion (Johnston and Packer 1987). The higher education community is increasingly and desperately needed to fill that gap. Yet, it often has to fight to get into prison, fight to stay in prison, fight for inmates to retain Pell Grant eligibility so that they can pay for their education, and fight negative publicity generated by legislators, the media, and the general public.

Despite the uphill battles, correctional postsecondary programs have proliferated since the first college program was introduced into a prison in 1953 (Wolford and Littlefield 1983). Today, an estimated five percent of the almost 800,000 inmates in state and federal prisons are enrolled in postsecondary academic and/or vocational programs (Cohen 1991; Norton and Simms 1988; Ryan and Woodard 1987). Since the federal government first provided money for prisoner college programs in 1967, in its demonstration Project Newgate, and with the subsequent flow of Pell Grants and state grants, a substantial investment has been made by society in college education for inmates (Seashore et al. 1976). This investment, however, has remained controversial. During the last reauthorization (1992) of the Higher Education Act, for example, Pell Grants for inmates barely survived, and new restrictions were imposed barring inmates with life sentences and those on death row from participating. Should the federal government withdraw Pell Grant privileges from inmates, 38 percent of all prison college programs would disappear overnight, probably with serious impact on recidivism and at great cost to society (Coffey 1982). It is interesting to note, however, that while the future of inmate Pell Grants was hanging in the balance in U.S. congressional committees, colleges were lobbying and advocating Congress on behalf of inmates, but correctional systems—which stood to lose the most—were silent and passive. There should have been a partnership and a united front. To date, neither corrections nor the higher education community has been effective in selling college education for inmates to the public, legislatures, and the media. As a matter of fact, those who work in postsecondary education in correctional institutions often have a tough job selling their programs to their own college community as well as to correctional staff.

This chapter is based on the premise that the correctional system needs a closer linkage with the postsecondary community and more of the services it can provide. It is also based on the premise that postsecondary education can—and has proven that it can—contribute substantially toward the habilitation, socialization, empowerment, and job readiness of inmates and to reduced recidivism, at substantial cost savings to the taxpayers (Ayers et al. 1980; Blackburn 1979; Duguid 1984; Taylor 1992; Thorpe et al. 1984; Werner 1990; Zimring and Hawkins 1988). The first and to date most substantial evaluation of prison college programs (that of Project Newgate and some other early postsecondary prison programs) found a number of positive effects. Although the study was inconclusive in terms of any impact on recidivism, it did show that graduates experienced increased employment, job stability, and continued schooling, along with less alcohol and drug abuse. According to the researchers, "The most important finding to emerge from the research is that prison college education programs pay for themselves" through increased tax dollars (Seashore et al. 1976). However, over the 40 years of experience with postsecondary prison programs, there has been a paucity of research and an even greater paucity of solid research. Furthermore, there has been inadequate dissemination and use of the small body of good research that does exist and that strongly indicates that prison college programs can reduce recidivism, increase employment, and substantially more than pay for themselves through increased tax revenue and reduced costs for crime, unemployment, and welfare. This failure to increase research and heed findings continues to do injustice to both corrections and higher education, and only a closer partnership will ameliorate the situation.[1]

---

[1] There is great controversy over recidivism as a measure of correctional education program success. I believe that it is an inappropriate measure in terms of basic academic and vocational programs. Although the programs are necessary as a base for further education and training, they do not yet provide an adequate base for employment. Furthermore, they may not provide adequate training in cognitive or higher reasoning skills. These programs should be measured strictly in terms of the achievement of educational goals and standards. Higher education, however, and particularly as supported by Pell Grants at considerable cost to American taxpayers, needs to be measured—as one measure only—as a cost-effective approach to keeping offenders from returning to prison. Hence, in this case I believe that recidivism is an important evaluation variable.

This chapter is primarily addressed to college staff charged with the
responsibility of setting up and running a college program in a prison setting
who are new, or relatively new, to the job. It will, perhaps, also be helpful to
those who are experiencing problems in their current relationship with
correctional staff and to correctional staff charged with the responsibility of
facilitating and supervising college programs. This chapter addresses selec-
tively a few critical problem areas that affect not only the prison/college
relationship but the support for prison higher education programs from the
general public and the federal government. The focus is on five problem areas
that seem to pose the greatest obstacles to successful prison college programming. These are: (1) the inadequate knowledge of college staff about criminal
justice, criminals, and, most of all, the correctional environment; (2) correctional line officer resistance to college programs for inmates; (3) inadequacies
and lack of rationales in the selection of college curricula in prisons; (4) lack
of equity in standards and expectations between prison and college campus
programs; and (5) the risks involved in the inappropriate use of Pell Grants for
inmates.

These observations and points are derived from practical experience and a
rather unique perspective. I served for several years as superintendent of the
Virginia Department of Correctional Education. This agency is unique in the
United States in that it is the only totally separate state agency set up to
deliver education programs to all adult and juvenile correctional agencies in
the state. The Virginia Department of Corrections functions as the landlord,
not the boss, of the adult correctional schools. In this unique setup, the
Department of Correctional Education served as a mediator between corrections and higher education in the course of bringing postsecondary education
into the institutions. In the process, we worked with eight different colleges;
only one, Southside Virginia Community College under the leadership of its
president, John Cavan, was at the time both experienced in and totally
committed to a mission in corrections (Gendron and Cavan 1990). One
private college, Mary Baldwin College, offered to bring a humanities model
into the Women's Prison and did so successfully. The others had to be enticed
and cajoled into corrections, with varying degrees of success. As I worked with
these colleges, I became increasingly aware of the need for not only a mediator
but an interpreter between corrections and higher education. At the start,
there were a great deal of misconceptions on the part of both as to the other's
mission and goals, operational procedures, philosophy, and role in corrections. Only through a process of communications and negotiations were
corrections and higher education able to reach a point of mutually supportive
operations and maximum benefits to all—inmates, college and correctional
staff, and taxpayers. The suggestions made in this chapter are based on the
experiences gained during that process.

KNOWLEDGE OF CORRECTIONS

Correctional institutions are often at the opposite extreme from colleges and universities. The former are closed, often hidden in a state's backwaters, seldom visited by the general public. They are organized into military hierarchies, emphasize discipline, foster conformity and obedience. Security, hence control, is their main concern. On the other hand, colleges are wide open, often the center of a community, the hub. They foster inquiry, free speech, individuality, and growth. They often appear undisciplined and disordered. Knowledge, and empowerment through knowledge, is their main concern. Thus it is not surprising that when two such totally different institutions try to join in partnership, problems will occur. Correctional staff often believe that outsiders, such as college staff, neither know nor understand corrections and are thus likely to create problems or endanger security when they come into correctional facilities. Quite frankly, they are often right. Although most people know something about college life, most know virtually nothing about prisons. It is, therefore, essential that all college staff who are to work on a prison college program become informed about corrections, both generally and specifically. Deans, even college presidents, should visit the prison and the warden before starting programs and assigning instructors. They should learn firsthand about the particular problems and concerns of the correctional administration. Overcrowding, litigation, budget cuts, staff turnover and vacancies—these are problems that prison administrators have to handle every day and that impact enormously on the entire institutional operation, including education programs.

College administrators should be willing to allow instructional staff adequate time and pay for preservice orientation and training and negotiate with corrections for the provision of some of that training. The more college staff learn about corrections, the better they will be accepted by corrections and function well in a correctional setting. Colleges with criminal justice departments could use their own staff for some introductory presentations of information about criminal justice and criminals. However, the more important thing is for college staff to listen to all kinds of correctional staff—counselors, teachers, correctional officers, psychologists—and visit all areas of the correctional facility, not just the education area and library. The goal is to get a basic understanding of how the institution is run, how inmates move within it, how the correctional clock of shifts, counts, distribution of medications, and meals ticks. The instructional staff members also need to learn about the con games before they are conned. They need to know the staff on the correctional side who can either help or hurt the program. All of this preparation takes time on the part of both the college and the correctional facility. Colleges need to invest in staff who are full time and committed to the program in the long run. Unfortunately, many colleges use mostly adjunct instructors in their prison programs. No doubt many of these are excellent instructors, but they seldom have the kind of time and commitment that make them fully vested in either their college or corrections.

Security is by necessity a primary concern of correctional staff, and college staff members need to be aware not only of the rules pertaining to security but the rationale for these rules, which are seldom as arbitrary as they may seem to outsiders. In Virginia lock-downs, in which all inmates were confined to their cell blocks, inmate movements were restricted, and programs were temporarily shut down (usually for a few days but sometimes longer) occurred fairly frequently. During this time, cells were searched for contraband. Had college staff members known the history of violence in Virginia prisons and the extent to which lock-downs reduced that violence—with the result being increased security for everyone, including college staff—they may have had a different attitude toward them. Correctional staff, on the other hand, needed to have a better system for notifying the college as soon as a lock-down had occurred to prevent its staff from driving the frequently long distances in vain. This is but one example of the need for both communication between the two bodies and a system of developing knowledge and understanding on the part of college staff for correctional operations.

DEALING WITH CORRECTIONAL STAFF

One of the most frequent complaints from college personnel in prisons is that correctional officers are neither supportive nor cooperative, and are frequently downright hostile and obstructive. Yet, for a college program in prison to work, the cooperation of correctional staff—especially correctional officers—is absolutely necessary. If not, as many have found out, students will not arrive on time, classrooms will not be open, equipment will not be functioning. Often these small acts of sabotage are a nonverbal expression of officers' negative attitudes toward college programs for inmates in general rather than toward any one program or instructor.

College staff should try to understand the underlying reasons behind this resistance in order to work out strategies to overcome it, vest correctional staff members in the college programs, and gain their support. Correctional officers are not required to have college degrees. As a matter of fact, it was not too long ago that correctional officers did not even have to have a high school diploma or a GED. Most come from urban and rural working-class communities. Many come from homes and communities where college education is neither common nor easily obtained, nor, perhaps, a high priority. Many, however, would like college education for their children but find it hard to do so on correctional officer pay. Their law-abiding children are usually not eligible for

Pell Grants and often have to work their way through college if they get there at all. Correctional officers often feel that inmates "get something for nothing" and do not "deserve" a college education. It is not hard to see why correctional officers so often feel envy and resentment toward inmate college students and the college providers. They also frequently perceive the better educated inmates as a particular threat to their authority and self-esteem, and they often believe—unfortunately, often justifiably so—that college staff looks down upon the entire correctional officer profession. They further often perceive college instructors as dangerous liberals or "bleeding hearts," who see inmates as victims rather than perpetrators and take their side against the correctional staff.

Prison college administrators and instructors need to become very sensitive to these issues, invite open discussion about feelings and perceptions among correctional staff, and develop strategies to overcome the resistance to and resentment of inmate college programs. The first step is to acknowledge that correctional staff have a good point. How do you justify giving a criminal a "free" college education when many law-abiding youngsters do not have that same opportunity? If you can convince a correctional officer, you can probably also convince members of the U.S. Congress. How? By doing your homework, knowing your facts, and sharing your information with them. Show them that research indicates that college-level programs have the greatest positive impact of any correctional programs on reducing recidivism and they pay for themselves over time. Show them that this saves them, as well as others, taxpayer money. Arguing that society must "pay now or pay more later" is more readily understood than arguing the intrinsic value of higher education on character, inmates' right to a second chance, or their legal entitlement to participating in the Pell Grant program. Some correctional officers, like many people in the community and in legislatures, still prefer to punish inmates by keeping them off the streets for long periods of time, and with the fewest "perks" possible—at whatever the cost. Respect the correctional officers' right to this view even if you do not share it.

There are two additional approaches to getting and keeping correctional staff support of the college programs. First, be sure that to the greatest extent possible the staff will benefit from the prison/college connection directly and personally. Many colleges provide courses for staff as well as inmates, with such additional perks as being able to take courses at the prison rather than traveling to the home college, and, if possible, at reduced fees per credit hour. Line staff who aspire to higher positions in the correctional hierarchy know that they need to work toward a degree. The days when one could rise through the ranks to become warden with nothing but a GED are over. The old "wardens" are being replaced with professionally trained "correctional managers." Most college staff have found that just inviting correctional staff to take a course with inmates is not a good idea. Officers are usually not comfortable in a class setting in which they are temporarily peers with those whom they have to control and supervise at all other times. They also fear that because the inmates have far more free time to study and often possess street smarts, they will make the correctional officers look intellectually inferior by comparison.

The second approach is to make sure, through negotiation with the prison administration, that staff members favorable to the college program are allowed to volunteer for duty in that area and are made to feel indispensable to the program. Usually, a college program assignment is considered a soft assignment, in part because inmates generally behave better in school (because they get kicked out if they don't). The atmosphere in the school area is usually much more pleasant than in many other parts of the prison, and, compared to the dining hall, yard, and cell blocks, it is a safe zone.

College education may not be a frill, but in the prison setting at least, it is a form of privilege. Unfortunately, we usually do not ask much, if anything, in return from inmate students. This is a mistake. It accentuates the feeling of a "free ride" that grates on staff and creates unrealistic expectations on the part of inmate students. Inmate college students should be obligated to pay back, in services if not in money. For example, prison college students could be required to serve as tutors in basic skills and GED classes. They could be expected to use some of their earnings toward books and materials. They should be required to work, at least part time. Behavior infractions should lead to at least temporary suspensions from the college program. Only the correctional system can make such policies; however, college staff needs to support them rather than see them as time-consuming hindrances in the education process.

THE PRISON COLLEGE CURRICULUM

Another common source for controversy in prison higher education programs is the choice of courses, curricula, majors, and degrees. Some persons believe that a junior/community college associate degree is appropriate for inmates but not a four-year or graduate degree. Some feel that courses that have a real *vocational* content are fine for inmates but not something as esoteric as Philosophy 101. Because the number of college-eligible students in a prison is finite and the range of what can be offered is equally closely circumscribed, the selection of specific prison college programs becomes extremely important. Unfortunately, many colleges, in coordination with prison staff, have chosen the path of least resistance and permit inmate interest to be the ruling, if not sole, principle in program and course selections. The result is a proliferation of business courses and psychology/sociology/criminology courses, and, more recently, computer courses. One would have to ask, for example, whether having your own business or entering someone else's business on a managerial level are realistic opportunities for a just-released inmate. It should also be remembered that the desire to enter a criminal justice-related field after release may simply be a sign of an inmate's degree of institutionalization, from which it is sometimes difficult to cut the cord.

The college, in coordination with the appropriate correctional staff, should develop a prison higher education program based on the best knowledge available, for example, research findings from scientifically evaluated college programs for inmates, labor market forecasts, etc.; only then should inmate interest and aptitude be taken into consideration. Once the program has been developed, staff must "sell" it to all interested parties—potential students, correctional staff, the media, funding sources—by explaining its rationale. Many college programs have floundered either because they tried to offer the least objectionable curriculum instead of what would be good and appropriate or because they tried to be all things to all people. After programs have established a track record, they tend to sell themselves.

It is interesting to notice, for example, that some of the programs with the best track records as measured by reductions in recidivism in scientifically designed follow-up studies are those that, on the surface, sound the least vocational and the most humanistic; they are also the least likely to have shown up on inmate interest inventories (e.g., the Canadian University of Victoria's liberal arts prison program; Duguid 1984). It is true, as Stephen Duguid has pointed out, that,

> education in prison is controversial in its own right, but a call for a focus on the humanities raises objections even among prison educators. Taking their cue from trends in education across North America, many correctional educators have focused on vocational training or academic courses aimed at occupational enhancement. This has assumed, of course, that education is in some way the same as or inextricably tied to employment preparation and further, that employability is an important factor in criminality. Both assumptions are highly suspect.

However, in a follow-up study of 65 men released from this program, all but one were employed, and most attributed this to their educational experience while in prison (Ayers, et al. 1980). Duguid deduced that "the key factor in employment may not be skills or training, but the ability of the individual to sustain a stable employment record, and that is more concerned with self-esteem, communications skills, the development of good work habits, and cognitive abilities associated with a liberal education than a result of vocational training" (Duguid 1984).

The point here is not to advocate liberal arts over vocational training, or a Kohlbergian cognitive/moral reasoning approach over behaviorism. After all, it is quite possible that the fact that the most positive outcomes of prison college programs to date are to be found in the Canadian studies is due to the greater number of serious evaluations conducted by the Canadians on humanities type programs rather than to the superiority of their approach. The point is that the college must develop its prison program *deliberately*, based on the best knowledge and resources available, then evaluate it to see whether it meets its goals. Some programs and approaches will be hard to sell, but it is much harder to sell something for which there is no real, clearly stated rationale.

STANDARDS AND EXPECTATIONS OF ACHIEVEMENT

Another common criticism of college programs for inmates is that they are not truly equivalent to "real" (i.e., on-campus) programs: Inmates do not need to meet strict requirements for admission. The programs consist of a lot of remedial courses. Inmate-students are not asked to do as much in each course as their counterparts on campus. Grades are inflated to keep inmates motivated and/or pacified. The colleges send second-class instructors to the prison, a lot of adjuncts who would never get college teaching jobs elsewhere. These are commonly heard complaints and frequently voiced suspicions. Unfortunately, these criticisms are all too often justified. Frequently, inmate-students are inadequately prepared for college when they are admitted under a Pell Grant. Many have just finished a GED while incarcerated and still have marginal reading, writing, communications, and computational skills. Many need remedial work before they take college classes, just as many students in the community need remedial courses after high school and before college. Inmates should be held to the same standards as other students in all regards, whether it be for admission, enrollment in specific courses, attendance, assignments and requirements in individual courses, or for grades and degrees. The watered-down prison college program is not only dishonest but potentially damaging to students in the long run. Many find after release, when they try to complete their degrees on a campus, that the standards are higher there than in prison and that they are unable to keep up. As a result many either fail or drop out. For an ex-offender, this kind of failure can have disastrous consequences. Only the college can keep the program honest, which means that on occasion, it will have to deny admission to, fail, or drop from the program students who do not measure up.

The inmates who, as consumers, buy a college education through Pell or state grants while incarcerated have a right to the same quality programming as students in the community, and the taxpayers who make the investment have an equal right to a fair return on their dollars.

THE USE AND ABUSE OF PELL GRANTS

The Pell Grant has been for inmates what the G.I. Bill was for returning veterans after World War II. Pell Grants have provided the opportunity for thousands of inmates to go to college while behind bars. Many of these inmates would probably not have done so while on the streets. The prison higher education programs became a turning point in many lives. I remember a mother telling me at one prison graduation, with extreme pride, "He is the first in our family to graduate from college," then adding wistfully, "Too bad it had to be in a place like this."

The Pell Grant program is critical to the provision of higher education in prisons; yet, every time the Higher Education Act is up for reauthorization, bills are introduced to bar inmates from access. But for the continuous support of Senator Claiborne Pell from Rhode Island for correctional education in general, and Pell Grants for inmates specifically, corrections might well have lost this important resource. Should inmates be barred from using Pell Grants while incarcerated, it will be primarily due to the imprudent and inappropriate use of Pell Grants by corrections and the willingness of proprietary schools and state colleges to become coopted for monetary gain.[2] Furthermore, it will also be due to the lack of any serious advocacy or lobbying on the part of corrections for Pell Grants and the frequently unwise, emotional, "bleeding heart" approach to such advocacy by the college community. Because the college is vested with responsibility for financial aid, it needs to take a firm stance in how the aid is to be used and resist pressure from corrections for less than appropriate uses.

College administrations that either already provide services in correctional facilities or are planning to do so need to develop their own policy in terms of the services they would provide in corrections under Pell Grants. They should further be aware of and understand the pressures they may come under from corrections for a variety of Pell Grant uses which—while not illegal—

---

[2] In the late 1970s and early 1980s, the prison Pell Grant program was wracked by scandals, and investigations were conducted by the General Accounting Office. Several proprietary schools that had feasted on Pell-funded inmate-students closed. Several officials from such institutions went to prison. The adverse publicity led to the introduction of three separate bills to bar inmates from Pell Grant eligibility at the time of the reauthorization in 1982. Recent activities suggest that the historical memory has been lost and that similar imprudent actions once again are putting Pell Grants in jeopardy.

basically are not in accordance with the intent of the federal act and might well jeopardize the program in the long term.

As a result of the financial constraints that have hit almost all states and the federal government, correctional budgets have been severely slashed even though inmate populations keep increasing. In correctional agencies where education is funded directly out of corrections allocations, administrators often "borrow" these dollars to pay for necessities such as food, housing, and security. Because there is no constitutional right to education for inmates and because states seldom have such legal mandates, education is frequently perceived as desirable but dispensable in a pinch. Recently, several states have seized on a new strategy—to unload their traditional (secondary academic and vocational) programs on Pell Grants through outside providers. Often these programs are not postsecondary in the true sense but admit almost anyone under a loose interpretation of "ability to benefit." For example, the state of Florida has virtually handed over the responsibility for its program to Branell College, a proprietary school that runs the program exclusively on Pell Grants. What is even more disturbing is that this "college" is an offshoot of the Corrections Corporation of American (CCA), a private company specializing in running prisons for profit. One way of cutting costs is to require students in CCA-operated institutions to apply for Pell Grants in order to participate in Branell College programs, the only education programs offered (Blumenstyk 1991). If this practice spreads, as it is likely to do, it is equally likely to lead to the abolishment of Pell Grants for inmates just as CETA programs for inmates were lost in the late 1970s due to similar abuses. College and university administrators can prevent this from happening only by refusing to be coopted by corrections in this regard.

The college program for inmates is usually the first step of a college's involvement in corrections. It need not, and should not, be the last. But much depends on the success of this first step in terms of convincing correctional staff that the college can become an indispensable partner in many aspects of corrections. Usually, once the barriers have been broken down, through mutual accommodations and through a successful inmate program, other college/prison partnerships can occur. Many states have found it advantageous to contract for a number of inmate education programs with local community colleges. For example, the Vienna Correctional Center in Illinois has contracted out of all its vocational courses to a college that, over the years, has developed one of the best prison vocational programs in the country. Some states like Washington and Iowa have successfully contracted out all of the responsibility for inmate education programs, from basic literacy programming through postsecondary, to their community college systems. In one of the institutions in the state of Washington, Clallam Bay Correctional Center, the college recently also absorbed the responsibility for correctional staff training. This move minimized any antecedent controversy over the introduction of inmate college-level programs because many of the same college staff served both inmates and staff separately.

Postsecondary education belongs in prison, whether it is invited by correctional staff and greeted with open arms or it must push its way in, making accommodations and gradually proving that it can be a great partner in a mutual effort to assist inmates in getting out and staying out. I believe with David Werner that "prison education must be removed from the punishment structure and seen as an independent force operating within the confines of the institution with benefits open to all" (1990). It can do so only when education staff members make a concerted effort to understand corrections, develop good communications, and dedicate themselves to providing the same quality programs as on any campus. Then perhaps corrections and the college community can jointly convince the public that postsecondary education serves not only inmates but the public interest as well.

A View from Higher Education

by George G. Carey

· · · · · · · · · ·

1230 hrs: A Tuesday in early May. I look out from a window on the second floor of the main building at the North Central Correctional Institution in Gardner, Massachusetts. The view to the west scans across a run of low-lying wooded hills that pile up upon one another, but my gaze is drawn not so much to the hills beyond as to what is directly below me—a dozen men planting vegetables in the two rows of 10-by-20-foot plots. From my perspective, the prisoners look as if they are working on huge grave sites, but come summer their work will furnish enough fresh produce to break up the monotony of their refectory food.

Unlike the men below me, I am not doing time. I have arrived at the prison half an hour early to teach one of the three remaining sessions of a college-level course: English 386, American Folklore.

This room is my classroom. Two doors, six windows, and on the north wall a small chalkboard. That is all there is to break up the brick decor. Two rectangular tables stand athwart one another in the middle of the room. Twenty plastic chairs are set in two stacks against the east wall. Everything resonates. Whispers echo. Before the correctional institution at Gardner became a state prison, it was a mental hospital.

Back in December, I signed on to teach English 386 for the spring semester in the Massachusetts prison system. To do that I have to moonlight from my professorial post in the English department at the University of Massachusetts in Amherst. I can't say I volunteered for this job out of any high moral

---

George G. Carey is professor of English at the University of Massachusetts, Amherst.

purpose. I am not a reformer by inclination, though I am aware that reform has been at the heart of prison education in this country ever since the Quakers opened the first prison school at the Walnut Street Jail in Philadelphia in 1798. Nor was money the inducement. Four thousand dollars to teach one session each of English 386 at two different prisons doesn't exactly bounce one into another tax bracket. I undertook the job more out of curiosity than anything else, the challenge of teaching individuals with a different set of associations and assumptions than those I share with undergraduates. The students I encountered every Tuesday at Lancaster and Gardner—bank robbers, murderers, prostitutes, pimps, drug hustlers, rapists—provided environmental variety enough to keep a jaundiced professor on his mettle. And not a single member of either class took off for Daytona Beach over spring break.

Lancaster, 35 miles west of Boston, is a minimum-security prerelease coed institution where 200 prisoners live in a community without walls. Many of them move off the grounds daily to work. Gardner, 15 miles farther west, is a medium-security institution, heavily guarded. Here 720 men live in dormitories, not cell blocks, and at prescribed times are free to roam the grounds. But to this innocent outsider the word *medium* seems a qualifiable term. There is a great deal of security. High double fences with rolled razor wire surround the place, interrupted periodically by glass-topped turrets that provide the guards a 365-degree view. To move in and out of the prison, I must go through what is called the trap, a narrow hallway with sliding metal doors at either end. Inside the trap is a metal detector and a guard who makes sure you are "clean" before you pass into the prison proper. (On my first visit I was relieved of my jackknife and my heart pills.)

That first visit I did not teach. I drove to Gardner with Walter Silva, the prison education project director, for an indoctrination that turned out to be an hour's session with the education supervisor. He handed me a set of regulations, then led me through the dos and don'ts of the institution. Mostly don'ts. Don't bring in any contraband, don't wear large belt buckles or hats, don't get yourself into any compromising situations that might lead to a setup. Then I was given a sheet entitled "Guidelines for Hostages," things to do should an uprising occur and I end up on the prisoners' side of the defense line.

- Be cautious of heroics. Don't act foolishly.
- Look for a protected place where you could dive or roll if either authorities or inmates attempt to assault your location with force.
- Keep your cool. Attempt to relax by thinking about pleasant scenes or memories. You might try to recollect the plots of books or movies. This will help you remain functional.

Reading this list I suddenly imagined myself shoved up against the brick wall by a giant convict who has me by the throat while I'm trying desperately to recall a few lyrics from *My Fair Lady*—"With a little bit of luck, with a little bit of luck. . . ."

1255 hrs: The students begin to trickle into the classroom singly and in pairs for a class that will last two hours. They have just come from chow. At this point in the semester, there are 13 men in attendance, down from the original 18 who signed up for the course. Most of them give me some sort of greeting. Even this late in the semester I have no idea how much they are getting out of the course. Several have mentioned to me that what we've talked about in class has made them more aware of cultural diversity, others expressed surprise when they realized how thoroughly folklore was laced into their own backgrounds. I don't really feel I've done much to angle them toward hard thinking, but that says more about my style as a teacher.

The class ranges in age from about 22 to 53, not exactly your conventional undergraduate spread. Officially I do not know why any of them are in prison, but word gets around, and some of the convicts are quite frank about their backgrounds. In a brief essay I asked the students to prepare about themselves at the outset of the course, one man wrote, "I have spent the last 18 years and six months straight in prison for the death of my stepfather. The men that know me well call me [Shotgun] so we should know how my stepfather died." Others were less direct when describing their past. When I asked Bill C. what he had done on the outside, he told me that he had been in the banking business. I subsequently learned that he had stepped into a federal bank with an automatic weapon and made a withdrawal. This caper landed him an 80-year sentence, with no parole until three quarters of it is served. At 42, Bill is only a third of the way there.

Bill may have more time to do than many of his classmates, but like the others he is aware that taking courses toward a college degree can help him in practical ways. All of the prisoners know that if they complete the course, they can shorten their sentence. Some are also aware that if they leave prison with a college degree they have only a 10 percent chance of returning; with simply the high school equivalency, their chances rise to 28 percent. (A more specific example: As of 1987, more than 40 students have graduated from the Boston University Prison Program; only one has returned to prison.) Beyond that, a good many prisoners enroll simply because these courses give them a momentary reprieve from the tedium of their lives. So much time spent in prison is slack time. There are the lucky few (about 25 percent) who have secured jobs that keep them busy, but for the majority, the terrain is very flat and very boring and it stretches away, day after day to the point of release. Education offers a detour.

1330 hrs: We are half an hour into the class. It is hard to keep the students' attention this afternoon. It is May after all, pleasant outside. The windows are open. We hear the voices of the men working their gardens. My students would rather be hanging around on the grounds. To counter what I knew would be a difficult teaching day, I have brought in an article about a bizarre rite, common among burglars.

I now have their attention, or as much of it as I'm going to get. We discuss the rite of the thief's calling card, known to folklorists as the "grumus merdae." Five members of the class have heard of the tradition, but they have certainly *never* practiced it. I point out to the class something of the dissemination of this singular custom. I trace the tradition back to eighteenth-century Europe. I suggest psychological interpretations, criminologists' opinions.

1400 hrs: Most of the class is still with me. We move the discussion out to examine comparable prison traditions and rituals. One student who spent five years in "the hole" at Walpole describes some of the unspeakable practical jokes (many of them scatalogical) played on the guards in that grim setting. Another mentions the story of the prisoner at Gardner who rebelled because he thought one roll of toilet paper per man per week insufficient. He too wound up in the hole when he placed a bag of his own excrement on an authority's desk. His star has begun to rise in prison legend.

In an attempt to make students aware that folklore is available to them if they will take the time to look, I try over the course of the semester to get them to write about the customs and rituals they know best. The papers I receive tell me that these convicts, like most of us, write with conviction and clarity about their own sphere of experience. During the semester, I receive provocative essays on the routines of street gangs in Boston, the initiation rites of bikers, the rituals of prostitutes. One student provided me with a glimpse into the nether world of pimping, its economics, its protocol, even its long narrative oral poetry known on the street as "toasts." An excerpt:

> And I was known as the most adequate male,
> But I curse the day I made my play
> For that side-walking Jezabelle.
> Now she was a brown-skinned mama like a China doll
> Who walked in the ways of sin.
> Up and down she trod
> With a wink and a nod
> To the nearest whorehouse den.
> Through hail, sleet and snow
> She'd follow that almighty dollar to hell if she had to go.

From out of the tightly knit community of the institution come papers on the convict's argot and the way it changes from place to place. In Massachusetts prisons, for instance, a marijuana cigarette is a "joint," in Pennsylvania it's a "bone," while in New York it's a "stick." Likewise, Massachusetts has "fags," which in Georgia are called "girls" or "boy-girls," in Leavenworth, "homos," in New York, "bitches." Other writers turned in commentaries on the perversity of the screws (guards) and spoke with affection about the prisoners' own folk heroes.

In the Massachusetts prisons, one hero almost every convict has heard of is Walter Eliot. Back in the 1970s, Eliot was doing a life sentence at Norfolk for murder. His wife visited him regularly. When she did, she was constantly harassed by a guard who "wanted to crack on her." When Eliot got wind of this, he was furious and he had his wife smuggle in two pistols (this was before the days of metal detectors, and according to prison lore it was this event that necessitated those devices). No sooner did he have his hands on the weapons than Eliot drew down on the screws, killing two (one being the man who was bothering his wife) and wounding three others. Then he grabbed his wife and headed inside the prison, where he holed up in a building that was immediately surrounded. He had sex with his wife for several hours before he turned the gun on her and then on himself.

For the average prisoner, there is weight to the Eliot story. As one man explained:

> There are legends in our own group which encompass many qualities of the hero. I think Walter Eliot exemplifies almost all. He was a murderer, the most respected criminal in the convict hierarchy. He killed the screw who was tormenting him. He was honorable in that he stood up for the honor of his wife. He was able to get a piece of ass in the prison before he died, a way of redeeming his manhood that the prison experience attempts to deny. And he did not allow the authorities the pleasure of making someone else pay for the crime because he killed himself. His story makes a convict feel whole again and thus serves a useful purpose.

When I came into the prison to teach I expected to find considerable alienation on the part of the convicts. I did not expect them to like me at all, and at first they didn't. But I believe their bias issued from the general suspicion they have for authority in any guise, not just a distaste for educators in general. Once those initial qualms were partially set aside, I got the impression these students accepted my presence, appreciated my willingness to do what I was doing. I'm not sure I handled those initial sessions with great success, but at one level anyway, I made the class believe that all professors did not necessarily fit the stereotype.

At the indoctrination meeting in January, I had been warned about dress and how that would affect the students. Inside the prison, I was led to believe, clothes do in fact make the man and my personal image would have a great deal to do with how the prisoners perceived me. Because I generally teach in a billed cap, khakis, L.L. Bean boots, and an open shirt, it was going to be difficult to come up with this "other" person I was to drag into class. But for the first meeting I knuckled under and wore a sports coat. I introduced myself, then very deliberately took off the coat, held it up for display and said, "Now that you have seen the professorial coat, we can get rid of this crap," and I threw it into a corner of the room. There was some muffled laughter. I have no idea what this did for the students; for me it was a great release and eased my feelings of alienation.

So it was not with the prisoners I felt uncomfortable. The real alienation I encountered came from the prison personnel. I wasn't sure they wanted me to be there at all. Ever since reformers and educators have moved into the prisons with their lofty notions of rehabilitation, they have come up hard against institutional authorities whose main concern, understandably, has always been control. In the eighteenth and early nineteenth centuries it was the convict's soul the reformers were after. Later on it was his psyche. But no matter what kind of religious practice or psychological premise got talked about by those who came in from outside, it was discipline that ultimately got carried out inside. As soon as the educators left the grounds, the control curtain dropped back down.

Each Tuesday when I showed up at the front counter with my books and notes, the correctional staff met me with looks of gray, grim resignation. It was not that I expected to be ushered into the prison with flags and panoply. Nor did I underestimate the complexity of establishing the tight security necessary to keep a medium-security institution functioning smoothly. Still, I was constantly aware that my presence was in some way an intrusion, a run in the knit of institutional life. When I mentioned this to the prisoners, they nodded and chuckled knowingly—just another level of harassment, they claimed.

At Lancaster, every week two students turned up 20 minutes late to class. When I inquired about their delay, I was told that the guard in their building would not release them without official word that I was on the grounds ready to teach the course. That meant a call to the building to free these people for instruction. When I asked the class about it, they interpreted it as a kind of paranoia on the guard's part, his lingering fear that education might set the prisoner outside the ranks of "good convict." From the staff perspective, the good cons were the ones who had resigned themselves to a life without economic or social status. They were content with menial jobs, happy to spend their time watching television and talking sports. The good cons, as the phrase had it, "knew their places" (Jones 1992a). Removed from this role—and education could do that—the student/convict became a problem in arrogance and disorder, a miscreant who was tripping up the system and pretending to be someone he was not. Such deviance demanded tighter controls, more stringent harassment. From my perspective as someone trying to conduct a coherent classroom, this nonsense seemed absurd—but then again, I was working inside the institution only one day a week for two short hours.

What I came to see through this personal experiment was that it was ridiculous to take sides, though equilibrium was sometimes difficult to maintain because the inmates had my ear much more than did the correctional staff. And I was a good American; I wanted to side with those who seemed oppressed. But the point was, I was there to try and bring higher education, whatever that was, into the prison, and I had to forget about reform and rehabilitation, good guys and bad guys. If an introductory course in folklore could leave in the minds of these students some residue of cultural awareness, some sense of how traditional values had shaped their lives, then perhaps I might make the small boast of bringing illumination. But as anyone in the teaching profession knows, it is difficult to test the returns, hard to locate the impact of your endeavor except in the vacant numbers of statistical charts.

Quantifying results in education has always been a tricky business, although perhaps less so with inmates because you can simply point to recidivism and say, up or down. Still, funding for convict instruction has always been a source of controversy. It presently costs the Massachusetts taxpayer $1,300 to keep a student enrolled in the UMass/Amherst program for a semester. Justifiably, a good many people complain about the high cost of education in general and question why it is that men and women who have not treated society all that well to begin with should be allowed this free ride at society's expense. Only in retrospect did I come to recognize the jealousy and frustration some of the prison guards must have felt over this situation. Here are men and women from lower socioeconomic levels of society who dream of college degrees for their children but face the outrageous expense of such education. Each day they come to work and witness murderers, thieves, pimps, and prostitutes entering upper-level classrooms for free instruction that they, as taxpayers, are indirectly supporting. The gray, biting looks I so often got from the correctional staff may have been aimed at someone they saw as contributing to an educational miscarriage. And I must admit to some personal anxieties on this matter. Each Tuesday, on the hour's drive back from Lancaster in the early evening after a long afternoon of teaching, I'd begin to think about the $20,000 a year my daughter's education was soaking up at her Ivy League university. I'd wonder if perhaps we wouldn't have been better off if she'd gone on the streets as a teenager, hustled drugs and herself, and wound up in prison, where she could have pressed through to a B.A. and saved me $80,000. But these qualms gave way to admiration for those prisoners who were earnestly pursuing education as an instrument to something they believed would lift them out of their self-imposed quagmire. For them, the taxpayer's dollar seemed a sound investment, especially when compared to the $32,750 the commonwealth spends each year to incarcerate a single inmate.

When all was said and done, when the final grades had been tallied and sent off and I was once more secure behind the ivied walls of the academy, I kept coming back to what this educational foray into the prison had done for me as a professor. It had not, that I could see, reshaped my vision of higher education, nor would I return to the undergraduate classroom at the University of Massachusetts ready to restructure my methods or retool my curriculum based on my teaching in the correctional system. But I definitely was both motivated and enlightened by the students with whom I came in contact during the 14 weeks of that spring semester of 1989. One star in particular comes to mind.

Fourteen years ago, at the age of 19, Rich Johnson went to prison, convicted of second-degree murder. In his first four years in the system he did little besides establish himself as a hard-core convict. Then gradually as he moved from one prison to another (10 in all), he began to take isolated courses, three credits here, four there. By the time he arrived at Lancaster, where he knew he'd be spending a long stretch of time, he discovered he'd accumulated 45 credits over a seven-year period. A fellow convict in the UMass program suggested he enroll and start putting those credits to work. Within three years, Johnson had an associate's degree and most of the credits he would need for a B.A. In May 1990, he graduated *cum laude* from the University of Massachusetts. In the fall of that same year, he was released on parole and began working toward an M.A. degree at Boston University.

For Johnson, the personal impetus came from within the program, more precisely within the classroom itself. The number and range of courses offered excited him, and he found the people who taught them sensitive to the kind of education he was looking for. "Just by the fact that these professors had agreed to teach in the prison," he told me, "I had the feeling they would be different and willing to take chances in ways more conventional teachers wouldn't. I didn't want education by dictation. I wanted education by development, and most of the people who came to teach in the prison taught with that in mind."

When Rich Johnson took my course in the spring of 1989, he was near the end of his course work for the B.A. degree. He was also singularly one of the most intelligent students I have ever taught. His mind was at once receptive and analytical. No more than three weeks into the course, Johnson seemed to know exactly where we were going. And it was obvious he was extremely savvy about prison life, understanding it at several different levels. He knew full well what it could do to an individual, but it was obvious that a liberal education and some diverse thinking had helped him set aside some of the resignation that had previously ruled his life.

Though I did not discover another mind quite so finely honed as Johnson's in my short tour of duty in the prison, I'm sure there are a great many very smart people who are biding their time behind all that mortar and barbed wire. Wouldn't it be nice to think higher education might touch those minds the way it did Johnson's. For many of the convicts I taught, there is, if not the dream of immediate release, hope—a hope that the program, if it continues, may work for them the way it has for Rich Johnson—as a means to open up their thinking and help ease them back into the outside community as productive citizens. For others, there is only time.

1502 hrs: The classroom empties of all but one student; Eric C. Eric approaches me and begins to discuss a paper that was due the week before, one he didn't hand in. "I'm sorry, Professor," he says. "I meant to get to it, but I had some other things on my mind, and I just didn't have the time."

Eric is doing three consecutive life sentences for a crime I don't even want to think about as I stand alone with him in the classroom, the nearest guard a floor below us.

"No problem, Eric. Next week perhaps?"

"OK," he says, "I'll try."

Three Perspectives on the Problems and Promise of Teaching in Prison

· · · · · · · · ·

EDITOR'S INTRODUCTION

This chapter comprises three articles that relate the experiences of those who have taught within the prison. Renée Heberle and William Rose offer insights gleaned from their teaching of political science courses at two Massachusetts prisons. They came away from their experience with a firm sense of the challenges inherent in teaching within the prisons. They report on that experience, in their own words, "complicated by the inmates' particular relationship to the state, the wealth of their life experiences, their relatively unsystematic educational background, and, perhaps most insidiously, by the mostly unreflective, contradictory attitudes of those who work with the students . . . as counselors, administrators and bureaucrats."

Throughout prison higher education, the appropriate curriculum is a continuing concern. June Licence describes an experiment at the State University of New York (SUNY) at Buffalo in offering a master of arts degree in American Studies. The experiment demonstrates the difficulties of instituting, within the prison, educational programs that have no vocational focus. She succinctly describes the development, success, and ultimate end of this program for human renewal. Like Heberle and Rose, her experience within the prison was shaped in the tension between the competing missions of higher education and the prison.

The final contribution to this chapter is made by Jane Richards-Allerton, who offers a critique of distance education based on her experience teaching English in prison via the Indiana Higher Education Telecommunications System. Her contribution emphasizes the gulf between the traditional classroom and the virtual classroom of distance education, and suggests that this gulf requires significant adjustments for teachers and students alike. Neither has distance technology transcended the shadow prison security casts over the traditional classroom. Instead, the introduction of this technology suggested a whole new set of intrusions and necessary accommodations. Perhaps more important, she reports that distance technologies, as they currently stand, thwart timely student-teacher interactions, make it difficult to build the classroom rapport essential to some types of learning, and leave prisoner-students less opportunity to interact with outsiders who do not necessarily share corrections' negative assumptions about their nature and potential.

. . . .

Teaching within the Contradictions of Prison Education

by Renée Heberle and William Rose

· · · · · · · · · · ·

INTRODUCTION

We teach courses that are marginal to, yet identified with, a traditional political science curriculum (i.e., "The Politics of Law" and "The Politics of Race, Class, and Gender"). We have brought these courses into the prisons in Massachusetts. As students and teachers of politics and political theory, we tend to view social life as a highly politicized field of power relationships. In classes at the main campus of our university, the principal task is to help students understand this aspect of the social; to come to view conventional notions of politics as essentially contested, or contestable, concepts. Moreover, we strive to identify and articulate the "thick" nature of politics in the United States; we teach that the study of politics entails something more than simply understanding the nature and role of our civic institutions or the behavior of our elected representatives "out there." As teachers of politics, we constantly attempt to encourage our students to engage in a sustained and informed political study of their worlds, including the world of daily life and the social world beyond. We attempt to help them think in a critical, yet systematic, way. On the main campus, this task is often complicated by the

Renée Heberle is an instructor in the Social Thought and Political Economy Program and has taught in the Prison Education Program at the University of Massachusetts, Amherst.

William Rose is an instructor for the Prison Education Program and is working on his Ph.D. in political science at the University of Massachusetts, Amherst.

relative youth, the limited life experiences and the (often willful) apolitical nature of our students. In the prison, this task is complicated by the inmates' particular relationship to the state; the wealth of their life experiences; their relatively unsystematic educational background; and, perhaps most insidiously, the mostly unreflective, contradictory attitudes of those who work with the students in the prison education program as counselors, administrators, and bureaucrats. We take up this last element first as it is common to our experiences. We will then discuss the former points as they relate to our particular experiences.

During an orientation session for new instructors, a counselor in a prison in which we both taught, in one breath, dismissed distinctions between students on the outside and students who are inmates as irrelevant to our project in the program *and* reminded us that we are working with "rapists and murderers." We assumed at the start, and confirmed in the course of our experience in the prison, that he was wrong on both counts—which did not mean that we watered down our courses or assumed that our students were innocent of the crimes for which they were convicted.

He was wrong on the first count because, as should be obvious, whatever the academic merit of individual students, their very institutional location suggests great differences from students on the outside. First, the prison students have a much more diverse educational background than our main campus students. Many prison students matriculate into the program with GEDs and extensive work in community college prison programs of widely uneven quality. Students on the main campus generally have four years of high school education and matriculate directly into the four-year college system.

In addition, the second part of the counselor's statement points to the fact that inmates are subject to the diminished expectations of a society that comes to identify them by the fact that they have broken the law. The effects of being identified in this way, of having their lives essentially and externally shaped by the moment of criminal activity, make inmates a very unique set of students. The diminished expectations that society may have of inmates or ex-inmates are symptomatic of the deeper structures within which prisons operate to control the sensibilities not only of prisoners but of noninmates as well. We often felt ourselves succumbing in an almost physical way to a pressurized sense of cynicism about the project we were engaged in with the students.

Moreover, life in the correctional institution itself presents day-to-day obstacles to learning that teachers and students unfamiliar with the details of incarceration have trouble imagining. The lack of reference materials impedes independent, systematic research. Further, although the students, many of whom read constantly, come to the classroom with widely diverse knowledge and interpretations gleaned from many different disciplinary sources, their knowledge and interpretations are the products of random interest that seeks, but has yet to find, direction. This randomness is compounded by the generally inconsistent quality of the holdings in the prison libraries, where romance novels challenge more scholarly, if dated, texts for shelf space. Moreover, problems of overcrowding and the concomitant lack of privacy inhibit study, although the static, tightly organized prison-life schedule structures the inmates' days in a way poorly organized students on the outside would envy. Finally, the prison guards generally (and perhaps understandably) resent that "privileges" are accorded to prisoners in the shape of federal funds (usually inadequate and currently under fire from law and order conservative forces in Congress) for education that they, as state workers, may not have access to for themselves or for their children. This makes for a fundamentally different atmosphere than that which exists on campus where, presumably, every resource is put toward encouraging students to learn in the most effective way possible.

When one puts the first half of the counselor's statement together with the second half, that is, that we should not forget that the students are "rapists and murderers," one gets a sense of the inadequacy of the introduction we received from those who should know better. On the one hand, we were to treat the students neutrally, to present the material in a neutral manner, and to view our intended audience apart from the prison context. On the other hand, we were to "remember" the identity of the students as being defined by their crime and behave accordingly in the classroom.

"They are just like the other students," we were told, "but keep your guard up. Do not speak in terms of human or individual relationships." The message was always: "Students are cons and guards are blue-shirts." That left teachers as at best potential pawns (or sitting ducks) and at worst as interlopers in the fragile system of power relations constructed and reconstructed on a daily basis between cons and blue-shirts. The implicit message received on a daily basis in our interaction with the guards and DOC administrators was that we were being trained as part of the disciplinary apparatus. The desired relationship was to be "us" (corrections personnel *and* teachers) against "them" (inmates). The public message remained: "Do not treat the inmates any differently from other students."

Our discussion of the counselor's statement is not meant to imply that we believe that it is possible or even desirable to create a prison world wherein the rules are clear, the personality types complementary, and the goals noncontradictory. If that vision of what corrections should be about were even close to the reality, we would have a truly closed system of domination and delusion as to human creativity. Seen in the light cast by our discussion, the contradictions embedded in the prison system may actually sow the seeds of creativity, flexibility, and political savvy on the part of inmates and workers. The perpetual sense of negotiation of rules and power structures and the intensely fragile sense of stability makes everyone's embeddedness in a disciplined and conformist society more apparent in prison than on the outside, where the negotiations are more obscure, less overt, and in some ways, more insidious. For us, as students of politics, this was the most important difference between our experience teaching inmates and our experience teaching students on the outside.

Given this understanding of our project as teachers of politics, the many-layered significance of the counselor's statement became ever more clear as the semesters wore on. The statement characterized the contradictory attitude of the majority of the workers in the DOC educational system. It represented, simultaneously, formidable obstacles and invaluable material to us as teachers. The statement represents a classic liberal, North American attitude toward crime and corrections and gave us a framework in which to address the politics of law and the politics of race, class, and gender in the United States as directly experienced by these students in their contradictory social location as "people just like everyone else" *and* as "rapists and murderers."

TEACHING THROUGH THE EXPERIENCE OF THE STUDENTS

The course on the "Politics of Race, Class, and Gender" attempted to develop an understanding of how the politics of what we like to call "special interest groups"—African Americans, women, workers, to name a few—are critical to the political culture of our nation. We argued that our present public institutions are inadequate to the task of reconciling the contradictions exposed as these groups come to recognize themselves as political subjects and make demands as such. The course explored such contradictions and sought to teach students to think critically about the capacity of particular groups to make it, to be recognized as relevant players in the historical task of constructing a just society.

The inmates had a well-developed sense of what it meant to be used in the service of state and social welfare and control. This sense was often sharper than that of the most astute students at the university. University students may be struggling with identity crises and with how to be useful in the world, but the everyday struggle for self-determination is nowhere so sharply defined as in a prison. One can see it in action in the most transparent of ways in the prisons wherein each level of administrators—budgeting, politicking, guarding, and inmate relations—pull and push prisoners into roles, determining just what manner of self the inmate will be permitted to develop and, perhaps, leave the prison with. In the short time in which we taught this course, the rules of the game appeared to be always changing. This was primarily due to political careers being built around the image and quality of the security system in Massachusetts, but can also be attributed, at the more particular level (and this is where we focused in class discussion), to different inmates' different interactions with the system.

At a prerelease facility where the course was first taught, four women and five men were enrolled in the class. The students were generally receptive to the ideas in the class, but it was apparent that there was a certain impatience among the students with politics and with theory. A couple of different things were going on with the students in the class. These became even more clear later, when the same course was taught at minimum- and medium-security facilities at a different institutional site.

As in most coed classrooms, the women at the prerelease facility tended to be more inhibited in their participation than the men. In addition, most of the women seemed less concerned with establishing themselves, either in the instructor's eyes or in their own eyes, outside of the inmate identity imposed by their present context. There were two possible reasons for this. Three of the four women had killed men whom they allege sexually or physically abused them. All of the women could claim, for different reasons, that their actions were taken in self-defense. Clearly we did not undertake to test these claims. For our purposes here it is enough that there was a general acceptance of them among the students. As far as we knew, the men had less access to a claim of self-defense in the traditional sense of the term as a means of explaining their crimes to society. In addition, perhaps because the system does not have an infrastructure developed for women parallel to that developed for the male population, the women in the class seemed less embedded in the system. Within the context of this classroom, that put them at a distinct disadvantage.

Teaching a course on the politics of class, race, and gender is always a challenge because students tend to have a personal stake in their political opinions, which are informed by their political histories. Whether we are teaching within the prison or at the university, we maintain a deliberate naiveté upon entering the classroom. We cling to the assumption that students are there out of their personal interest in learning and exploring and challenging their given opinions because it helps us sustain a dynamic interest in the process of learning. However, we also assume that presented in the abstract, political theory will have little to say to students. We never assume they want to learn theory purely for the sake of it. Political theory is not understood by students as instrumental or useful in the way computer science or business classes are. In addition, as pointed out above, most students in prison learn on their own, taking advantage of sparse and arbitrary collections of books and documents found in the libraries or borrowed from friends. They have a given, albeit often incoherent (by traditional academic standards), set of knowledge through which they filter material for class discussion. Sometimes it feels like a hopeless enterprise to try to engage with this knowledge with which they come to class; yet it is generally best to hold to the belief that institutionally structured, paradigmatic theory will be more effectively integrated if connections are made through responding directly to comments rather than letting them float out in the air while rushing on to the next set of presorted arguments. However, the emphasis on dialogue often leaves one with a sense of being engaged more in an exercise of persuasion than in one of teaching.

To better persuade, in addition to respecting the varied knowledge of the students, the discussion was often framed around questions directly related to what students also knew well, that is, the prison system, and then extrapolated to larger social and political problems. For example, how do prisons work to improve our sense of social security in light of social relations of race, class, and gender? What do they do to sustain these systems and formations? How can we dissect the technologies of control operating within prison walls and the relationship to an increasingly violent and fragmented outside world? How does this process constitute the convict even as an ex-con? How is this process of identification related to identities constructed in and around race, class, and gender?

Of the three areas of the course, gender was always the most difficult. The women had immediate sympathy for the material and acknowledged more readily than the men that there is, indeed, a politics to gender relations that is different from that which informs or imbues other social relationships. The men, on the other hand, tended to resist the claims made in feminist theory and research that women have a second-class or second-sex status, particularly in Western cultures. These were the weeks where absolutely nothing was taken for granted regarding student attitudes and arguments constructed specifically around avoiding unnecessarily alienating the male students. The hope was to draw them into a project of thinking critically about themselves and others as gendered political subjects. Gender politics is one of the hardest politics to see on a day-to-day basis. Because the course focuses on the politics that we live every day of our lives and the relationship between that politics and the larger structures of power, getting students to ask questions different from those they are accustomed to is central to the learning process. Some typical questions about gender tended to be: Why do feminists hate men? Aren't men oppressed as well? Aren't women favored over men if men have to work harder to make a living and experience more violence? What about women's power over men, that is, sexually and emotionally, as a mother? Isn't that kind of power more useful than whatever powers men have over women? Why don't women try to use that form of power in order to achieve their ends?

Why don't feminists talk about humankind? Why are they so obsessed with what it means to be female?

These are all questions that students ask out of (usually) genuine interest. And they are confronted in this instance with a teacher, a woman and a noninmate, telling them that women's power over them is basically phantasmatic, ideological, amorphous, and is defined by men, through men, and, sometimes, for men. The general argument was that women negotiate a very different set of sexual power relations in our everyday lives than men do. "But what," they asked, "about female prison guards?" The response was something like the following: No prison guard, regardless of sex, is immune from becoming what they called a control freak, but the students might want to reflect on how they judge women prison guards differently than men and analyze these guards' behavior in light of a larger social critique of gendered roles we perform in all kinds of social settings. For example, why do women prison guards often seem to be overcompensating and unnecessarily brutal in their attitudes toward the men? This way of thinking politically about gender does not claim that women prison guards should be understood in the sense of being let off the hook. Rather it suggests that the students can ask questions about their everyday encounters with women, with authority, with each other, that will allow them to negotiate the craziness of prison politics with some level of dignity and self-possession.

"The Politics of Law" was taught to many of the same students as the "The Politics of Race, Class, and Gender," and like the latter class, was profoundly complicated by the facts of the students' personal experience—in this case, their intimate association with the criminal justice system. The course itself was an attempt to treat seriously the claim that "all law is politics"—to try and understand *how* law is political. First, we studied various jurisprudential traditions to provide some background about how people give meaning to the law. The primary focus of the course, however, was on the interaction between law and politics in its institutional context. Specifically, we examined how institutions such as courts, the judiciary, and the legal profession shape legal consciousness and, in turn, how such institutions respond to social and political demands. Further, a good deal of attention was given to understanding the American reverence for the Constitution, the trial process, and the rule of law in our political culture. Consequently, a unifying theme for the course was the faith in the ideal of the rule of law, a faith many Americans maintain in the face of overwhelming evidence that the legal system does not, and never has, served as a neutral, objective, or fair mechanism for the adjudication of legal claims. This ideal was traced through the historic role and symbolic nature of the courts, their elite participants (i.e., judges and lawyers), and the trial process itself.

Clearly all of us are aware, to some extent, of the role of both criminal and civil law in our legal system. Yet few of us experience the criminal justice system in a direct manner. Rather, our understanding is usually mediated through media representations. The prison students, obviously, experience the law in a much more direct way. They understand the very real violence of its sanctions through the seizure and incarceration of their bodies. Such personal, physical experience generally issues an extraordinarily cynical attitude toward the law and the legal system. This experiential knowledge and the resulting cynicism serves to inhibit the systematic and critical analysis of the legal system.

The refrain "all law is politics" is a familiar one that seems to challenge the ideal image of the law as being somehow autonomous, separate from the world of politics. It makes problematical the traditional understanding of the judge as a neutral arbiter in a dispute, objectively identifying and applying the law to a given factual situation. It undermines the legitimacy of that professional class—lawyers—whose authority rests on their monopoly over a highly technical language that presumably derives its meaning independent of a prior political context. Yet, the notion that "all law is politics" is often simply asserted in the negative. The tone is one of betrayal. Beneath the assertion usually lies a sense that a good system unfortunately has been perverted by the actions of a few. "All law is politics" is used then, not as the first step in debunking a mythology, but as a lament for what has been lost.

The suggestion is that this view is common to students both inside and outside the prison. The latter group may be understood to articulate a general malaise regarding the present nature of the legal system (i.e., something is wrong and it probably has to do with the improper transgression of politics into the sphere of the law). The former group of students, because of their more intense relationship with the criminal justice system, evince a more dramatic response. The distinction between the two groups, however, is generally one of degree rather than of kind. That is, for all their cynicism, the prison students maintain an allegiance to the fundamental tenets of the American legal system; they merely view the problem as one of corruption.

For most students in the prisons, the assertions of a corrupt legal system are grounded in racial or class analyses. The system, it is often maintained, is susceptible to the manipulations of a wealthy, predominantly white class within a hierarchical structure of power. The perceived benefits that the American legal system ideally promises to all are thereby understood to have been undermined by the interventions of a few. Again, the characterization is articulated in terms of betrayal, which accounts for the overriding cynicism. Such an attitude tends to inhibit extended and systematic analysis because it denies the efficacy of the very project of inquiry. As pointed out, this attitude is more pronounced among inmates than among students with a more distant knowledge of the legal system, and must be overcome before the project of a vigorous examination of the nature of the "politics of law" can begin.

CONCLUSION: WHY PRISON EDUCATION?

In its ideal form, teaching is the sharing or imparting of knowledge and information in an effort to bring students into a semistructured state of understanding. Teaching adults of many varied ages and experiences, as one does in the prison, gives this project a whole new meaning. It often feels that the art of persuasion is the more valuable one than the art of teaching conceptualized in some pure form. We try to resist the feeling that we are dragging minds along behind our words, trying to lace them into harness so that we can leave the room feeling as if something had been accomplished. We know intellectually, and because students tell us, that this is not what is going on, but it is a personal and intuitive sense that weighs on our commitment to teaching as a project. In general, because students in the prison education program tend to be much more forthright with their opinions and acquired knowledge than university students, we are challenged to explain, argue, persuade, and generally think more critically about each piece of what we teach than in the university.

In reflecting about our experiences in teaching in the prisons, it becomes clear that the balancing act we engage in involves many different edges. One edge is that given by our decision to teach the way we do, using dialogue rather than lecture to draw out arguments and ideas. Another edge, for those teachers who are women, is that of being female in a (usually) all-male place and negotiating the gender politics that often emerge, front and center in the classroom. Another edge is our affinity with the students, as opposed to the corrections system. And yet another is our personal struggle to develop ever more compelling ways to talk about the politics of the law, race, class, and gender that will bring the urgency we feel for understanding the subjects home to the students. All of these edges act as contradictions, irreducible to any one "fact of the matter" or insight into the nature of the project of prison education. And all of these edges function to keep us interested in teaching in the program. We don't harbor any illusions about the importance of our presence in the prisons. We remain keenly aware of the momentary importance of what we offer relative to the importance of the other kinds of relationships inmates negotiate on a daily basis. However, in spite of our worst moments of wondering what the hell we were trying to do, we usually believe that strong and diversely situated prison education programs are worth struggling for.

Generally, as a society, we believe that we engage in fantasies about the quality of our modern-day, socially enlightened benevolence as we allow those we have decided are deviants (criminals) to be treated like humans "in spite of what they did." Prison education is a part of upholding that system of legitimacy and should be looked at in the context of the criminal justice system in which it is permitted to function. However, the interactions between inmates and people not invested in a full-time capacity in the correctional system can keep prisons from remaining completely outside the popular sphere of awareness. Prisons in the United States are a great sphere of mystery and otherness. Although people prefer to sustain the myth that prison life is but an aberration in an otherwise well-ordered and free society, prisons remain loaded with significance in the popular imagination. We believe that no one should be complaisant about the concrete realities of prisons and of the population that inhabits them and works in them. They are a constant reminder of how concrete means of enforcing social order usually supersede abstract ideas about justice and freedom. Prisons are a constant reminder of the negotiations in which we all engage, the many different ways that we try to be "good" and remain on the consensual side of the social contract in order to avoid ending up like "them," who exist under the coercive shadow of the state. Prison education can and should function—as the name implies—on both sides of the walls, educating outsiders about prisons and educating inmates about different possibilities for change.

An Experiment in Liberal Studies

by June Licence

· · · · · · · · · · ·

On May 1, 1986, the State University of New York at Buffalo held a graduation ceremony at Auburn Correctional Facility (CF) to recognize those who had graduated with an M.A. degree in American Studies since the inception of its program in 1979-80. Held in the facility chapel, the ceremony involved a dozen students in caps and gowns (two of whom gave outstanding addresses); representatives of the SUNY/Buffalo Graduate School and American Studies faculty; a poet laureate from SUNY/Buffalo's English department; Auburn administrators; graduates' families; diplomas; recognition gifts; flowers; and a "yearbook," *Concrete Garden*, containing the writings of the men in the graduate program. A reception, catered by the prison, was held in the facility library, capping one of our most memorable prison education events.

For all those years, faculty and students and staff from Buffalo had made the six-hour round-trip drive to Auburn (near Syracuse), New York, delivering lectures and resource materials and administrative forms. They did this not because they received additional funding, but because the educational experience, not only for men in Auburn but for faculty and students in the outside American Studies program, was exceptional:

> Our experience has convinced every participating faculty member that prison students can do the work—often superlatively—and that they bring an enthusiasm, dedication, and commitment that make teaching in such a setting not an act of charity but a rewarding professional experience. (National Endowment for the Humanities [NEH] grant application)

June Licence is program coordinator, Department of American Studies, State University of New York, Buffalo.

We sensed that we were also having a broader impact on our students, as they were often tutors in other educational and social programs within the prison; they were frequently considered leaders by us and, we learned, high-profile troublemakers by corrections administrators.

We had begun at Auburn with one person who wanted to do graduate work and had admitted additional students in an ad hoc fashion, maneuvering within the facility without any official administrative structure. There were no tuition or other moneys available at the graduate level, such as Pell Grants at the undergraduate level, to underwrite such programs. Our lack of financial resources made us realize early on that we could either do it (actually teach and offer the degree) or talk about it to SUNY, State Education Department, and Department of Corrections (DOC) officials to propose and become a program on paper; we chose to do the teaching, assuming that, once proved as a positive program for human renewal, official approval would follow.

When the New York State Department of Correctional Services Education Department created a statewide graduate plan—for an M.S. in Social Sciences at Eastern Correctional Facility, an M.P.S. in Theological Studies at Sing Sing, and an M.A. in Humanities "in the western part of the state"—we took the opportunity for recognition and to move closer to Buffalo (Wende Correctional Facility was a maximum-security facility 20 minutes from campus). We applied for funding to institutionalize/stabilize our program, which would now be a four-night-a-week operation with more curricular structure than the one-night-a-week program at Auburn.

Preparing an NEH grant application provided us an opportunity to express why we thought the education we had been offering was particularly appropriate:

> Humanities programming in particular, rather than narrowly vocational education, has special importance for such a setting, given the complex personal histories of prisoners and the formidable cultural challenges facing them within a correctional facility and upon release. The basic focus of humanistic disciplines on the relation between self and society, the central tension involved in humanities as at once bearer of traditional values and source of critical reflection on those values and institutions— these speak directly to the dilemma of prisoners who need better to understand themselves, their world, and most crucially, the relation between these. The process of humanities teaching, with its focus on values and thoughtful reflection, on writing, research, critical reading, addresses as well the urgent need prisoners have for analytic skills and tools for making informed judgments in demanding contexts.

American Studies is an especially good vehicle for such an experiment in humanities education. As the field has evolved over the past two decades, it has moved from an initial concentration on orthodox history, literature, and national character in a somewhat narrow sense to a more diverse and inclusive approach to cultural analysis, one grounded in many disciplines and seeing American culture as an amalgam of peoples, values, and experiences within a complex national and world setting.

Our approach (at SUNY/Buffalo's American Studies Department) is well-suited to the needs and opportunities of highly motivated and intellectually qualified students drawn to graduate study in prison. These are men hungry to understand themselves and their society more usefully through concrete, relevant research and application. More than traditional programs, our approach can support this by addressing the realities that inform their lives (we include autonomous components on Puerto Rican Studies, Native American Studies, Women's Studies, Intercultural Studies, and are affiliated with the African-American Studies Department) and the histories that have produced these realities. At the same time, our approach helps them move beyond the limits of this experience and to examine their world in new ways from diverse vantages and in terms of different values. In this way, we hope to provide skills, knowledge, and insight for helping students deal constructively with the problematic past, a pressured present, and the uncertain future. (NEH grant application)

Although our application received an excellent peer review rating, we fell victim to the politics of an agency that seemed to think that prisoners would benefit from a rather narrow, unquestioning acceptance of their failures and recognition of the vocational world as their home; the critical and culturally sensitive writings in our curriculum would only confuse their understanding (in the words of one prisoner, "They build us basketball courts, but we'd better not ask for tennis courts!") We were unable also to make our interdisciplinary program "legible" within current rubrics: Although everyone seemed to find our arguments and offerings compelling, they had no bureaucratic structures in place to take advantage of it—or they thought that because we had operated so successfully for so long, we didn't need funding now.

Despite not receiving outside funding, we did obtain two teaching assistantships and a graduate assistantship from the university to help faculty and staff carry the program. At Wende, we had an official office with a computer, library, etc., none of which we had had at Auburn; two of our inmate graduates from Auburn also were moved to Wende in order to serve as inside staff for us.

Because our Ph.D. program (on campus) also was approved—without additional resources—during this period, we found ourselves stretched beyond the limits of our "volunteerism." Although still able to provide courses, we were unable to spend the excessive amount of time required trying to make real the Department of Correctional Services' edict (as well as our fundamental requirement) that education programs inside were to be of the same quality as any on outside campuses. Every day seemed to bring new, "nonnegotiable" challenges by prison officials clearly aimed at preventing our efforts to operate a sound and responsible educational program. Supervisory staff seemed unable or unwilling to countermand often arbitrary edicts by line officers or to tailor any general rule to meet educational requirements. (We discovered underlying dynamics, such as the deputy superintendent of programs' having received a failing grade in graduate school years earlier from the retiring faculty member who donated a large part of his library to us; only when the "Dep" referred to this basically African-American Studies collection as "trash" did we begin to sense the depth of our problem.)

There was never any argument made that our students, faculty, administrators, courses, etc., breached security in any real sense. But as they define security in contradictory rules and regulations, not only hostile to education but racist as well, security staff showed uneasiness and a concern all too common: that the administration could not tolerate the fact that inmates were being legitimized as leaders, thus threatening the time-honored hierarchy and clearly defined roles of authority. If this underlying attitude were made clear, perhaps accommodation might be made.

Within the year, the Wende administration closed the program down. Thus a nine-year-old program ended, although we have kept working with students who were then enrolled, as they had completed course work and were at their M.A. project state. Not only did Wende have no reputation (as Auburn had) as an education or programs facility, it was half a reception center at that time, which seemed to increase its security bent. It had also become a place both for previous Attica officers[1] and minority officers to bid for assignments. (The racial tensions among the Wende corrections staff were legendary, and included "duking it out in the parking lot.")

The racial and gender aspects of the discord were significant and often blatantly expressed—for example, corrections officers snarling, "Oh, here come the *Masters*," when referring to our students entering "South Africa block," where they were housed, or the chair of the American Studies

---

[1] On September 9, 1971, inmates of Attica prison took over the prison demanding better conditions and human rights. By September 13, New York State Troopers ended the takeover in which 43 persons were killed including 10 corrections officers.

department being told by the superintendent that he had ended the program because "she (the program coordinator) doesn't smile enough when she walks down the hall!" Inherent in the endemic racism and sexism of the facility was the implication that homage had not been paid, authority not recognized, hegemony ignored; this program was running like a "university program," not a "prison program."

The inability to implement the Department of Corrections official position that "the same education" should be provided within correctional facilities as on the home campuses of the colleges and university was caused by the lack of any official administrative structure to make that possible. At Auburn, any success we enjoyed was on the strength of a superintendent of long tenure who administered a facility with a sense of mission—education and programs—a luxury probably afforded by the relatively low turnover of staff and prisoners. The stability of its general operations seemed to allow greater flexibility and innovation.

Although a visionary and supportive superintendent will always strengthen any prison-university educational arrangement, the existence or operation of an education program should not rely totally on such a situation. And while the goodwill and efforts of dedicated students who desperately want education also will help greatly, more is required.

As long as we have prisons, we must ensure that programming can take place to the same, if not to a greater, measure than it does on the outside. What would it take, organizationally, for any program (especially one conducted by a college or university) to be able to operate with a modicum of success within a correctional setting?

1. There must be societal and legislative/executive recognition that imprisonment should be the sanction of last resort and that the fundamental purpose of a correctional system is to correct or, more accurately, to empower people to understand their actions and to provide resources to enable them to reenter society as contributors and to act in noncriminal ways. The goals of producing income for the facility/state or jobs for economically depressed communities should never take priority over the public safety goal of returning people enabled to participate constructively in their communities.

2. There must be an administrative organizational structure or team (one at the governor's level, one at the Department of Correctional Services, and one at each facility) that reflects the above-mentioned priority. Policy should be determined by representatives of all the programs in the prisons (job training, mental health, health, education, social services, etc.), with the presumption that these programs will operate as they do outside of prisons. Under this structure, the

primary function of facility staff, from superintendent on down, is to determine *how* to enable programs to operate effectively; any exceptions would have to be argued to this interagency policy team. There should also be a corrections staff reward/merit system built into each facility correlated with the number of prisoners who successfully complete both mandated and voluntary programming.

3. There should be no disqualifications for entrance into an academic program except those used on campus, although priority lists for limited space may be set by the college program; there should be no capricious transfer of any students (except to parole, etc.) for the duration of their program (usually one to two years at the graduate level) unless they are able to transfer into a comparable program that accepts earned credits if transferred.

4. Educational programming should carry at least equal pay to that of vocational/job assignments so that prisoners don't suffer by choosing programs of human renewal.

5. It is hoped there would be regular linkages between the inside and outside programs and community support for people being released. For example, a local church supported our students with a program called GIFT (Good Investments For Tomorrow) by arranging for individuals to relate either financially or personally (or both) to one of our students, helping with educational resources and, possibly, with reconnecting to society upon release. Students who are released should be able to come out directly into a corresponding academic program (if they have not completed their academic work) or to a career-placement/job training program coordinated with social service agencies.

We all experienced a sense of human renewal by offering our M.A. degree program inside New York State prisons. Despite all the frustrations, we came to understand the world more fully and to recognize that education could not only empower individuals but could (and did) bring people of diverse perspectives and backgrounds together in a celebration of understanding. We even have some hope that we diminished the systemic racism and gender bias that can lead to violence.

Technology and Progress: A Questionable Experience

by Jane Richards-Allerton

• • • • • • • • • •

Imagine the talking head of Big Brother from *1984* looking in at you three times a week for 50 minutes. That was distance learning in its early stages, until new facilities allowed for a new concept. Instead of a TV studio, Ball State University provided state-of-the-art classrooms, equipped with cameras and microphones connected to a statewide network, so that students at distant locations could complete their general studies requirements as part of a class presented on campus. As part of the new distance learning program on the Indiana Higher Education Telecommunications System (IHETS), Ball State joined three other state universities to provide satellite and phone hookups to more than 200 sites quite distant from the traditional classroom setting: in hospitals, factories, high schools, and prisons.

These advances in technology offer new horizons in education. In the very near future, anyone with a television set and a telephone will be able to participate in classes at home, from primary education through master's degree programs. Anyone with a computer and a modem will be able to attend class, conference with a teacher, and do small group work in real time with live video feeds on split screen monitors. However, even though technology has advanced from the original "talking heads" to interactive audio and video components, distance learning still has several major drawbacks that must be considered before it is offered as the only option in every situation. First and foremost is the idea that education is the imparting of knowledge. To learn, students must be part of an interactive, friendly environment that offers them

Jane Richards-Allerton is an instructor in the English department and teaches in the Prison Education Program, Ball State University, Muncie, Indiana.

the benefits of the teacher's pedagogy; in addition, we must consider the constraints of logistics and attitudes to analyze how they will affect the students' ability to learn. One very important part of imparting knowledge is that the technology must not overshadow the students' and teacher's needs.

When my colleague and I agreed to team teach the first English class on IHETS in the spring of 1989, we had one semester to prepare it, so we were quickly immersed in the design, production, and teaching of the Composition sequence of classes (English 103 and 104 are "Composition" and "Composition and Literature," respectively). Both Mike, the other member of the team, and I felt comfortable teaching in the traditional classroom, so we felt confident and excited about the transition to the televised class. The design stage taught us to use the technology that IHETS offered us to make video a more integrated part of the classroom. We learned to create video from an idea to a finished product, working with an instructional designer to generate ideas that the director and artists could then turn into graphs, charts, still photos, and video "roll-ins" to make our presentations more interactive. What this planning stage did not prepare us for were the challenges of teaching composition skills at a distance and overcoming the changes needed in teaching methods, logistics, and attitudes.

Distance learning is an efficient choice for technical professionals like engineers who want to stay current in their particular field, but it may not fit the needs of those classes that wish to engage the students interactively in new ways of viewing the world. The traditional liberal arts education seeks to train and exercise students in the three main branches of learning: the humanities, the hard sciences, and the social sciences. Pedagogically, it seeks to expose students to the various disciplines, to make them free thinkers. Therein lies the most poignant problem of distance learning: Can students in their living room, in a small group in a factory, or in a classroom in a prison learn effectively if the teacher is removed from the students' immediate experience or if this free thinking is contradicted by the environment in which they must live?

My experience suggests that this is not an effective teaching tool in situations where the teacher wants to engage the students' minds immediately. Current technology, which allows for one-way video and limited two-way audio contact, is not yet at the level where students can overcome the distance that televised interface places between teacher and student. This is especially true for students who are not highly motivated and for beginning students. Learning to think, read, and write demands interaction and the presence of a teacher before and after class to answer questions and respond to the feedback of students. It demands that the students have access to the teacher that distance learning does not allow; additionally, for such a personal subject as writing, the students need to be able to drop by the teacher's office for a one-on-one conference on an assignment or for help in revising drafts.

Because distance learning classes are produced using the same planning methods as television news, each class must be carefully organized to the second in a script that tells the producer/director precisely how much time to allow before starting a roll-in or when to pan over the class; the technology requires this type of orchestration. In the six weeks of designing our courses, we struggled against this rigid control of time because writing classes are not content-laden classes but rather courses that encourage originality and thinking skills from class interaction and opinion. In writing classes, students deal with personal opinions and interpretations, so it is vital that the entire class and teacher build a strong sense of rapport. As we begin reading materials for essays, the students develop their thinking and writing skills through often lively discussions that force them to open their minds to consider new points of view. These spontaneous discussions often illuminate the students' thinking, so if the time constraints of the script are adhered to, the students miss part of the learning and critical thinking because there is not enough time to expand their dialogue. Compounding this problem was the limited telephone access for the students at the sites. The technology for the telephone hookup allowed for only four sites to call in at a time; because we had six sites in English 104 and seven in 103, it was impossible for all sites to be on-line at once.

Many of the methods and practices that we take for granted in the traditional classroom, those tried and true ways of helping our students with writing, did not work as well in prison settings primarily due to time and movement restrictions. Some adapted well once we understood the constraints, but some had to be reevaluated and discarded. Small-group work, peer evaluation, emphasis on content and organization rather than grammar, topic selection, library research, and journals were particular areas where I quickly learned to adapt my teaching methods.

Small-group work and peer evaluation offer the students a chance to read and comment on each others' writing as they evaluate essays at different stages; writers gain confidence in their own skills as they offer suggestions to their peers; and class rapport is strengthened as they learn to trust themselves and each other as they work together both in and out of class. All of this created problems in the prison setting due to the students' need in confinement to look out for themselves; the Department of Correction's discouragement of friendships among the inmates made the problem worse. The students at the Reformatory had a more difficult time than those at other sites because once they did begin to work together and depend on each other, they had no access to each other outside of class. If they wanted to give a classmate an essay to peer evaluate, they would not get it back for at least two days, when it might be due at that class meeting.

Because those in our 104 class had just finished a 103 class in a traditional prison classroom, they knew that individual, personal attention, as well as small-group work, was an important part of the writing process. In English 103, we had arranged for extra weekly visits to have conferences with students out of class. I continued the practice into 104; accompanied by a student tutor, I made four more visits. This proved to be a great way to build rapport with the students, to earn their trust, and to tutor them on their writing, but it was a very time-consuming process. In order to meet with them for two hours, we had to schedule the visit around our classes (we were each teaching two other composition classes) as well as around their full class schedule and institutional countdowns; this often meant going to the prison according to our schedule and meeting with as many as were free at that time. It was an administrative headache, also, because the director had to write them extra passes, get us gate releases, and walk up to meet us when the guards at the front desk called, sometimes taking away from our time spent with the students.

Though I traveled to the Reformatory for my 103 class, I adapted the peer evaluation to the time and distance constraints of distance learning by allowing 20 minutes of class time to peer evaluate each assignment with the students at the sites able to call in questions as I moved from group to group in the classroom. At first, most of them felt unprepared to make suggestions to fellow writers because they did not yet believe in their own writing abilities; once they began to receive feedback on their own writing, however, many of them gained the necessary confidence to make suggestions to others and learned to accept suggestions as a part of their writing process.

In addition to their lack of confidence in their abilities to evaluate others' papers, the Reformatory students believed that the purpose of an English class was to learn grammar and mechanics; thus, if they could only understand where to put the punctuation, how to spell the words, and how to write complete sentences, writing would be easy. This was especially true in my 103 class because their most recent classes—study for their GED—emphasized grammar. On the first day of class, I explained my grading criteria, in order of importance: content, organization, style, and mechanics, with the emphasis on having something to say and making a point. They had a hard time believing this, especially when they received their first papers back with a low grade and many punctuation errors marked, but they did eventually learn the importance of communicating an idea in the way that an audience would understand and using a standardized language for doing so. They worked hard to do this, and though they complained during the class, they were very happy with the results at the end of the semester.

Because English 104 dealt with reading literature and understanding its meaning, we selected a number of readings centered on the theme of gender issues. It was an excellent choice because we were able to use the strengths of stereotypes and prejudice to draw all of the students in on equal footing. It certainly sparked some lively discussions and strong writing as they developed their essays. Because it was an issue with which they were all familiar, we didn't have any problems with an attitude I had discovered in my 103 class: "This topic won't work for us because it doesn't apply to us, so we do not need to know this information." This was one of the most difficult attitudes that I had to overcome as I stressed that we could not do all of our papers on prison-related issues and that, because the purpose of a college education was to stretch their minds, they needed to open them and consider all possibilities.

The topics that were the most difficult to deal with were ones that involved research of any kind. Though the institution had a library, its main resources were legal books and various older reference books that were needed by GED students, that program having received several more years of financial support than the fledgling college program. As a result, materials were at a premium, periodicals were sparse, and most current ones had missing pages and volumes. The students did not have access to Interlibrary Loan, and what they did have available was too expensive for them to use. The 104 research paper component requires use of the library; if we wanted research done, we had to provide the materials, a matter we had not realized soon enough to remedy by ordering casebooks on a specific topic. Our syllabus allowed the students to submit three proposed topics from which we would select one. Though the Reformatory students came up with a variety of interesting topics, none of the possibilities were even remotely related. Mike and I made a deal with them: Narrow the options to two choices and we would search for and compile relevant materials, copying pertinent data to bring to them. This seemed like a logical option, but it limited their interest in the subject matter immediately, and they found it difficult to write the papers. In addition, this was a time-consuming, expensive process for Mike and me because this funding had not been built into the class.

The planning stage of the writing process is crucial to success, so our students were required to keep a daily journal, including subjects that dealt with their everyday life, our writing topic materials, their views on the writing process, or anything else of interest to them. This journal writing taught me about the bureaucracy and red tape involved in teaching in a prison setting. It began rather simply with the list of supplies required for the class: a spiral notebook for four weekly journal entries. This was forbidden because the metal wire might be used for a weapon. The solution? Loose-leaf notebook paper in a two-pocket folder.

The logistics of teaching in the prison are often complicated by a lack of discussion between the teacher and DOC as to what restrictions are necessary for the DOC to maintain control in a maximum-security prison. This is further complicated by the DOC's inability to completely understand the needs of a classroom setting. Often the strict control prohibits instructors from going into the prison to work with the students, and even when it is allowed, the situation calls for the instructor to be aware of the practices of that institution. Both the classroom setting and the teacher and students' actions are restricted; in addition, the problems that do occur take on a more frightening tone and sometimes can threaten the rest of the class.

The journal assignments taught me that although we must fight our irrational fears (stereotypes), there sometimes is a truth to them. I assigned open-topic, journal entries as part of their course work. A student I'll call John decided that I was a subject of interest to him about halfway through the semester when he wrote an evaluation of the class in his journal describing how much he was learning about writing; the entry ended with "all this— brains, beauty, and legs!" My first reaction was to write a flippant "thanks!" at the end of the entry and ignore it, in part because I knew they had little contact with females. However, as I read on, I found 15 more pages of fantasies that included me as the main attraction. For the first time, I was afraid for my own safety as I remembered all of the scary prison scenes from television. His journal showed an increasingly more graphic and irrational view of reality, to the extent that when I came into the classroom, I found myself glancing furtively at him, which, to him, probably implied a special recognition; I was just plain scared!

I called the director at home that evening and explained what I had found. His response was that if I could send him copies of the journal, he would take it up with his supervisor, and, if I agreed, John would not be allowed to attend class again until we resolved the problem because this behavior was unacceptable and could jeopardize the program. I agreed, but on the condition that he not be punished until we had discussed the outcome. I wanted to deal with the problem as I would with any other student, but I wasn't sure how. The next day I learned how crucial my reaction would be to the other Reformatory students when another student, Jeff, asked if he could speak with me at the end of class; he apologized for John's journal entries and asked me to not give up on the rest of the class because they were not all like John.

Later in the week, I received a call from the DOC asking if I would file charges against John for sexual harassment so he could be punished and removed from the college program; it seems that this was not his first problem. Still unsure how to deal with this, I consulted with my department chair, who agreed that because it was so late in the semester (early November), the best way to handle the situation was to keep him out of class, but allow him to finish his assignments on his own to attempt to get credit for the class. From the time I had read the entries to this inquiry, the original director of the College Program had resigned and a new director had assumed the office. The new director allowed John to return to class and to attend the next tutoring session because no charges had been filed against him. As we entered the room, I knew the meaning of the phrase "feeling my blood run cold" as I saw John sitting in the back corner of the room. Though I wanted to turn and run, I calmed myself and began to answer student questions.

In the next two hours, the tension in the room became palpable as the other students allowed John to ask but one question. After we finished, the director told the students it was time to leave, but several, including John, made their way toward the desk. John stood about 6' 4" and weighed about 220 pounds. To say that I was afraid is an understatement. However, Jeff and three other students actually formed a physical barrier between me and John until he left the room with his questions unanswered. They then apologized again for what had happened and assured me that they would not let him bother me again. Though I appreciated their assurances and knew that this episode was somewhat more dramatic because of the environment in which it took place, my fear was very real and undoubtedly exacerbated by the walls, bars, guards, and my inability to escape a frightening situation. When I am asked if I'm afraid to teach in a prison, I remember John's journals before I reply that, though there is some danger, it is not my primary concern when I walk in the prison classroom: my students are.

Security at the Reformatory was something of a problem because, in order for me to meet with my students, the administration had to schedule an extra guard to stand outside the door to "protect" me. I was one of the very few women in the institution and the only one allowed to teach. Because our class did not meet on-site on a regular basis, Mike and I were given whatever room was available. It was an often embarrassing walk to a classroom because the toilets were located in the education office and library but were without walls for security reasons; sometimes I would walk into the room and have to quickly avert my eyes or turn around. Because our students were very protective, they didn't want other students bothering us; on those occasions when I was in a room with windows facing into a corridor, I usually had an audience lined up at the windows. This was a bit unnerving, so one day when the sounds of catcalls and knocks on the windows were particularly disturbing, one of my students pulled the blind down and said calmly, "Ignore those babies. They don't know what they're doin'."

Exchanging assignments and essays was an administrative headache that we tried to resolve before class started because we knew that we would have six essays, a research paper plus its drafts, and weekly assignments to send and receive. We argued the importance of speedily receiving essays and returning them to our students for revision, for that would be the only way for students to improve their writing ability. Though we explored the possibilities of a fax machine, computer links, Federal Express, and the U.S. mail, the only option for the prison class was the U.S. mail because of security. The problem, we soon learned, was that it often took a week or more for mail to pass through security and travel the 30 miles to campus. Luckily the director lived about 10 minutes from me and agreed that it would be more efficient for him to collect essays and trade weekly assignments. Many evenings I left him packages in his front door and found the same in my own. I'm not sure we would have succeeded nearly as well with the distance learning experience without him. As a matter of fact, when he resigned as director near the end of the 103 class, paper exchanges became laborious.

One essential component of a composition class is attendance and participation in the class discussion. Unfortunately, this was controlled by the rigid scheduling of the DOC to ensure security. Because both classes were scheduled to air from 1:00 to 1:50 p.m., three days per week, the inmates' lunch and count preceded the class; count was often late due to a delay in lunch, so the students rarely made it to class until 1:15, which meant the students frequently interrupted class to ask questions to catch up. The original director always informed us that they were late and taped the class for them to view later. Unfortunately, they often missed changes in due dates, quizzes, or vital discussion of the reading assignments, which allowed them to engage the other students in discussion to help generate ideas for their essays.

After class ended at 1:50, we had open air time until 2:00, when the network cut us off, so the students could phone in with questions. Because the 104 students had experience in the classroom, they understood classroom etiquette and shared time and questions accordingly; in contrast, because the 103 students were first-semester students taking their first class over television, they had little concept of this etiquette, often breaking in on conversations or dominating the phone lines so no one else could call in. Because there were 17 inmates in this small classroom, they believed that they had priority over the other groups, and with 45 other students in class, it was frequently frustrating for the students at the other sites. Fortunately, the students at the other sites learned quickly that the prisoners had no other chance to ask questions, so they generally conceded air time to the Reformatory.

Stereotypical attitudes and expectations about prison and prisoners are an important consideration in a prison setting. Teachers walking in will be in the same situation Mike and I were on our first visit, having never been inside a prison and knowing little about what is necessary to maintain control. We were uncomfortable when we walked through the metal detector and through our first gate. Because the Reformatory is maximum security, we had to go through three more gates, a cell block, across the yard, and through a locked door into the school building. As we walked with a guard, all of the stereotypes and pictures I had ever seen of beady-eyed, menacing figures came to mind; the day before, I heard on the news of a stabbing outside the school building, so the fear and questions concerning our safety were foremost on my mind. Though I could see the guards in the hallways, all of the clichés related to prisons I had ever heard were kept in mind.

This fear and societal attitudes about prison life are the first issues that we as educators must address when we agree to teach in a prison setting. Knowing how we are influenced by the media, we must force ourselves to explore and address our own attitudes before we can begin to deal with our students as students with special needs. As a woman entering this all-male environment, I knew I had to deal with my fears quickly so my students would not pick up on them. The students are aware of these fears and stereotypes: Two upperclassmen who were clerks in the education office were quick to reassure me that because the prisoners valued this program, they would protect us in the event that there were any problems. We were reassured of this when we talked with our link to the students, the director of the College Program.

The realization of the damage these stereotypes cause became obvious when we began to discern who and what our students were: They asked what we thought of prison life, what our expectations were for them, and if we saw them as any different from our other students. As we got to know them while they were in the classroom, the stereotypes slipped away because the students truly wanted to learn how to communicate in writing. Though we had been warned that our students might have a difficult time trusting us because of their environmental practice of looking out for themselves first, the very nature of writing created an atmosphere of trust and openness that soon made them comfortable talking to us and asking us questions. We learned that though they had committed some foolish, some terrible crimes, they still had other redeeming qualities.

As the second semester progressed, I began to see patterns emerging in the types of problems and pressures the prisoner-students were having, especially with time constraints and attitudes. I continued to carefully document the successes and problems we encountered dealing with administrative and individual needs of our prison students until, at the end of the second semester, I convinced my department chair and the dean of Continuing Education that these students were a special case because their lack of education required smaller classes in a more individualized setting where they could have more direct contact with their instructor. We recognized that they were affected by a classroom situation that offered them high-tech materials without the benefit of the necessary teaching methods, logistics, and attitudes to make use of them. As educators in the liberal arts, our job is to help all students open their minds to see new ways to communicate and support their ideas in their own voice. We must find the methods that work, given constraints of prisoner students, to help them learn. Unfortunately, as educators working in a prison setting, we must also open the minds of those in the Department of Corrections to change their belief that education is not a top priority because to them (and to society) rehabilitation is only a word, not a practice that should be encouraged.

Fortunately, not all of the prisoners fall prey to this negative pressure. There was a bearded, long-haired, tattooed biker I had for two courses, who had entered the first semester with a negative and challenging attitude, but who came to me at the beginning of the following term after summer break to ask if I thought he could become an English major. His changes made me realize that we must not allow learned fears to let us lose track of or discourage a student's desire to learn. These classes are certainly the most challenging and demanding I have ever had the pleasure to teach. The life experiences, environment, and attitudes of these students motivate them, generally, to excel as writers and thinkers—far beyond what one would expect if considering only the stereotypes.

Two Prisoners' Views of Prison Higher Education

Editor's Introduction

Prisoners have a vested interest in the scope and quality of programs of education in the prisons. They have knowledge of the forces that shaped their criminal pasts. They have been drawn to the promise of higher education, and they have experienced the problems of learning within a punitive confinement. What prisoners have not had is a significant voice about the aims, goals, and structure of the education that rationalized itself as a response to their needs.

This chapter offers two examples of prisoners speaking of their experience of learning within confinement. Jon Marc Taylor writes of his past and its relation to his struggle to obtain undergraduate and graduate degrees while incarcerated. Catherine Mason also writes of learning within the structure of confinement, an experience she defines as "multiemotional." That she finds it noteworthy that "professors did not act as if we were ignorant" speaks volumes about her other experiences as student and prisoner, and about the broad role prison higher education can play in the life of a prisoner.

These two voices, grounded in the real experience of learning within the prison, are authoritative articulations of the importance of the philosophical position adopted by prison higher education programs. It is one thing to say, in academic prose, that corrections and higher education have antithetical roles and differing regard for prisoners who seek to learn. It is quite another to hear from prisoners themselves about the hardships of learning in an atmosphere structured to degrade and defile. Prison higher education programs, in the minds of many offenders, are an alternative to corrections and the damage it inflicts. When prison education programs, in their anxiety to survive, come to adopt or accommodate the attitudes and values of corrections, they may be risking one of the precise bases for their appeal to prisoners themselves and, therefore, the ultimate reason for their past successes.

. . . .

Cogito, Ergo Sum

by Jon Marc Taylor

· · · · · · · · · · ·

Our aspirations are our possibilities.

Robert Browning

In the waning summer days of 1980, the judge's gavel fell for the final time in my criminal case before the county court. At the ripe old age of 19, I was sentenced to 71 years in the state's penal system. Words cannot convey my utter despondency. On more than one occasion, I was tempted to commit suicide. Through turbulent choices made and unalterable actions taken, I had irrevocably changed by life, and society had now decreed that most, if not all, of my remaining existence was to be spent behind bars. Simply put, the community said I was worthless, beyond redemption. Except for the small yet monumental consolation that no one had died by my hands, I found it difficult to object to their assessment.

For the next two years, I bounced through the system from diagnostic center to prison, back to the courts, and once again to my new home, the penitentiary. While in the prison, I moved from orientation units to cell houses to dormitories, and from work as a kitchen helper to bricklayer to janitor. Nothing, except the cloaking monotony and the cold gray walls enclosing the prison, was consistent. The only things I learned were that I could survive the crucible of the penitentiary, that my family still loved and supported me, and that maintaining my remaining tenuous sanity required a long-term goal, a quest to strive for, a reason to live.

Jon Marc Taylor is a graduate student in Ball State University's correctional education program at the Indiana Reformatory.

The man who removes a mountain begins by carrying away small stones.

Chinese proverb

In the autumn of 1982, with the encouragement and financial support of my family combined with a Pell Grant, my odyssey through the gauntlet of postsecondary correctional education began when I matriculated into Ball State University's (BSU) extension program at the Indiana State Reformatory (ISR). My goal at that point was to earn, sometime before the end of the decade, a baccalaureate degree. At that juncture, the institution's college program had existed for six years, enrolled approximately 30 full-time students out of 1,600 inmates, and had conferred a single bachelor's degree.[1] Three classes a quarter, for three academic quarters, I worked my way through an eclectic mix of courses in English composition and literature, psychology, anthropology, political science, sociology, and physical earth sciences. Due to our small enrollment and "stepchild" status with campus faculty, students at ISR were limited to this mishmash of liberal arts offerings, mainly from the English and history departments. Thus, at that time most students, because of the de facto curriculum availability, minored in these areas.[2]

At last I had found my lifeline, the exploration and development of my intellect. I thrived on the positive challenge and surprised myself with my academic savoir faire. I could actually witness the results of my cognitive growth in my test scores and term paper grades. For the next five years, every dean's list printed would include my name. The journey, though, was at times frustrating, painful, and even maddening, as all growth can be. I struggled to improve my poor composition skills, sometimes rewriting papers five or six times before accepting a final grade. I developed, through trial and error, practical penitentiary study skills, such as studying with radio headphones on to drown out the cell house's roar, napping by day and reading late at night, and minutely organizing out-of-cell academic chores so as to maximize those restricted opportunities. I formed study groups that quizzed each other over meals at the chow hall, tutored each other in brief snatches of conversation on the walks, or debated issues in roundtable discussions at recreation, but always with a Bible prominently displayed.[3]

---

[1] By 1990, the program had expanded to over 150 full-time undergraduate students, due primarily to a federal court ruling ordering inmate access to state student aid grants in addition to federal Pell Grants. The university also conferred 100 associate's and a dozen bachelor's degrees by 1991 to inmate-students at the prison.

[2] Later, as the enrollment grew, so did the diversity of possible minors.

[3] Any meeting of over three or more offenders in a nonsport activity, even at recreation, was considered an "illegal gathering." However, as long as a Bible was displayed and conversation of a religious nature was heard when guards approached, such groups were left alone.

Grades were everything; it was *the* competition played by half of the student body. Getting As was not enough to win; there had to be 97s, 98s, even 99s for one to triumph. Academic excellence was our way to prove our own self-worth and demonstrate our growing reasoning abilities.

By late 1984, I had received both an appellate court-ordered sentence modification mandating a 15-year term until mandatory parole and my Associate of Arts degree. One provided hope for a life one day beyond the walls, while the other provided hope of an enriched existence no matter where I resided. At last I began to comprehend the design behind the seemingly divergent curriculum. Literature classes resounded with examples from history, psychology, even anthropology. In one poignant memory, I recall a Russian literature class where the striking realization dawned on me that all imprisoned men, no matter what the dungeon may be called in the society's popular lexicon, shared a brotherhood in the all-too-similar experience of survival in the gulag.

In other cases, geography, political science, and art history courses blended with the cross-pollination of wide-ranging studies. On more than one occasion, coalescing ideas from disparate sources, a student or students built erudite rationalizations challenging conventional prescripts presented in class. Lively, often raucous debates resulted, sometimes including the professor, fueling self-empowerment and self-discovery. Once, during a lecture on Picasso's work *Guernica*, the students pushed beyond the limited confines of the artist's expressive choice of mode and medium being presented by the lecturer, and expounded upon the painter's insight in presaging the horrors of the London Blitz, the bombings of Hamburg and Dresden, and the nuclear devastation of Hiroshima and Nagasaki—all to the professor's consternated delight. What I realized from all the dynamic experiences was that the varying schools of thought, philosophies, and subjects approached from differing perspectives taught the essence of what a college education is all about: how to question, how to think.

> *Education's purpose is to replace an empty mind with an open one.*
>
> Malcolm Forbes

By 1987, with the attainment of senior status, I had an increasingly difficult time enrolling in on-site classes from the narrow curriculum available that would fulfill my history major's requirements. Thus, while I took whatever courses seemed interesting—which were nearly all of them—to fill out my credit hours, senior-level correspondence courses were required to meet the department's graduation criteria.

At this point in my life, I loathed correspondence courses. The workload seemed more demanding than in-class course work. A typical lesson required

12 to 15 single-spaced typed pages to perfect. There were no professors to answer direct questions and to set weekly deadlines, thus no sounding boards for complex or confusing ideas and no immediate incentive not to procrastinate. And tests, at times, addressed issues that had not been queried in the assignments. In other words, in spite of ambiguous or obtuse questions, I was forced to learn the material more thoroughly than before when classmate discussions and professorial lectures filled the textbook void. In retrospect, this experience was another enlightening step in my evolution as a confident, self-motivating student.

Concomitantly with these developments, Dr. Ross H. Van Ness began teaching at the Reformatory. A very personable man and a staunch advocate of adult and continuing education, he audaciously suggested I pursue graduate work. "What a preposterous idea!" was my initial reaction. It had never been done before in our state or, as far as anyone could tell me, in any other state either.[4] Yet I had stretched out my bachelor's degree curriculum by two semesters, delaying my graduation and subsequent transfer out of the college program—my intellectual and spiritual oasis in the desert of the modern penitentiary.

Patiently and persistently, Dr. Van Ness worked with me to create a program of graduate study, the cornerstone of which was to be set by the Indiana Higher Education Telecommunications System (IHETS), which BSU used to telecast an interactive, fully accredited M.B.A. program. Now a Master of Business Administration was what I wanted; an M.B.A. meant BIG BUCKS. The "fallback" program was an M.A. in Executive Development for Public Service (EDPS), a degree program from the Department of Lifelong Education. This program permitted a student wide latitude in designing an interdisciplinary public service management degree to meet individual needs. It also had the advantage of including a broad range of courses from nearly a dozen university departments. Initially, I was not as interested in the latter option; it was not as prestigious as an M.B.A. and I saw no real future for an ex-con in public service.

In early 1987, the Indiana Department of Correction (DOC) and BSU entered negotiations on installation of the IHET system equipment at the Reformatory. After a series of frustrating delays, I took the opportunity at the 10-year anniversary convocation of the BSU program at the prison to introduce the dean of Continuing Education to the commissioner of Corrections and opened discussion of the IHETS installation by these two key players. This discussion speeded completion and helped overcome bureaucratic road-

---

[4]This assumption was incorrect. States such as New York and Texas have graduate programs in their correctional systems and have graduated well over 150 inmate-students with master's degrees.

blocks. Dr. Van Ness also pushed the issue and was mildly censured by university administrators for overstepping his position. Eighteen confounding months and many thousands of dollars later, the system was operational.

During the interim between conception and operation, the feasibility of earning an M.B.A. diminished due to the undergraduate and graduate prerequisite requirements of that program, none of which had previously been available at the penitentiary "campus." The core requirements added to the graduate courses increased a 33-semester-hour degree program to nearly an 80-hour program. Even more damaging was the fact that the M.B.A. courses were telecast during the evening and on Saturdays, when inmates were not permitted (at that time) to take classes.[5] While the IHET system's installation hung in bureaucratic limbo, I completed three combination undergraduate-graduate level courses for graduate credit, the maximum permissible for an undergraduate. My intention then became to earn the Executive Development degree by combining the M.B.A.'s core requirements with a combination of other courses that could be scheduled at the Reformatory or taken on an individually arranged basis.

> If one advances confidently in the direction of his dreams, and endeavors to live the life which he has imagined, he will meet with success unexpected in common hours.
>
> Henry David Thoreau

The history of corrections is replete with noble plans and grand programs gone awry, and once again this story is an epistle to Murphy's Law. December of 1988 witnessed the bestowing of my Bachelor of Science degree, *cum laude*, with departmental honors in history and three national or international honor society distinctions. At the time of presumed elation for accomplishing my original goal, the devastating news that ISR policy did not recognize my graduate student standing —thus necessitating my reclassification out of the college program—was imparted the same week as my diploma.

The original ISR-BSU college program policy, written more than a decade before, had never addressed the possibility of graduate study. The then-director of education at the Reformatory, ironically a BSU adult and community education doctoral student, could not be persuaded either to grant an exemption or request an amended policy allowing for such academic growth. Even phone calls to and a personal meeting with the superintendent by my mother failed to create an allowance. In effect, I was expelled from the

---

[5]During the 1989-90 academic year, the Reformatory switched to an afternoon-evening class schedule (1:00 to 8:00 P.M.). This still did not make IHET-MBA classes available because they ended at 8:30 P.M. The next academic year, the program was returned to its traditional day schedule (8:00 A.M. to 3:00 P.M.).

institution's college program, told to find a job within the Reformatory in 30 days or lose my housing unit assignment where I had resided for six years, and left to complete nine prepaid graduate credit hours the best way possible.

In a classic case of adult and community education troubleshooting, Dr. Van Ness was able to negotiate a special one-semester dispensation with the College of Business, waiving the live viewing and interactive requirements for televised classes and allowing me to view taped classes instead. All this was with the proviso that by the next term the "supervision issue" would be resolved and participation in the live, interactive televised classes would be possible. However, because I was no longer classified as a college student, I had to find a work assignment where the supervisor would grant me an absence three mornings a week to use the college office's VCR unit to watch six to eight hours of taped classes per week.

After 13 employment rejections (due to the course work necessities), I felt like the proverbial doctor of medieval studies who was forced to drive a cab, except the Ph.D. had a job and I did not! Fortunately, a friend located a work assignment opening for me in the music theory program, conveniently located two floors below the college office and classrooms. Thus, while I studied organizational behavior and macroeconomics, I also learned scales and came to the depressing realization that I possessed no talent for the trombone.

The semester's ordeal, moreover, was just beginning. The education director then informed me during a mutually heated discussion that there was no classroom space available for me to use the VCR, and therefore I could not view my class tapes. Recalling a technique learned in a political science class in international negotiations, I elicited authorization to use the VCR if I could find the space. Smugly, the director, assuming no offender could make such an arrangement, consented to my request. The next day, I sat in the corner of the college area's eight-by-ten-foot bathroom with the VCR cabinet pinning me in one nook while the students used the facilities in the opposite corner.

Suffering good-humored ribbings and not-so-good-natured flatulence, I studied class tapes and scribed lecture notes. I juggled a four-day delay of class tapes because the education director would not permit classes to be recorded as they were being broadcast, forcing BSU to mail them to me. Along with the music theory classes, instrument practice, and the regular restrictive institutional schedules, I was required to meet deadlines for course papers and comply with campus test dates. At one point, the management professor, out of frustration, threatened to eject me from his class after he called the prison to personally comment on one of my papers, only to be informed that no graduate college program existed at the Reformatory.

With the administrative assistance of Dr. Van Ness, I managed to earn an A in the management class and missed the same grade by a single percentage point in the abstract science of economics. After this semester's series of glitches and frustrations, I realized that the IHETS was not going to be allowed for graduate study at the prison. The rest of my degree would have to be completed via "arrangement," a euphemism for modified correspondence courses, a form of distance learning.

The ultimate goal of the educational system is to shift to the individual the burden of pursuing his own education.

John Gardner

After this traumatic semester, completion of my graduate degree became totally dependent on specially arranged classes from cooperative professors in the departments of adult education, journalism, and political science to round out the flexible Executive Development degree requirements. This solution, however, was not without its own inherent problems. There would be restricted direct contact with professors, no classmates with whom to tutor, and an administration that actively failed to support my program of study.

Perhaps, though, the greatest problem facing any inmate-student, but especially the inmate-graduate student, is the lack of adequate access to research material. Most prison libraries fall woefully short in providing sufficient depth and diversity for even undergraduate study. The solution in my situation was a threefold strategy. First, professors were advised of my research limitations and asked to provide additional texts, either by borrowing them from their own libraries or from university library stacks. Second, professors sought to collect pieces of current research that could be mined for research papers (a practice becoming a common occurrence for many on-campus classes) that could be collated into course-specific supplemental texts. Third, because the remainder of my courses either focused on adult and community education issues or could have their research projects reflect information from this area, I began collecting my own library, concentrating on correctional issues, especially postsecondary correctional education, as my field of specialty.

The structure of arranged classes varied but usually included assignments of several texts with paper readings, review of audio- and/or videotapes, short and long research papers, two or three direct consultations with the professor, and one or two proctored exams. In many ways, the arranged graduate classes resembled the standard correspondence course, though one on steroids. The overall work load was easily double any undergraduate correspondence class I had taken. What I learned to appreciate the most about such a pedagogy is that it allowed me to concentrate on developing knowledge in-depth and to participate in a varying element of teacher-student negotiation over content and direction of each course. Each class became a custom-crafted learning experience, while retaining a core body of knowledge expected of any student

in that particular area. In essence, the program reflected the practical fulfill-
ment of the tenet of flexibility in the philosophy of adult education.

Still, though, there was concern by my advisor over the watered-down
learning experience. Between the hodgepodge of research material and isola-
tion from other graduate students, there was concern among university
officials and myself that I was earning a second-class degree. On every
occasion of comparison, however, I learned this simply was not so. Professors
sent me student papers as assignment examples, and upon comparison, my
work equaled or excelled that of my classmates.

On another occasion, in a judicious twist of fate, the ISR education
director and I were concurrently enrolled in two different classes taught by the
same professor—who also happened to be my official graduate advisor. In the
course of fulfilling my graduate thesis requirement, I enrolled in this professor's
grantsmanship class, researching and writing an 80-page grant proposal to
fund the prison's graduate program. The professor was not only impressed
enough with the quality of the work to use it as an example in future classes,
he presented a copy of the thesis to the education director before his class,
explaining its outstanding qualities and commenting to the director how
proud he must be of my efforts. The class then applauded the director's
"farseeing adult education programming" at the prison.

After completing the music theory program, to circumvent ISR's regula-
tion concerning work assignments and dormitory housing status, I registered
for a second baccalaureate in general studies funded by a consortium of church
groups and friends. This option solved two problems: (1) it provided a job
assignment, and, (2) by declaring a criminology and criminal justice minor, I
qualified to enter national student paper competitions in the criminal justice
concentration field. Thus, while I took one or two undergraduate classes a
semester, the remainder of my graduate degree was completed as well.

Eight years after beginning my postsecondary odyssey, I was granted the
first graduate degree conferred to an Indiana inmate. ISR, however, refused to
allow the presentation of the actual degree, and later "lost" the withheld
diploma. In the fall of 1990, encouraged by Dr. Van Ness, I applied for and was
accepted into the university's doctoral program in adult and community
education, although with the understanding that my incarceration would
preclude my completing the required semesters or fulfilling the degree's two-
semester residency requirement. Nevertheless, in eight years I had progressed
from an undirected freshman to a focused doctoral student, all within the
misanthropic wasteland of the penitentiary.

> Education is what remains after you have forgotten everything you have learned
> in school.
>
>   Albert Einstein

The postsecondary attainments made by men and women in prison have not been without controversy. Critics of my education (as well as other inmate-students) have claimed my degrees are worthless, alleging that by the time I am released, I will have forgotten the knowledge gained and skills learned. Obviously, I do not agree with this skewed assessment. The value of education well exceeds what I have learned about a particular subject; it is about opening the mind, invigorating the spirit, and extending the vistas of human possibility.

Upon reflection, there is virtually no comparison between the lost, frightened teenager who entered the back gate of the Reformatory a dozen years ago and the focused, confident man who now resides in this institution. Physical and mental aging are not the only differences separating the two men; more important is the educationally induced, maturing cognitive and moral mindset that recognizes the severity of past transgressions and accepts their consequences, limitations, and life-shaping forces. I now see myself as a man who recognizes his own self-worth and potential to be a positively contributing member of his community instead of the destabilizing and self-defacing predator he once was. Education has helped me to become a person who can unconditionally but not uncritically love and respect himself for all his failures and successes. From this foundation I can begin to truly accept love and respect others, including all of their foibles and strengths. And as Senator Bill Bradley comments, "Ultimately, respect is what it's all about."

To date, I have not achieved my original graduate dream of earning an M.B.A. Somehow, it just does not seem as important, although, one day I would like to fulfill that dream as well. As an adherent of the doctrine of Karma, I believe it was my fate to complete the public service degree before any others. A repetitive theme through those classes was the inherent value of people—valuing them for their potentiality, uniqueness, and worth as human beings. Through its humanistic philosophy, this degree imparted moral precepts by example and perhaps by osmosis. The lessons, though subtle, were psychologically penetrating and powerful. Today, I find myself reflexively evaluating my thoughts and actions by the barometer of what is fair, just, and right. In my opinion, these seeds were sown by my undergraduate liberal arts curriculum, then cultivated by the course work of the public service graduate study.

> Throughout the centuries, there were men who took the first step down new roads armed with nothing but their own vision.
>
> Ayn Rand

To make graduate study a success in the penal environment (at least *this* one) takes the cooperation of highly motivated, patient students; a flexible university; and professionally imaginative as well as caring instructors. Also essential are creative planning and problem solving in providing research resources, delivering courses, and working through the restrictive milieu of institutional roadblocks. Finally, the cooperation, if not the unflagging support, of the correctional system becomes necessary for such an opportunity to succeed and thrive beyond an individual guerrilla academic insurgency. Although much less adjustment is required of schools already delivering postsecondary correctional education programs, their mechanisms too must be supportive of graduate study to be successfully implemented. A healthy dose of humor will also go a long way in relieving the stress inevitably experienced in such circumstances.

The central element that allowed me to survive all the assaults on my dream was my unwavering will to succeed. Never did I believe my goal, once established, was impossible to achieve. No matter what occurred, no matter what obstacles were placed in my path, I found a way to reach the next objective. With the support of faculty, family, and friends, my dreams became reality. My next quest is to earn a doctorate in adult and community education and to one day return to the Indiana State Reformatory and teach a class in the very classrooms where I once sat with a number on my chest. One day, I will.

> *Everything can be taken from a man but one thing; the last of human freedoms—to choose one's attitude in any given set of circumstances, to choose one's own way.*
>
> Victor Frankl

A Prisoner's View

by Catherine Mason

· · · · · · · · · · ·

Higher education in prison is a multiemotional experience. It is both frustrating and rewarding. Within your first two weeks in prison, you realize that the environment is oppressive. If you are fortunate enough to have access to higher education while incarcerated then you will have intellectual stimulation that you will not find anywhere else in the system.

My story begins in February of 1988 when I was incarcerated for writing bad checks. Pregnant at the time with my first child, I was sentenced to nine years. For the first eighteen months of my sentence, I was limited to, through the Department of Correctional Education (DOCE) school, business and cosmetology classes that did not stimulate me. There was also the occasional night course offered by the local community college, but the only degree it offered was Executive Housekeeping, and I had higher aspirations than that.

Then it happened. In August of 1989, the first meeting of the Mary Baldwin College Goochland Campus came to order in the library of the DOCE school. We were excited. There was a mixture of high school graduates, those who had recently gotten their GEDs, previous college participants, those who had never attended college, young, old, and somewhere in between. The only thing we had in common was jail, and that is enough to solidify any group of women. There was nervous laughter among us. What are we getting ourselves into? What is it going to be like? Can we make it? Will the instructors treat us as if we are ignorant merely because of our surroundings? In that initial meeting most of our fears were laid to rest and most of our

---

Catherine Mason lives with her daughter in Roanoke, Virginia, where she works in medical billing and is a student in Mary Baldwin College's Adult Degree Program.

questions (at that moment) were answered. I was excited, but the real work lay ahead.

In the next meeting, we learned more about the college process. There were papers to fill out, forms to sign, courses to request. But these were minor hurdles compared to what was to come.

As the beginning of the semester neared, we found out that the gym basement would be sectioned off into our classrooms. The floors and walls were freshly painted. Chalkboards were hung and desks furnished. The Department of Correctional Education seemed willing to do their part; they would furnish our books. It all seemed easy enough—sign up, get the books, and start studying. What we didn't count on was the opposition we would get from the staff.

Prison is not a place to foster self-esteem. It seemed that the administration was saying, "We don't want them educated." The officers were angry because we were getting something they couldn't afford and getting it "free." We heard that enough to know exactly how they felt about us educating ourselves.

By now we were about three weeks into the great endeavor, the "fresh" gray paint on the concrete floor was about half gone, we had no supplies, and the gym basement was hotter than Hades in the middle of a heat wave even though the rest of the school was air-conditioned. I was getting the idea that the Department of Correctional Education was not really supportive of the program. But we persevered.

The education was truly stimulating. The professors did not act as if we were ignorant, but listened intently to what we had to say and adapted their teaching methods to relate to us as adults who were knowledgeable in other areas of life. That is not to say that they allowed us to be slack in our academics; the classes were rigorous, and the majority of us were in there to learn and to learn all that we could.

We had now learned a lot about Tina Wilson, our program coordinator, wonderful teacher, and all-around special person. She had to be, to deal with us in the midst of these trying times. Don Wells, the Director of Continuous Education, was the man behind the setup of this program; he spent a lot of time and effort to make sure that the program succeeded. He was a corner-stone and was fondly referred to as "Uncle Don." Then there was Dr. Dave Cary, an excellent professor and teacher, bar none, from whom we learned a lot about both sociology and life. Dr. Virginia Francisco took over when Don Wells retired. These were the people who were there for us whether we had an academic or a personal problem—they listened well and helped if they could. They took time with us and treated us as if we were human.

As our first semester was drawing to a close, we reacted as most college students across the country do—with panic at the thought of upcoming exams. We studied intently, took our exams, and finished with only a few minor scrapes, bumps, and bruises. But our reward was coming. Grades? No, that's not it. Sure, they were important, but what we were really anticipating was the Christmas party that Don and the professors had set up for us, complete with Mary Baldwin College sweatshirts and "real" food catered straight from the college campus.

With the arrival of January 1990, we were about to begin our second semester. Again we went through the class schedule and sign-up, but this time the Department of Correctional Education told us they couldn't provide books, the money isn't there. It isn't there at Mary Baldwin either, but somehow Don and Tina scrambled to get us books. Our survival rate must have had a magnetic effect on the officers' radios, because it seemed the more we studied, the louder their radios got. At first this was a little distracting, and, as the semester progressed, it became extremely irritating.

During this time there had been talk of having a "Mary Baldwin" hall to house all of the Mary Baldwin College students. This sounded great. We could encourage each other, there could be quiet study time and a host of other things that would enable us to feel more like students. The living conditions at that time were not conducive to learning. Most halls housed 70 to 75 women in space designed to hold 38 to 40 women. Seventy women on a hall can make a lot of noise even if you are in a room by yourself or with one other person. Eventually there would be a place to house all of the college students at once, but for now we lived scattered across the campus.

Finally the spring semester ended. During our first two semesters, we had taken courses that most college freshmen take—English, sociology, western civilization, literature, art. We were building a good foundation with instructors who were flexible but serious about learning. We were learning the college process with a little added stress from the living conditions. For the most part, we were good students, not in the greatest environment, but what else did we have to do? There weren't exactly groups of dates lined up outside our buildings waiting to take us out. That is not to say that we weren't serious about our studies—we were, but in part because we had the time to be. A small summer session came and went without any major mishaps—we were finished for the semester. And that is where my real problems began.

During the past year, the prison had become filled to overflowing. Something needed to be done and done quickly. The Department of Corrections' solution was to bring in four trailers, one of which was to be a Work Release trailer, to house the women. Before there was a Mary Baldwin program, I had signed up for Work Release. The Work Release program had been on hold for some time, but now the Department of Corrections was reimplementing it. I was chosen for the Work Release program along with 23 other suitable candidates, and, in June 1990, we were moved into the trailer. What an adjustment! Most of us had been in the system for at least two years, and some for longer than that. We had achieved enough steps (awarded for good behavior and cumulative time) to have single rooms. Now, all at once we were thrown together, 24 of us, in one double-wide trailer. These were cramped conditions, to say the least. In addition to the 24 beds, the trailer housed showers, sinks and commodes, a washer and dryer, a recreation dining room, and an office for the officer. There was 16 inches of space between the bunk beds.

It was also time for me to go up for parole. With a parole answer pending and having learned more about the Work Release program, I decided it was not for me. After much thought I decided to turn down Work Release and return to the Mary Baldwin program. Getting out of Work Release was difficult. Once the prison administration had decided you were a "suitable" candidate, they didn't want to let you go.

Finally, after much proverbial red tape, I was allowed to leave the program, but not to return to the single room for which I was eligible. Instead, I was put in the new trailer set up for the college students—exactly the same setup I described before, a mess. If I thought that a single room with 70 women outside my door was loud, I was wrong. That did not compare to trying to study with 23 women in the room with me. How would I do it? Perhaps by studying in the afternoon when some were gone and others were taking naps. That worked pretty well until we got an officer who liked to watch soap operas at 80 decibels. Now what? My cassette player with Luther VanDross at a semi-low level might work. The semester had just begun, and already I was feeling overwhelmed. Living in a trailer full of womenwith a pending parole answer, I didn't think that I could handle a semester of classes. Fortunately, two weeks into the semester, I received a parole answer and a release date. My time in prison was over.

After being released in September 1990, I took about a year and a half off from my studies to get my life in order. I returned to the Mary Baldwin Adult Degree Program in April 1992. Despite the obstacles I encountered while a student in prison, the Mary Baldwin program was the best thing that happened to me. It gave me motivation and self-esteem that I couldn't get anywhere else. That program is the reason I'm in school today. With an anticipated graduation date of May 1994, I am pursuing placement in a graduate program in clinical psychology.

Women Offenders: A Population Overlooked

by Christine Ennulat Wilson

· · · · · · · · · ·

EDITOR'S INTRODUCTION

This chapter addresses a population forgotten. Women prisoners have largely been overlooked in the literature of prison higher education. This fact may be no more than an accurate representation of the reality that they have also been overlooked in the actual delivery of opportunities for higher education within the prison. From the outset, prison higher education programs have tended to emphasize on the education of male prisoners. Why have women received so little attention as both offenders and candidates for reform? How is it possible, in an era that celebrates women's increased freedom and equalities, that women prisoners suffer substantive inequality in relation to male prisoners?

Christine Ennulat Wilson argues that an array of circumstances are responsible. On the one hand, the relatively small number of women prisoners makes them an easy population to overlook and also hinders efforts to develop and sustain programs that meet their needs. On the other hand, higher education's role in the lives of women prisoners is shaped by misperceptions regarding women offenders and by sexism in higher education, the prison, and the larger society.

The educational opportunities afforded to women prisoners tend to reflect the gender inequality and occupational role segregation that is deeply imbedded in our culture and society. Wilson points out, for example, that although

---

Christine Ennulat Wilson is a freelance writer and editor living with her family in Virginia.

the ratio of programs for women to the number of institutions for women is actually greater than that for men, the programs themselves are limited to preparation for gender-suggestive roles, provide opportunities for lower levels of academic work, and are less likely to lead to the acquisition of a college degree.

· · · · · · · · ·

"And one of the assistant wardens tells her, 'We just want to make things hard for you while you're here so you won't want to come back.'"

One of the psychologists at the women's prison where I coordinate a college degree program has just recounted a conversation with an inmate about the institution's delay in completing the remodeling of some rooms in the facility where most of the programs take place. The college classes have been slogging away in the gymnasium and whatever other space we can find, but these as well as treatment and religious programs have been on hold for months. The psychologist concludes, "The thing is, these women already know how to survive absurd circumstances. It's what they're used to."

Women offenders have been overlooked since the beginnings of incarceration as punishment for crime. But the word *overlooked* has a deceptive lack of connotation (as in "Oops! We forgot the women again!") that belies the complexity of the web of forces at work against equality of opportunity in general within women's prisons. This web includes, and is sometimes especially true for, attempts at implementing higher education programs.

Most of the material on prison higher education programs has been drawn from experience and research in men's prisons, and the majority of it seems to be about the capacity of liberal arts programs to move inmates up through stages defined by developmental psychology. Comparatively little has been written about women and crime, much less about women prisoners and postsecondary education. What exists is mostly anecdotal material about the experience of teaching in a women's prison, about instructors having been pleasantly surprised at how literate the women were, about difficulties getting calculators or string or eyedrops past security, about the lack of space and the disruptiveness of the institutional environment itself. None of the literature draws connections between these small, annoying symptoms and what they manifest, phenomena that are described in the recent, more general literature on women in prison: misperceptions regarding women offenders, and the sexism that pervades the system. In male institutions, there is an average of 10 vocational programs for inmates as compared to three in women's institutions (Flowers 1987) . The dearth of programs in women's prisons is all too well known to those who have had educational responsibilities in the field of corrections for women; it is a reverberation of a policy of neglect from the beginnings of incarceration as a way to deal with crime by women. Of course, it affects efforts in education:

> It is important to note that many of the demands for reform have come from outside the criminal justice system, often from groups with widely divergent interests and concerns. This often means that many new proposals for reform are acted upon simultaneously, although they may conflict with one another, and often when they are greatly at odds with the philosophy of the existing system. In effect, this means that model programs are frequently superimposed on a system whose basic purpose is antithetical to the goals of the model, and this lack of consistency dooms the projects to failure. (Glick and Neto 1977)

For most incarcerated women, not only the circumstances of their lives before and after incarceration but the system itself is hostile to education. If postsecondary programs are to succeed in women's institutions, they need to be designed with more in mind than the sensibilities of the system, its purposes and perceptions with regard to the women in its charge. They must take into account, as well, the women's perceptions of themselves, and their needs, during and after incarceration.

THE AGENDA OF THE SYSTEM

Prior to the penal reform movement of the late 1800s, the popular belief was that, because "men were created by God to be aggressive and women were created by God to be passive and domestic . . . the female offender [must have] gone against her natural tendencies. As such, women in prison were not deemed capable of reform and redemption"(Feinman 1983). Feinman goes on to state that they were incarcerated in institutions with men and left at the mercy of male residents and staff, often abused to the point of death. Of course, they were also denied opportunities for instruction or recreation.

After the first reformatory for women was built in 1873 in Indiana, the perpetuation of sexual stereotypes in women's corrections continued. The system was "a matriarchy where 'good' staff women, acting as mothers, would teach the inmate-children to be proper women in a simulated homelike environment in the prison" (Feinman 1983). Even the architecture, often cottages on a country hillside among trees and flowers, reflected these homey values (Flowers 1987).

Today, most programs for women continue to try to teach women offenders to be "honest, law-abiding members of society as wives/mothers or homemakers who have husbands to support them" (Feinman 1983). These programs fall into five categories: (1) institutional maintenance, including clerical work, food service for the institution, general cleaning, and maintenance of the grounds; (2) education, which is mostly remedial; (3) vocational training, most often toward stereotypical jobs; (4) treatment, including therapy, Alcoholics Anonymous, Narcotics Anonymous, etc.; and (5) medical care (Pollock-Byrne 1990).

Work in women's prisons tends to be concerned with domestic upkeep, and the institutions often categorize these work assignments as treatment, implying that "if the treatment is housewifery, the sickness, it is implied, is being an inadequate and incompetent housewife" (Dobash, Dobash, and Gutteridge 1986). Vocational training typically covers traditionally female tasks including cosmetology, sewing, food service, and clerical skills (Flowers 1987), and this list repeats itself again and again in the literature on women's programs. Carp and Schade (1992) suggest that the job training women receive in prison is of the same kind that "led to them being underemployed or unemployed in the first place, and their educational deficits are left unaddressed." Also ubiquitous is the list of reasons for the lack of vocational and rehabilitative programs for women: (1) Programs are not cost-effective because there are so few female prisoners (currently only 5.7 percent of the total incarcerated population); (2) such finances are "unwarranted" for females, who are less of a threat to society than males; (3) program participation is low; (4) many women's facilities, usually one institution per state, are inaccessible, located in remote, rural areas; and (5) women are still perceived mostly in the role of homemaker, not breadwinner. So "legislators and corrections officials give full priority to men's programs, . . . [giving] women few or no opportunities to learn new skills or earn enough money to aid their families on the outside" (Flowers 1987), much less themselves. The average percentage of state correctional budgets allotted for female offenders in 1984 was 5.08 percent, individual state budget allocations ranged from 1.3 to 12.3 percent (Ryan 1984). Allocating an average of 5.08 percent of the correctional budget for what was, at the time that figure was recorded, about 4.4 percent of the incarcerated population does not sound inconsistent; however, because the female population is so small, it is less cost-effective to run programs on the same scale for them as for men.

Other theorists suggest that the women themselves have not made enough noise to draw public attention to their situation (Alpert 1982). It is said that "male inmates are far more apt to stand together to redress a grievance than women are. Women complain but endure" (Harris 1992). Apparently, when they do complain or express legal concerns, those in power believe that the women's concerns are "not that keenly felt and [are] largely 'emotional'" (Chesney-Lind 1986).

THE POPULATION: DISENTANGLING MISPERCEPTIONS

Ironically, criminologist Freda Adler set forth in 1975 a theory of women's criminality that became popular with the media (Chapman 1980) and supported the sexist modus operandi of women's penal institutions: "The phenomenon of female criminality is but one wave in this rising tide of female assertiveness—a wave which has not yet crested and may even be seeking its level uncomfortably close to the high-water mark set by male violence." Adler went on to analyze what she thought was a burgeoning of white-collar crime by women:

> A trend which will arch its way upward for at least another generation and shatter the stereotypes of both women and criminals before it levels off. In this development we are witnessing the decline of femininity as we knew it, or thought we knew it, and the rise of a type of woman whose lack of traditional role models makes her as unfamiliar to her parents as she is to herself, a social experiment in unisexual modes of normalcy and deviancy. (Adler 1975)

Women want to be like men, and "crime is a vehicle for exhibiting traditional masculine qualities . . . it is fun, it involves a spirit of liberation, of risk-taking." Rita Simon (1975) came to the related conclusion, in less florid language, that the increases in property crime by women were directly related to increases in women's labor force participation. Confusingly, earlier in her book she had pointed out the lack of change in the degree of women's participation in the labor force (Naffine 1987).

Opposing arguments did not enjoy such exposure and apparently still have not filtered from academia into correctional circles, although they make much better sense. In a 1976 article, in addition to toppling Adler's statistical argument by using some simple calculations, Laura Crites found in her study of the demographics of American female offenders that most were from minority groups, were poor and worked in low-status jobs, were undereducated, and had children to provide for. She concluded that

> employment benefits derived from the feminist push for equal employment opportunities accrue predominantly to white, middle-class females. The women's rights movement has largely swept over the subpopulation group of poor, minority females, into which the female offender falls. These women, rather than being recipients of expanded rights and

opportunities gained by the women's movement, are, instead, witnessing
declining survival options.

Jane Roberts Chapman (1980) agrees that the situation of poor women
may have worsened because of a generalized shift of economic responsibilities.
"A large proportion of women with children under age 18 now work; support
payments from absent fathers are seldom made, even in middle-class families,
and there is a more widespread expectation that women will be financially
self-sufficient." Chapman suggests the term "frayed-collar crime" as more
descriptive of the economic crime that becomes more frequent whenever the
economy is in decline, rather than in response to any increased opportunity
brought about by liberation.

Some may interpret this economic argument as discounting the offender's
responsibility for her crime and failing to take into account members of higher
socioeconomic classes, but the facts as drawn from U.S. Bureau of Justice
Statistics are as follows: Women are less likely than men to be working in the
month before their arrest, 47.1 percent to 70.1 percent of the men. Sixty
percent of the women have been on welfare, and the highest salaries earned
from the jobs they have had range from $3.36-$6.50 per hour (American
Correctional Association 1990). Mothers with children under 18 make up
67.5 percent of the prison population, 84.9 percent of whom had legal custody
of those children prior to entering prison, and 85.2 percent of whom plan to
live with their children upon release. Only 20.1 percent of women in prison
are married. Circumstances after incarceration are much the same as circumstances before incarceration, often worse. And, no matter from which side of
the tracks they hail, they leave prison no better equipped to face their
circumstances—social or economic—than they were when they entered.
They leave with nothing that might make it more possible for them to take
responsibility for their lives in less damaging ways.

Glick and Neto (1977) found that female offenders generally advocate
traditional roles for women: "It is important for women to have children and
for men to be hard workers and primary support of the family." Chesney-Lind
and Rodriguez (1983) heard again and again in their series of interviews with
incarcerated women "the desire to work at straight, respectable female jobs
('be a secretary with an important boss') and have a fairy-tale marriage with
the 'right' man." The top 12 vocational areas of interest in one women's
institution, for the most part, reflect this leaning toward pink-collar jobs; they
are, in descending order, child care center aide, keypunch operator, nurse's
aide, typist, cosmetologist, computer programmer, data processor, medical or
dental assistant, photographer, clothing designer, cashier, and correctional or

parole officer. Older women gravitated more toward traditional areas while younger women gravitated toward less traditional areas (Sorenson 1981).

Why are traditional attitudes so much more common in this fragment of the female population? It makes perfect sense that most of these women have not had time in their lives for "identity crises and exercises in assertiveness training" (Adler's aforementioned "rising tide" notwithstanding). Having missed out on the economic gains made by the women's movement, they have to support themselves and, most likely, their children in an inflation economy (Crites 1976). This is a nearly impossible feat under traditional sex role definitions, because occupations that are "acceptable" for women, by those definitions, do not pay well enough. To differentiate traditional from nontraditional sex roles or occupations implies an implicit value judgment; to talk of liberation connotes rejection of the traditional end of the spectrum of sex roles, which would be a mistake. The danger lies in skewing the spectrum—in pigeonholing women into those roles, in women limiting themselves to them. When women do so, they often must find alternative ways to survive within those roles.

Interestingly, the survival skills, "assertive and even aggressive attributes" that made it possible for these women to support themselves are a source of ambivalence for them. They regret having become tough, streetwise survivors (Chesney-Lind and Rodriguez 1983). The very character traits that enabled these women to be independent (even though this particular type of independence may have made them capable of performing their crimes) become reasons for self-castigation. I have often heard about and remarked upon the generally low self-esteem that prevails in the women's prison setting; their conservative values about rules for women may help explain why this is so.

Chapman (1980) suggests that another way to interpret poor self-esteem is that it points to dependent status. Chesney-Lind and Rodriguez (1983) echo this idea, saying that "one suspects that the search for the 'right man' and the desire to establish an 'appropriate' dependency relationship with him is a greater source of female criminality than the desire for independence." Chapman cites Center for Women Policy Studies surveys that revealed "pervasive and many-leveled dependency found among women offenders" and goes on to describe how dependencies may interact—a woman "drinks because of a dependent-abusive relationship with a spouse." Because of this she becomes "a person unlikely to benefit from a specific opportunity—such as job training [or college programming]—if her self-perception is that she is unable to achieve anything on her own."

THE PRISON ENVIRONMENT

This dependent behavior is generally not addressed in women's institutions; in fact, it is reinforced by the institutional environment. Jean Harris (1992), former resident of Bedford Hills, shows this in action:

> The arbitrary, often childish, even paranoid little rules change constantly, serving only as ubiquitous reminders that virtually every move we make when not locked in a cell is controlled by others. One day we can wear colored blouses into the visiting room. Then we can wear only white ones, and some of the colored ones are sent home. Later it changes again. . . .
> "Dental floss is important to use at every brushing," the prison dentist assures the women. She gives them dental floss. Suddenly, "No more dental floss. Dental floss is now contraband. If you are found with dental floss you will receive a Charge Sheet." The beat goes on. 'You can. You can't. You must. You mustn't. Who said you could do that? Well, from now on you can't.' Reduced to an errant two-year-old, you find yourself wondering, 'Will I ever be able to function outside again? Will I be able to cross a street by myself?'

"Walls are replaced by personnel, guns are replaced by stringent rules, bars are replaced by constant vigilance" (Gibson 1976). Contrary to the common belief that women's prisons are more cushy than men's, most are more custody oriented than treatment oriented (Pollock-Byrne 1990), with rules often more strict than in men's institutions (Flowers 1987). These infantilizing, even dehumanizing rules exist because there are usually only one or two facilities for women in each state; thus a single facility must house minimum, medium-, and maximum-security inmates. Most of the women live under the medium- and maximum-security policies, regardless of whether they merit them, because of the few for whom they are designed (Pollock-Byrne 1990); "only 24 percent of state facilities . . . recognize those differences [in security grading] and use specific systems for women" (American Correctional Association 1990).

Labeling theory, in sociology, examines how those in power "make labels . . . and apply them with such efficacy to the powerless that the latter internalize the message and reconstruct their self-image and behavior accordingly" (Naffine 1987). Presumably, policymakers in women's prisons are at least somewhat educated in criminology; however, criminology textbooks are noted for their omission of women criminals in spite of the publication of relevant research. This is for the usual reasons, including the underrepresentation of females in the total population of offenders, authors' views of female crimes as no real threat to the "moral fiber" of society, the view that women's crimes are less violent and disruptive, and the "interdisciplinary nature of women and crime topics" which might be discouraging to authors (Wright 1987).

The operation of many women's prisons then is based on that of male institutions, and there has been nothing with which to replace the old labels for women; they are ready-made and applied in abundance (if not with "efficacy"). Negative, belittling clichés about women fill the air and become self-fulfilling prophecies: "Women are passive" (they are rewarded for behaving in that manner); "Women are devious" (treated as such, they must become so in order to protect themselves); "Women gossip" and "women backbite" (one of the first things they are told during intake is that they should "snitch" on anyone they see breaking the rules—they are rewarded when they do so). Just as most of these women had no time to become "liberated" before being incarcerated, they have no space in which to do so while incarcerated. Not only have they become survivors (i.e., less than feminine, exhibiting characteristics that are wrong because they do not conform to the image of the traditional woman), they are now inmates (i.e., less than human, even more pigeonholed than before). In such an environment, where the safest way to function is to have no voice, it is difficult to be one's best self, let alone discover, or even remember, who that might be.

HIGHER EDUCATION IN WOMEN'S PRISONS

Many of the women with whom I have worked, in a four-year, liberal arts B.A. program, see their college experience as an opportunity to explore and assert their identity, sometimes for the first time. "I never realized that I could actually *think*," one former student said to me just before her release. "I've realized that I'm able to think for myself, and that my ideas are worth a damn." Another student, a 13-year resident of the institution, wrote in an essay for a composition class,

> Most of my thinking is done for me. I'm told when to go inside, outside, when to eat, listen to the radio, etc., etc . . . I['ve] felt inadequate. I haven't been exposed to many new ideas or had anything to explore, just . . . rules, and more rules. The environment here has played a big part in language I've learned because it was all I've heard. All of this is why college has forced me to think for myself. Some might not want inmates to be involved in higher education, [because] it might teach us to challenge authority. The only one I challenge is myself, every single day.
>
> You might ask, what changed my mind? Where is the girl who knew it all? Some might call the change maturity or growth. I believe I discovered my soul. It was nearly lost in the black hole of prison life but kept striving for survival for some unknown reason. . . . (M. 1990)

This student defines *soul* as conscience, her inner voice, her own voice. She and others in the program have been free, in the college classrooms, to find their potentials, to exercise them, and to stretch them. One thing I have found surprising, and unsung in the literature, is how intelligent, schooled or not, most of the women are. No one seems to acknowledge it, least of all the women themselves. But awareness of and trust in the workings of one's own mind add up to empowerment of the type that leads to accuracy and clarity of self-image, to accuracy and solidity of self-esteem, and toward anchored decision making. This is independence—individual, if not yet economic—which may or may not be washed away by economic realities soon after the students step back out into the world. The classroom becomes an island on which they can experience themselves as students, an identity that, by definition, involves growth and change and openness to possibility.

But then they leave the classroom to go back to their living units, where it is well nigh impossible to study because of the noise level and/or poor lighting and/or because they are allowed to have in their living areas only certain materials, which may at any given moment be declared contraband (three-ring binders recently suffered this fate at my institution) and/or their chairs have disappeared from their rooms. Or they go to their floor-mopping or dishwashing jobs, often full time, because in some states the incentive pay for class attendance has been abolished . . . that is, if it ever existed; about one half of the institutions responding to a 1988 survey paid women for classroom attendance.

DIMENSIONS

With so little concrete incentive, it is not easy to be a college student in prison. Even so, the programs continue and the women sign up. In 1984, 72 percent (40 of 58) of women's institutions responding to T. A. Ryan's (1984) survey offered college programs. A 1989 preliminary survey by John Littlefield (1989) turned up what looks like another 72 percent figure, 49 programs in 68 institutions (some institutions may offer more than one type of college program). Neither of these surveys differentiated as to whether these were one-year, two-year, or four-year programs, or whether they were directed toward degrees.

U.S. Bureau of Justice Statistics from 1986 show that 28.4 percent of women in the state prisons had completed high school or obtained their GED and 14.8 percent had completed some college requirements, for a total of 43.2 percent of the female, state-incarcerated population who might be eligible for college, if possession of a diploma or GED constitutes eligibility. Ryan's 1984 figures on the educational level of women in prison, as well as in jails and detention centers, add up to 40.2 percent possible college candidates.

In 1984, only eight percent of Ryan's surveyed population participated in college programs. Littlefield's 1989 survey showed about twice as great a proportion of the female population participating. Only six percent of the male inmates in Littlefield's survey participated in the 444 programs offered in the 703 male institutions in his sample, but the difference may be accounted for by the relative abundance of other types of programs offered in those facilities in comparison to those offered in female facilities (e.g., 10 vocational programs for men, three for women; Flowers 1987).

It appears then that higher educational institutions have not overlooked the female population; in fact, the ratio of programs for women to women's institutions surveyed is greater than that for men. It is a safe bet, however, that the number of one-year certificate and two-year associate degree programs in women's institutions by far outstrips the number of bachelor's degree programs, a conclusion informally supported by what little prison higher education information I could gather by word of mouth. The main reason for this seems to be that the average stay in prison for women is only 16 months.

The difficulty of access to bachelor's degree programs and the proliferation of associate degree and certificate programs may unintentionally mirror the propagation of stereotypical sex roles already in place in the system. But when instability of population keeps the number of prospective clients small, the type of program that will draw the most bodies into the classroom is the program that most likely will be considered cost-effective and will not be canceled for lack of participation.

When a two-year program is the only postsecondary offering in an institution, it effectively shuts out the women who already have some college experience. Four-year programs, on the other hand, shut out many of those who have families to support, which significantly reduces the number who might take advantage of them. It is most likely the exception rather than the rule for a female prisoner-student to finish a bachelor's degree while incarcerated, but the hope is that she will finish after her release. Unfortunately, for the majority of female offenders, this is not the case. Apparently, four-year programs, which might lead their participants into more lucrative employment than other types of programs, once again can best serve only those who came from that kind of background in the first place.

Some women are transported to men's facilities in order to take upper-level courses. This opportunity is usually limited to minimum-security prisoners, however, which precludes homogeneity in the group and shuts out otherwise qualified students. Similarly, women who live in coeducational institutions often, in spite of having access to a greater variety of programs in general, fail to take advantage of them because "institutional anxiety regarding the presence of female inmates and the proportion of women in coed institutions" makes access to opportunities difficult (Flowers 1987).

TYPES OF PROGRAMS

Many prospective students are not willing to put themselves in the position of once again failing to finish something they start, whether it be a two-year or a four-year program. Others see college as a luxury, an environment in which they never imagined to find themselves, because early, negative academic experiences left them convinced that they could not possibly be college material. Or the alienation from such an educational possibility may be simply because life has not left them time for such pursuits.

A substantial majority of the mothers, most of whose children are young (the average age of the incarcerated female is about 30), are trying to prepare themselves to support their families upon release. For them, there is almost a sense of panic underlying the choices they make about which programs to undertake. They are more inclined toward something like a cosmetology certificate, because it is a specific, concrete skill they can have in their hands when they go back and face the world, more concrete in their view than an A.A. in general studies or a B.A. in humanities. Many of the majors offered in prison higher education seem to have similarly lofty titles—interdisciplinary studies; human services; letters, arts and sciences; and the like. This is not to decry the value of these courses of study, but to point out that the value of the content may be lost on those who may not wish to sit through lengthy explanations of the titles. Prospective college students' areas of interest have been found to include drug counseling, law, business administration, psychology, music, art, creative writing, speech communication, foreign languages, and home economics (Sorenson 1981). They want to know how they can do *those* things, and if they cannot, then why.

PREPARATIONS REQUIRED FOR SUCCESS

As with other nontraditional programs in women's institutions, those who offer them must be prepared to do some public relations work to get the women interested (Pollock-Byrne 1990). Women in prison need, more than anything else, a balanced variety of opportunity, and they need to be able to believe in the availability of what exists, however limited by the circumstances and atmosphere of women's corrections. They also need to believe that they will be encouraged by teachers, at least, should they undertake something as demanding as college, because they know they will not find support from guards or other prisoners outside of the classroom.

A significant portion of the clientele will be women who have just gotten their GEDs and who, on the momentum of this achievement, run right over and sign up for college programs. But because the GED test is not designed to measure critical thinking skills involved in college work, the student may be setting herself up, once again, for failure. This suggests a need for precollege preparation, for noncredit study skills seminars or writing workshops that may help forestall some of the attrition occurring in these programs. Instructors need to be tenacious and encouraging of their students, as it is "all too easy to intimidate [them]. Inmates, confronted with their endless . . . deficiencies, may opt to flee from further academic struggle" (Calisti 1986); they may cancel themselves out before experiencing themselves as learners, before conquering their fears of dog-paddling. To see a student discovering skills she did not know she had is a reward many instructors find worthy of any extra energy invested.

ACADEMY-PRISON STAFF RELATIONS

But, of course, financial aid does not support noncredit activities. This part of a program would have to be financed in some other way, at least initially. Then, perhaps, college preparatory programming could be passed on to other students by those who have already accumulated experience; more advanced students might operate a writing center or a study center, depending on the flexibility of the institution. This model exists informally in many programs as an outgrowth of the sense of community these programs engender. In many institutions, however, it may not be possible because "to help one another smacks of empowerment, which is the antithesis of prison policy. The system must have the power; the inmate must be rendered impotent" (Harris 1992).

Because security personnel have the most power over the women's lives while they are incarcerated, relations with them are important. Many of them, having worked in the system for awhile and having developed immutable images of their charges, tend to look askance at any program that places substantial demands on its participants: "Yeah, she's just in there to be with her friends. She falls out of everything she starts. I give her three weeks." College, an opportunity many officers have felt was unavailable to them, may be viewed even more negatively. Three and a half years of faculty smiling and politicking at my institution have alleviated this somewhat, but it is by no means gone. If we could extend to staff at least some of the educational benefits available to the prisoner-students, attitudes would probably improve. One program I know of invites staff to participate as students in the classes for free, with the prisoner-students welcoming them without equivocation. But when we suggested this possibility to the students at my institution a while ago, the response was a flat "No." They felt the idea was a threat to the one island in the institution where they did not feel like "inmates."

CLASSROOM VERSUS DISTANCE LEARNING

Not all course work takes place in classrooms, with flesh-and-blood instructors present. I have found no data on attrition rates in women's college programs, and of course none specifically comparing rate of attrition in person-to-person instruction versus other delivery systems, including learning contract, interactive television, or correspondence. It takes great motivation and focus for anyone to complete a program based on distance learning, even more so in the prison environment with all the opposing forces already described, not to mention the inevitably paltry library resources. Besides demanding a great deal of discipline and motivation, an overbalance of distance learning may also foster among the students a sense of distance from the college, impersonal service from an impersonal behemoth. Of course, sometimes it is not feasible to offer every course in a classroom, and alternative delivery systems become a necessary substitute. The best place for them may be in upper-level classes, which are usually smaller and attract students more secure in their identities as students and more confident in seeking out the help they may need. Outside-of-classroom learning may also allow for more choice as to majors.

CONCLUSION

A recurring theme in my conversations with coordinators of other prison college programs for women is that the greatest success happened in the classroom, where, as was quoted to me more than once and as I have heard the students in my program say, "we feel free." The classroom is safe, an environment where they can speak their minds, be "uppity" without fear of penalty. They can experience success and have the chance to recognize and understand it; they can make mistakes in a place where there is someone to encourage them through to the other side of those mistakes. They can experience themselves as resources, because they are, as one of my colleagues could not emphasize enough, "the greatest untapped resource that exists in our country . . . a gold mine."

The juxtaposition of what happens in the prison college classroom with the surroundings in which it persists, and the friction inherent in that juxtaposition, make the value of the enterprise that much more vivid. I have often thought of it as "real life plus funhouse mirrors," and it is the most alive teaching experience I can think of.

Evaluating Prison Higher Education: A Beginning

by Johnstone Campbell

· · · · · · · · · · ·

EDITOR'S INTRODUCTION

The final contribution to this book concerns the crucial matter of evaluating higher education's efforts in the prison. Johnstone Campbell argues that higher education practitioners in the prison must transcend the political and ideological forces that have dictated that recidivism—return to incarceration after release—constitutes the sole measure of program success or failure.

Much is at stake here. Higher education may wish to be more than the next click in the rotation of institutions—from religion to psychology—that have offered themselves to the prison as "corrective technologies" and therefore earned a share of the historic failure of the prison to acheive its stated aims. Higher education cannot do this unless it is all owed to function independent from the goals of corrections; so far, by and large, these goals have dictated what higher education in prisons should be and what the standards for success or failure ought to be.

Johnstone Campbell is interim director, Inquiry Program, and a member of the graduate faculty, Higher Education Program, and lecturer at the University of Massachusetts, Amherst.

Like education, scholarship is both a solitary and collaborative activity. I am indebted to the following colleagues and students for their direct and indirect contributions to my thinking about this topic: Charles Adams, Debra Anderson, Deborah Dugan-Burke, Raymond Jones, William Lauroesch, Mary Deane Sorcineli, and George Spiro.

Campbell argues, in fact, that in the face of myriad assessments of this outcome, there is a compelling need to emphasize evaluation. Assessment suggests that a course or program will be measured against some standard, perhaps one imposed by sociopolitical imperatives. He describes evaluation, however, as a self-reflective process that can and should be undertaken by all participants in a program. Unlike assessment, evaluation is a dynamic process that allows aims to become recognizable and develop throughout. If prison higher education is to have any hope of freeing itself from the political and social contexts that shape its possibilities, the business of evaluation must play a critical role in the realization of that freedom.

· · · · · · · · ·

This volume has identified how and explored the ways in which prison higher education has a distinct place at the periphery of the academy; it has also focused on the ways in which prisoners, already marginalized by society, are marginalized in yet another way to being college students. There is a delicious irony, perhaps even a poetic educational justice, here. Although the political and economic contexts are ever present and always important, in prison education it is possible to focus upon the educational issues and questions that are lost in the more traditional settings. Rather than worry about what easy measures can be devised to determine how well we are controlproducing the desired outcome, we can ask the more basic question: What are we doing in the classrooms and in the programs that sponsor the classes? In brief, we can shift our attention and energies from assessment to evaluation.

Evaluation begins with a set of inquiries into the education activities themselves. As every teacher knows in an active way, and students sense without necessarily having the language to describe it, evaluation begins at the beginning. Evaluation begins before the first day of class and occurs as an ongoing activity throughout the semester, in sharp contrast to outcome assessments, which are made after the fact. In addition to this self-reflection during the semester, evaluation also includes retrospective reviews and determinations by all the participants once a class or course of study is completed; the process of evaluation cannot be reduced to a seemingly straightforward test administered under a centralized authority.

Prison higher education casts the educational issues in bold relief. The quantified measures common in program assessment and institutional research assume a set of norms that are less and less valid for the academy as a whole and inappropriate for prison higher education from the start. If we think of prison higher education as an experiment, it is an experiment without a group. The normative measures of a department's or program's success (such as GPA at graduation, percentage and quality of graduate schools attended, percentage and salaries of entry-level employment have a secondary correlation to the variegated purposes, objectives, and outcomes of prison higher education, and they may not apply at all to the specifics of any given prisoner-student's circumstances.

Prison higher education also figures significantly in the expanding scope of higher education in which the driving question of the day is what it means to teach a population that is intellectually, racially, culturally, socially, economically, and sexually diverse. While politicians, the press, and the general public have been embroiled in debates about what should be taught, education research has made significant discoveries about how we teach and the impact of education upon student development. The debate about the importance and place of human renewal of prisoner-students is part and parcel of this new direction in educational inquiry.

This chapter raises and explores two questions: What should we evaluate and how should we evaluate?

TEACHERS EVALUATE THEIR TEACHING

Every conscientious teacher begins, conducts, and concludes a course with an expanding and contracting set of impelling questions that are specific to the particulars and peculiarities of the time, place, and participants of that course. Thanks to recent innovations, today there are two ways to think about and evaluate effective teaching. One is a synthesis of some 55 years of studying how teachers teach. The other turns our attention from teacher to learner. What they share is a primary concern with the teacher-learner interaction that acknowledges the importance of content while respecting the integrity of the participants without reducing them to stereotypical roles: faculty and undergraduate, do-gooder and prisoner-student.

"The center of all teaching and learning is the interaction between the teacher and the learner" (Eble 1988). Not too long ago, this idea was considered a radical challenge to the classic view of college teaching and was dismissed as the outrageousness of the fringes of the academy, such as prison higher education. In the early 1990s, the teacher-learner dialectic stands at the center of every scholarly discussion of effective teaching.

The "Faculty Inventory of the Seven Principles for Good Practice in Undergraduate Education" has articulated the components of the teacher-learner dialectic and provides an easily administered self-inventory that offers a quick and telling picture of how well an individual teacher is working with students. It is a distillation of the major research on effective teaching that identifies seven principles and the components and activities that make up effective work in each (Chickering and Gamson 1991). It focuses upon how teachers can better work with their students without drawing harsh judgments about the weaknesses it uncovers. Even first-rate, widely acknowledged, distinguished teachers can find the self-reflection and the suggestions beneficial because the focus is entirely upon improving the teacher's interactions with students. But although inventory is an invaluable tool, it addresses only one part of the teaching dialectic.

Angelo and Cross (1993) look at the other part of the dialectic, the learner. They have devised an extensive set of techniques that enable teachers to observe and evaluate how well and in what ways their students are engaging the material in the course.[1] As with the "Seven Principles," the purpose is not to measure students' successes and failures in the supposed mastery of the course's content but to understand the ways in which the students are pursuing their studies with an eye to helping them to do better as learners engaged in an active process.

These two methods of looking at teaching and learning provide practical means for observing and evaluating what is one of the basic tenets of prison higher education: The alpha and omega of education is the complex set of responsibilities that teacher and student have to themselves, each other, and the course activities and content that bring them together.

Prisoner-students inhabit an extraordinary world that is as new and initially inexplicable to them as it is foreign to the teachers. Weis (1985) argues that the African Americans she studied in an urban community college are caught between two cultural worlds. Prisoner-students are in an even more confusing predicament: Exiled from the cultural world of their upbringing, their commitment to their studies makes them deviants from the cultural world of the prison.

As a consequence, the characteristics and qualities of the specific interactions of teacher and prisoner-learner assume an importance unparalleled in traditional settings. In order to meet and work with each other, both teacher and prisoner-learner must step outside the known terrain of their respective worlds. Insight into and an understanding of what any given teacher does to

---

[1] Angelo and Cross call the techniques "Classroom Assessment Techniques." The purposes, objectives, and proposed uses, however, are instructional improvement for both teacher and learner. In effect, then, despite the nomenclature, they are talking about what I am calling "evaluation" in contrast to "assessment" in this chapter.

help or hinder the prisoner-learner's studies, therefore, is of fundamental importance and a prerequisite to and pentimento for all other evaluations, which combine both quantitative and qualitative methods.

TEACHERS EVALUATE STUDENTS

Grades (whether they are of the A–F, collegiate "4 point," or straight 0–100 percent form) are the assessment currency of the land. Criticisms (both specious and well-founded) have been raised, and a variety of alternatives have been proposed, but it is hard to imagine that grades will be replaced any time soon. Unfortunately, grades and grading are two of the most basic educational mysteries for students at all levels of school and college and in every type of institution. The fundamental educational mystification is that learning can be reduced to right answers; it cannot be so reduced, learning is nothing more than personal opinion. The fundamental cultural mystification is that grades are the measure of the student as a person. It is reasonable to assume that the vast majority of prisoner-students (not to mention the majority of prisoners in general) have suffered in and been penalized by an educational system built upon these insidious premises. Ironically, prison higher education's continued existence and growth present a compelling refutation of the cultural norms and misperceptions about higher education.

The prisoner-students who enroll in, make constructive use of (even without completing a program), and graduate from prison higher education programs of all types put the paradoxes of prison higher education as delineated in the essay by Jones and d'Errico (see above) and the contradictions discussed in the essay by Heberle and Rose (see above) as well as the assessment-evaluation distinction into the spotlight.

Consider this caricature:

> Learning is right answers. Grades measure the percentage of right answers. Good grades mean the student is smart. Smart students are good people.

> Learning that does not involve right answers is not as valid. Grades are a matter of rewarding or punishing effort, personal opinion, motivation, lady luck.

> Ergo: Successful prisoner-students and successful prison higher education programs must be breaking the rules. The prisoner-students cannot be as smart (that is, as good) and the programs cannot be as demanding (that is, as excellent) as their counterparts outside the prisons.

The immediate evaluative challenge in prison higher education is to assure our students and ourselves as faculty and administrators that they are indeed engaged in the best education possible, and that they are in fact becoming well educated, despite being in a sociocultural environment instituted to deny the prisoner-students the fundamental promises of higher education, that is, ready acceptance into society and marketable employment knowledge and skills.

The longer-term challenge is to gather an assortment of data and a variety of analyses that demonstrate the accomplishments of prison higher education to its supporters and provides the basis upon which to address its critics. To do so, it is necessary to make the evaluation of the students' work a central part of the educational process.

Because abandoning grades is neither possible nor in the best interests of the prisoner-students, it is necessary to embed them in a larger evaluative activity. Years of experience in a wide array of schools and colleges have shown that it is possible to combine written evaluations and grades in ways that are informative and instructional for all involved.

In the experimental fervor of the mid-1960s that lasted into the 1970s, an impressive number of variations were generated. Looking back from the beleaguered 1990s, it seems clear that there are two models and that they can be readily adopted and adapted by both individual faculty and entire programs (as well as schools and colleges) with relative ease as long as there is the commitment to evaluation over assessment. In the first model, the faculty member provides a written evaluation of each student's work in addition to the letter grade. In the second, the student submits a written self-evaluation (separate from the teacher and course evaluation) to which the instructor adds a written evaluation and the grade.

Prison higher education, by virtue of the motives and commitments of those who work in it as well as its distinctive characteristics, such as small classes, addresses the most common concerns and objections to the use of written evaluations of student work. Two concerns do require brief mention, nonetheless.

The first concern is the fear of piling yet another responsibility upon faculty who have already assumed an out-of-the-ordinary work load by participating in a prison higher education program. In practice, the work sounds more onerous than it is. The difficult part, the observations of and reflections upon each student, is done while teaching during the semester. Writing a paragraph takes time, to be sure, but is in actuality nothing more than writing a brief report of what has been "done."

The second concern is the now classic conflict of content versus process. What is to be evaluated? Reducing the question to an either/or dualism obfuscates the issue. Even in courses that rely exclusively upon tests of the student's mastery of content and/or job-specific skills, there are significant differences among students that deserve evaluative attention from the teachers. Three students who earned a C, for instance, might well have done so in very different ways. One may have simply earned a C on each and every test. Another may have started very poorly and ended very well. The third might have begun strong and then plummeted.

The use of written evaluations can be especially appropriate in the nonacademic culture of the prison. Events, such as lock-downs, that are independent of the prisoner-students and their faculty, can affect a day's work or an entire semester's. However, teachers and programs decide to respond to the disruptions in terms of final grades, evaluations can assist in keeping the prisoner-student's attention on the educational significance of their work. A considered paragraph for each student not only helps them in their studies but contributes to the general improvement, in time, of both the instructor's work and the quality of the program.

STUDENTS EVALUATE TEACHERS AND THEIR COURSES

Faculty folklore about student evaluations of teachers and their courses has never been published in a single place, but it is safe to say that there is enough to fill a chapter of a book, if not a monograph, and that most of the folklore is about the negative aspects of student reviews of their teachers "for the record." The principle mistake make by faculty and administrators is to think that student evaluations are a popularity contest not unlike American political elections. Kenneth Eble in his classic *The Craft of Teaching* (1988) has given the best expression to what he calls "the mythology of teaching," that is, 12 very mistaken assumptions. One of these assumptions is "that good and bad teaching cannot be identified." It easily follows, then, "that the popular teacher is a bad teacher" and that the persecuting teacher is the good teacher:

> Teachers who did everything wrong but were superb and. . .who were
> detested by students then but are revered now. "I hated old Dworp's guts,"
> a professor will say, "but I really learned from him."

Actually the identification of good and poor instructors is patently obvious. Even a brief period of time spent in a department or program talking informally with students and faculty invariably uncovers the consensus about how faculty are rated. In 27 years, I have never seen this system fail, but neither have I seen it trusted—nor should it be. Student evaluation of faculty deserves a more formal approach and should be accorded the same credibility that faculty evaluation of students is.

The need for an evenhanded, program-administered process to evaluate teaching is self-evident. Getting past the obvious common knowledge about teachers and establishing a reliable basis for evaluating instructors has proven difficult and time consuming.

There are two compelling questions. Can a quantifiable evaluation form be designed that will prove reliable both within a discipline or department and also across disciplines and departments? The second question concerns the addition of quantitative and qualitative questions that can address the distinctive particulars of any given course, instructor, department, or program.

The answer to both questions is a resounding yes. Bubble forms, as students call the computer answer sheets, have been used for a long time for teacher evaluations, long enough so that now there is reason to believe that certain questions are statistically reliable both within and across disciplines (Doyle 1983; Theall and Franklin 1991). Three questions seem to have a global applicability and validity:

1. What is your overall rating of this instructor's teaching effectiveness compared with other college instructors you have had?
2. Overall, how much do you feel you have learned in this course?
3. What is your overall rating of this course?

As simple and as seemingly vague as these questions read, in comparative contexts they are remarkably revelatory. Although it would be unreasonable to stop with these questions, it is safe to assume that they provide an accurate basis on which we can begin to compare a chemist and a Chaucerian, for example.

There are 10 other questions that have been found to be statistically reliable, although they are not quite as universally compelling. They ask for evaluative comments on the instructor, the course, and the student doing the evaluation. In practice and used consistently over time, they provide a remarkably informative comparative and quantitative picture that can be readily understood and explained.

But useful as this approach is, it omits as much if not more than it includes when the primary concern is instructional improvement rather than institutional measurement. It is an easy task, however, to supplement the so-called objective questions with specific or open-ended questions that ask the students to write brief comments.

The qualitative questions move the matter of student judgment from the narrower confines of assessment into the more open and educationally important area of evaluation. Student comments have a specificity and immediacy that no questionnaire can achieve. The students' written evaluations also have a usefulness that is widely undervalued.

While the faculty have been observing and evaluating their students' learning, the students have had an equally discerning eye on their instructors and courses. We do ourselves, our student and their successors, and the programs a disservice when we overlook student commentary. The issue is not the students' lack of qualifications to assess a teacher's scholarly competence and expertise. The issue is effective college teaching. Usually only students spend time with a teacher in the college classroom. Students have a wealth of observations, insights, and suggestions that can be astonishingly constructive when we make the effort to elicit them and learn how to read them.

Prisoner-students are no exception. In fact, their ambiguous status in the prison and in higher education accords them a unique perspective as participant-observers. They are pioneers exploring new territory, always conscious of the old world behind them and ever alert to both the subtleties and the broad picture of the new world before them.

PROGRAM EVALUATION

Just as the evaluation of teaching and learning by faculty and students begins at the beginning, program evaluation begins with inductive data and observations (in contrast to the deductive approach of externally driven program assessment). Program evaluation draws upon and should grow out of the previous types of evaluation. It is simplistic, however, to see program evaluation as either a combination or even a synthesis of the others.

Program evaluation has two closely related but separable components: instructional and institutional. The instructional component is principally internal; its purposes and objectives are to review and improve our work within any given program, from course revision through curriculum to teaching improvement. The wealth of evaluative information and insight that accrues in even two to three semesters can be staggering.

As valuable as this material is, it is incomplete until augmented by two retrospective sources of information and data: one from the faculty and staff, and the other from students. The first source is an annual, end-of-year review that is comparable to a student's end-of-semester evaluation. When time and care are invested at the end of an academic year to bring the principals together to discuss the program, the courses, the students, and the teaching, it is possible to develop a new perspective on the outstanding questions of "How is the program doing?" and "How are our students doing?" This year-end review is also the time to make creative use of the standard assessment feedback loop to clarify goals, collect information and data, analyze the results, make any necessary adjustments, and prepare to repeat the process at the next year-end review.

The second retrospective evaluation is an exit interview that can be done in writing shortly after each student completes a course of study. As with the teacher and course evaluations, the exit interview can mix and match quantifiable and qualitative questions; the questions can cover the full range of programmatic concerns that are important in the specific institutional setting. When the same questions are given to successive years of graduates, the results can provide confirmation of what is working well and suggestions for areas that need to be revised, dropped, or added.

The exit interviews are a bridge between the immediacy of instructional evaluation and the longer-term project of institutional measurement and assessment, the second component of program evaluation. Institutional measurement addresses multiple audiences, a large percentage of which think that the quality and accomplishments of prison higher education can be assessed through readily quantifiable measures of accountability. These efforts are misguided when directed at traditional institutions; when they are used to review prison higher education they border on the absurd. Given the present and foreseeable climate in which prisoner-students will have to study, however, the demands for this type of assessment must be addressed.

The conventional measures used in institutional research and program assessment have their place. Evaluation does not disregard quantitative data; evaluation puts the data in the context from which they were generated. Data about student grade point averages, attrition and perseverance, prison higher education's equivalent of choice of major, along with the array of follow-up studies dictated by the panoply of futures that face prisoner-students after they leave a program (whether or not they completed it) are fundamental. But simple comparisons with other college students and programs—even with other prison higher education programs—are not very fruitful if they rely upon these data alone.

Just as letter grades in a course need the "thick description" (to borrow Clifford Geertz's phrase) of teacher and student written evaluations, so do the data about a program need the multicontextual commentary of the evaluative material gathered over time from and by faculty and students in any given program. Neither quantified data nor contextual explanation alone can explain the richness of the experiences of teaching and studying in or the multidimensional outcomes and successes of prison higher education that keep and attract prisoner-student, faculty, and administrator alike.

CONCLUSION

Our efforts, as individual faculty and administrators, as faculties and staffs of specific programs, and as participants in the educational institution of prison higher education, have the potential to contribute to educational practices far removed from the confines of the prisoner-students we are committed to teaching. At the moment, the potential remains just that, a suggestion of things that may come. Before we can hold the mirror up to the larger institution of higher education we must look ourselves in the eye. The challenges of evaluating prison higher education are formidable, in part because of the nature of prison higher education and in part because so little basic research has been initiated. Let's first look at this lack of research.

The prisoner-student is an unknown member of the academy. Prisoner-students enroll in higher education courses and matriculate in programs for reasons more complex and elusive than the reasons for which traditional students attend college. Institutional researchers are only now coming to recognize that students attend community colleges for reasons and in patterns that cannot be explained by the models developed to understand full-time, residential students in four-year colleges. It remains to be seen if prisoner-students are different in degree or in kind from their closest cohorts, the community college students.

From the researcher's perspective, we know even less about the faculty and administrators who seek out the rewarding but often trying opportunities to work in prison higher education. What attracts them, what retains them, what happens to them over the course of several years are only three obvious questions about which we have little insight.

Similar questions can be asked about the colleges and universities that sponsor and sustain prison higher education programs. Programs emerge and evaporate with great frequency, while some enjoy a lengthy half-life. Although the concrete particulars may be known to the participants in any given program, very little is known about what factors are at play in prison higher education as a national institution.

The ongoing, inductive, programmatic self-evaluation outlined in this chapter cannot address these and other basic research questions, but it can assure us of our accomplishments, make us confident of our strengths, alert us to real and potential weaknesses and problems, and guide us toward constructive improvements. With this knowledge and insight, it is possible to meet our students with a legitimate sense that we know what we are doing and how well we are doing it, to explain our work to those who certify the programs, and to address the often uninformed and misinformed critics who challenge the very existence of prison higher education.

Afterword

· · · · · · · · ·

The foregoing chapters have dealt frequently with the difficulties that abound in two institutions, corrections and higher education, diametrically opposed in purpose—security and freedom—working together toward a common end. Yet the outlook is optimistic: The very fact that more than 50,000 prisoners (Jones 1992b) participate in higher education is a significant achievement that reflects well on both corrections and higher education. As the chapters reveal, prison higher education programs are proving to be a learning situation for everyone. Although both corrections and higher education see their own work through different lenses, each recognizes the necessity to adapt *without* violating the prison's or the academy's first responsibility. The road ahead is sure to be filled with land mines and potholes. But the groundwork is in place—diligence, openness, and hard work (and a little bit of luck!) will move it forward.

Appendix
one
· · · · · · · · ·
The Federal Pell Grant Program

by Anne Peramba

The Higher Education Act of 1965 formally brought a federally funded loan and work program to postsecondary education. But it was not until the 1972 Amendments that any grant funds were introduced. This was the Basic Educational Opportunity Grant Program (BEOG). The Education Amendments of 1980 changed it's name to the Pell Grant Program, in honor of Senator Claiborne Pell from Rhode Island. Unlike the other campus-based Title IV programs (where the determination of eligibility is made on campus by the aid administrator), the Pell Grant Program is centrally administered by the federal government. Application is made directly to the federal government, which then hires private agencies to process the information. A voucherlike payment system makes it somewhat transferable between institutions, and as its original name suggests, it is the foundation of funding when determining an aid package. Today, regulatory guidelines fill an encyclopedia of more than 1,000 pages and are under constant scrutiny and change.

The Pell Grant Program is the largest student grant program administered by the Department of Education. It differs from other campus-based programs in that, if students meet all necessary requirements, they are entitled to payment of a Pell Grant upon the institution's receipt of a valid, signed Student Aid Report. The purpose of this program is to award grants to help financially needy students meet the cost of their postsecondary education. Within the burrows of guidelines, the student must basically prove need, be

---

Anne Peramba is assistant director of financial aid at the University of Massachusetts, Amherst.

enrolled in an undergraduate program leading to a degree, and be making satisfactory academic progress.

The Federal Pell Grant Program, as it is now known, publishes regulations that address certain populations, but none as stringent as the 1992 Amendments, which restrict the eligibility of incarcerated students. Each state must now demonstrate to the U.S. Department of Education that federal Pell Grant awards will be used to supplement, not supplant, the state's level of postsecondary education for fiscal year 1988. The department will collect data annually from states about their expenditures for educational assistance pertaining to incarcerated students. Until a state has qualified its incarcerated students through the department, no incarcerated students in the state will be eligible for a federal Pell Grant.

It seems evident that the population of incarcerated students certainly meets the basic criteria established for the Pell Grant Program, the demonstration of need. Studies show a high percentage of these students come from the lowest economic levels. They would have no problems demonstrating maximum eligibility whether inside or outside of prison.

Appendix two

· · · · · · · · ·

Pell Grants for Prisoners

by Jon Marc Taylor

The winner of the third annual Nation Institute/I.F. Stone Award for Student Journalism, which carries a prize of $500 and is open to undergraduates in U.S. colleges, was Jon Marc Taylor, an inmate at the Indiana State Reformatory. Taylor is enrolled at Ball State University's college extension program, majoring in criminal justice, criminology, and psychology. His writings have appeared in The Angolite, *the* Journal of Correctional Education, *and other publications. His goal, after his release, is to "earn a doctorate in adult and community education, become a positive prisoner advocate, and one day return to teach in the very classrooms where I once sat with a number on my chest." His account of the attempt to deny prisoners Pell Grants for higher education is squarely in the I.F. Stone tradition of advocacy journalism.*

—The Editors

Prisoners are the black sheep of our societal family, and thus discussions of their treatment are relegated to back-room deliberations of how they should be punished. A common opinion is that we are too soft on criminals and that what ever rehabilitation (or lack thereof) they receive is more than they deserve. An example of this disposition was the Congressional effort to bar inmate eligibility for Pell Grant higher education financial assistance. Last year, both the Senate and the House of Representatives passed legislation prohibiting offenders from qualifying for such aid. Before surveying this attempt at *Capitol* punishment, a short history of college programs for prisoners is in order.

Taylor, J. M. 1993. Pell Grants for Prisoners. *The Nation*. The Nation Company, Inc. Reprinted with permission.

Not until 1953, when the University of Southern Illinois matriculated its first class of inmate-students, did higher education enter the nation's penal institutions. U.S.I.'s radical experiment was slow to take root, for, by 1965, there were only 12 postsecondary correctional education (P.S.C.E.) programs in the country. The largest constraint facing these programs was the same as for any type of rehabilitative program—lack of funding.

In 1965, however, Congress passed Title IV of the Higher Education Act, which contained the Pell Grant program entitling student-prisoners who met certain criteria to receive financial aid for college-level studies. With the implementation of this funding, P.S.C.E. opportunities flourished; by 1973, there were 182 programs, by 1976, 237 programs, and by 1982 (the last official count), 350 programs offered in 90 percent of the states. Yet with the continued growth of the nation's correctional population, at most 10 percent of the country's prisoners were enrolled in P.S.C.E.

Even so, prison officials could see the effectiveness of these programs. Correctional administrators, facing ever-growing numbers of offenders whom they had to house and control, found that those enrolled in the program were easier to manage and better behaved than the average prisoner, providing a calming effect on the rest of the population.

What is more, beginning in the mid-1970s, studies of inmate college students (especially those earning degrees) revealed that they recidivated at much lower rates than nonenrolled prisoners. Between 1974 and 1979, three programs in Alabama, Maryland, and New Jersey reported substantial reductions in offender-students' recidivism, compared with standard return rates. These reductions ranged from a drop of 57 to 37 percent in one case to a dramatic difference of from 80 to only 10 percent in another program.

Perhaps the most widely reported evaluation was published in *Psychology Today* in 1983. The study noted that "recidivism . . . among college classes at New Mexico State Penitentiary between 1967 and 1977 averaged 15.5 percent, while the general population averaged 68 percent recidivism."

The positive reports continue into this decade, with the District of Columbia's Lorton Prison College Program noting a recidivism rate for students of only six percent, compared with an average that exceeded 40 percent. In 1991, the New York Department of Correctional Services reported on its four-year study of the state's P.S.C.E.—the second largest program in the nation. The study found a "statistically significant" difference in the return rates of those who earned degrees and those who did not complete the college program.

Today it costs $25,000 annually to incarcerate an individual, whereas one year of P.S.C.E. programming can be purchased for $2,500. In other words, for only 10 percent of the cost of a single year of imprisonment, an offender can enroll for two semesters of postsecondary education. If such education is continued for two to four years, society more than likely will receive ex-offenders whose chances of recidivating are in the low double- or single-digit range, compared with a national recidivism range of 50 to 70 percent.

Besides providing substantial savings by reducing the costly rate of recidivism, prison college programs produced educated workers for the economy. Studies in New York and Ohio in the early 1980s, at the height of the Reagan recession, revealed that P.S.C.E. graduates were employed in substantially higher numbers than other parolees in the area (60 to 75 percent compared with only 40 percent), suggesting that the education earned by the offenders favorably influenced employers' decisions in hiring them and offset the social stigma attached to their ex-con status. Parolee unemployment is a prime contributor to recidivism, so any program that enhances an ex-offender's employability is of benefit to the community.

The Corrections Program of the College of Santa Fe, New Mexico, has had great success in turning around its inmate-students. Examples include a graduate who went on to become a physician, another who became a vice president of an international company, and others who became personnel directors and teachers. A former death-row inmate rose to the directorship of a state corrections industry department.

These success stories give added emphasis to the words of former Chief Justice Warren Burger: "We must accept the reality that to confine offenders behind walls without trying to change them is an expensive folly with short-term benefits—winning battles while losing the war."

On July 30, 1991, Senator Jesse Helms rose to introduce Amendment 938, which read: "No person incarcerated in a federal or state penal institution shall receive any funds appropriated to carry out subpart 1 of part A of Title IV of the Higher Education Act of 1965." Helms fulminated that "American taxpayers are being forced to pay taxes to provide free college tuition for prisoners at a time when so many law-abiding, taxpaying citizens are struggling to find enough money to send their children to college."

The Helms Amendment was grounded in two assumptions: (1) that a significant diversion of grants from needy young people to prisoners is occurring, resulting in a large percentage of traditional students failing to receive aid, and (2) that inmate-students are not "needy." Both are false. Only 1.2 percent of the total number of Pell Grants issued went to prisoners. By any stretch of the imagination, this is not a significant diversion of funds.

As for prisoners not being "needy," a 1986 Bureau of Justice Statistics bulletin noted that 60 percent of prison inmates had earned less than $10,000 the year previous to their incarceration. In other words, they would have been below the poverty line and thus eligible for educational financial aid had they not been imprisoned.

With African Americans, Latinos, and other minorities composing 55 percent of our country's prison population, and with 60 percent of inmates coming from the lowest economic levels of society and 41 percent having less than a ninth-grade education, compared with 16 percent of the nation's adult population, there can be little doubt that student-prisoners are "needy." "If you want to educate black men, if you want to reclaim the talent out there," observes Robert Powell, assistant vice president for academic affairs at Shaw University in North Carolina, "you have to go into the prison." The sad reality in the United States today is that P.S.C.E. is one of the few remaining means by which minority youth can receive a college education.

The same day Amendment 938 was introduced, it passed the Senate by a floor vote of 60 to 38 and was attached to an appropriations bill. Helms later attached his amendment to the Higher Education Reauthorization Act. By then, the legislative action had shifted to the floor of the House.

On March 26, 1992, Representatives Thomas Coleman and Bart Gordon presented a joint amendment that would prohibit "any individual who is incarcerated in any Federal or State penal institution" from qualifying for Pell Grant assistance. The basic argument propelling the measure was the same as the one Senator Helms had promulgated the previous July. Many "facts" and "figures" were bandied about during proponents' orations over the issue, most of them inaccurate.

Representative Coleman, for example, claimed 100,000 prisoners received Pell Grants. This figure would mean that one out of every eight inmates in the nation is a college student! Such a notion is preposterous. In 1982, researchers John Littlefield and Bruce Wolford estimated that 27,000 inmate-students were enrolled in 350 prison college programs, representing less than four percent of the national penal population. Another study conducted the same year reported that P.S.C.E. funding was arranged through a myriad of sources, but Pell Grants were the primary tuitional financing for 37 percent of the inmate-students. Even with prison populations doubling in the interim, projecting a matching increase of inmate-students and "guesstimating" a doubling in the percentage of Pell Grant use by this population, a reasonable assumption is that fewer than 40,000 offenders received federal higher-education assistance in 1991.

During the House debate, Representative Steve Gunderson tossed more false facts into the mix. He stated that only 3.1 million students out of 6.3 million applicants received Pell Grants, and that this imbalance of aid "to the most needy of students among us" could be substantially corrected by barring inmate eligibility.

Actually, 3.6 million students received Pell Grants, not 3.1 million. Furthermore, the Senate's version of the Higher Education Reauthorization Act significantly increased the appropriation for the Pell Grant program, enabling an additional 600,000 students to receive aid. The increased funding of the program will raise the family income ceiling from $30,000 to $50,000, with grant maximums raised as well, from $2,400 to $3,700 and eventually $4,500 by 1999. Ironically, Senator Helms cast the only dissenting vote against the very program he was so concerned about the year before.

The Coleman-Gordon Amendment easily passed, 351 to 39, and was sent to a joint House-Senate conference, whose duty it was to resolve the differences between it and the Senate's version.

Meanwhile, outside Congress, opposition to the Helms and Coleman-Gordon amendments was gathering. On July 31, 1991, the day after Senator Helms introduced his amendment, a one-page alert, headlined "HELMS AMENDMENT WOULD DROP INCARCERATED PELL GRANT PROGRAM," went out over the national postsecondary E-mail Network. The bulletin briefly explained the proposition and included some of the debate's highlights.

This rapid notification of the impending disaster facing postsecondary correctional education galvanized a wide array of institutions, organizations, and individuals. College presidents and university deans, professional associations and political action committees, friends and family of prisoners as well as prisoners themselves—all organized campaigns and lobbied Congress to vote against the prohibition of Pell Grants for prisoners.

In September 1991, the 14 universities and nine private colleges that compose New York's Inmate Higher Education Program (IHEP) convened their semiannual conference with the Pell Grant crisis as the main item on their agenda. They agreed to form a political action committee to oppose the amendments.

The newly formed PAC collected information and disseminated it both within and outside the New York IHEP association. It also cooperated with other concerned organizations including Educators for Social Responsibility, the Fortune Society, Literacy Volunteers, Minorities in Corrections, the National University Continuing Education Association, the N.A.A.C.P., the New York State Correctional Association, the Coalition for Criminal Justice, PEN, the Urban League, and Wilmington College. Additionally, the PAC contacted the offices of representatives who sat on the joint Congressional committees and provided extensive P.S.C.E. data.

Another group active in the fight was the Correctional Education Association. Founded in 1946 by Austin MacCormick, the man who established correctional education as a fundamental part of prison reform in the 1930s, the C.E.A. is the only professional association dedicated to serving educators and administrators who provide services to students in correctional settings. Steve Steurer, the C.E.A. executive director and legislative network chairman, organized the association's extensive response.

Also active was Citizens United for Rehabilitation of Errants (CURE), which was founded in Texas in 1972, was expanded nationally in 1985, and now has more than 7,000 members. The organization's position is that prisons should be used only for those who absolutely must be incarcerated and should have all the resources they need to turn prisoners' lives around. The national office in Washington has extensive contacts with Congressional representatives and worked closely with Senator Pell's staff.

Across the nation, inmate-students also worked to defeat their funding exclusion. On some prison-college campuses, such as in New York State, the faculty and institution staff organized the students' reaction, while on others the students themselves marshaled their response.

The men enrolled in Ball State University's extension program at the Indiana State Reformatory were such a self-motivated group. Members of the prison's debate team utilized the semester's various speech and communications classes, which had enrolled over 70 percent of the 138-member student body, as a forum to get the word out.

With the cooperation of the teaching staff, students in the speech classes were allowed to fashion presentations in accordance with the courses' structures to provide information on the Helms Amendment. These presentations ranged from simple lectures to round-table discussions to mock debates. The students imaginatively employed cost-comparison charts, experts on P.S.C.E., and audience participation as debate judges to bring home the point of the value of P.S.C.E. and the seriousness of the legislative threat. Other students wrote letters directly to the state's representatives, or to friends and relatives urging them to do so.

The combined efforts of the nation's colleges and universities, professional associations and political action committees, individual voters, as well as the erudite pleas of the prisoners themselves, effected the defeat of the Helms Amendment in two separate joint committees. The process was repeated against the Coleman-Gordon Amendment.

In this effort, incarcerated persons learned that they were not powerless. They could lobby Washington politicians just like any other special interest group. What the men and women who wear numbers on their chests lack in political clout and financial resources, they can make up in cunning and determination to succeed. Across the nation, the motto of prisoners needs to become *nec aspera terrant* (frightened by no difficulties).

[*The Coleman-Gordon Amendment was defeated. In the Higher Education Reauthorization Act of 1992, Pell Grants for prisoners were retained, with some changes. The most important of these were that grants are available only for tuition and fees and that prisoners on death row or sentenced to life without parole are ineligible.*

—*The Editors*]

Selected Bibliography

This listing includes all works cited as well as other relevant materials.

Adams, Stuart N. 1968. *College Level Instruction in U.S. Prisons: An Exploratory Survey*. Berkeley: University of California Press.

———. 1973. Higher learning behind bars. *Change* 5:45-50.

Adler, Freda. 1975. *Sisters in Crime: The Rise of the New Female Criminal*. New York: McGraw-Hill.

Allen, H. E., and C. E. Simonsen. 1992. *Corrections in America: An Introduction*. 6th ed. New York: Macmillan.

Alpert, Geoffrey. 1982. Women prisoners and the law: Which way will the pendulum swing? In *The Criminal Justice System and Women*, edited by Barbara Raffel Price and Natalie J. Sokoloff. New York: Clark Boardman Company, Ltd.

American Correctional Association Task Force on the Female Offender. 1990. *What Does the Future Hold?* American Correctional Association.

Angelo, Thomas A., and K. Patricia Cross. 1993. *Classroom Assessment Techniques: A Handbook for College Teachers*. 2nd ed. San Francisco: Jossey-Bass.

Angle, T. 1982. The development of educational programs in American adult prisons and juvenile reformatories during the nineteenth century. *Journal of Correctional Education* 33: 35-39.

Arcard, Thomas E., and Phyllis Watts-LaFontaine. 1983. They're here to follow orders, not to think: Some notes on academic freedom in penal institutions. *Journal of Correctional Education* 34 (3): 119-21.

Arts Degree Program. *Dissertation Abstracts International* 39: 1982A.

Arts-In-Corrections Program Report 1991-1992. 1992. California Department of Corrections.

Arts-In-Corrections Quarterly Report, Third Quarter. 1989. San Quentin State Prison: California Department of Corrections.

Astone, N. A. 1982. What helps rehabilitation? A survey of research findings. *International Journal of Offender Therapy and Comparative Criminology* 26: 109-20.

Ayers, J. D., et al. 1980. *Effect of University of Victoria Program: A Post Release Study*. Report prepared for the Corrections Service of Canada.

Bacon, Corrine, ed. 1917. *Prison Reform*. New York: H. W. Wilson Co.

Barker, Elizabeth. 1984. The liberal arts in a correctional setting. Paper presented to the 41st International Conference on Prison Abolition, Cincinnati, Ohio.

Barr, Norman, and Leonard Zunig. 1970. Community involvement, judicial administration and campus prisons. Paper presented at the Annual Congress of the American Correctional Association, Cincinnati, Ohio

Barrows, Samuel J. 1900. *The Reformatory System in the United States*. Washington, DC: U.S. Government Printing Office.

Bates, Sanford. 1936. *Prisons and Beyond*. New York: Macmillan.

Baughman, W. N. 1983. *Model Learning Center MLC Monthly Report*. Rockville, MD: W. N. Baughman.

Behar, J. 1986. Prison education. *Journal of Sociology and Social Welfare* 13: 366-84.

Bell, R. 1977. Correctional education programs for inmates: Summary report. Paper, School of Education, Lehigh University.

Beresford, Ingram. 1937. Education in prisons. *Journal of Adult Education* (September 10): 33-39.

Bisby, F. Lowell. 1931. Objectives in prison education. *Prison Journal*. (April 11): 11-13.

Blackburn, F. S. 1981. The relationship between recidivism and participation in a community college program for incarcerated offenders. *Journal of Correctional Education* 32: 23-25.

Blackburn, G. 1979. The relationship between recidivism and participation in community college associate of arts degree program for incarcerated offenders. Ph.D. diss., Virginia Polytechnic Institute and State University.

Blackwell, P. H. 1973. Higher education in prison: A study of the impact of college education upon selected inmates of Draper Correctional Center, Elmore, Alabama. *Dissertation Abstracts International* 34: 3080A.

Blumenstyk, G. 1991. Use of Pell Grants to educate inmates provokes criticism. *The Chronicle of Higher Education* (June 5): A1, 20.

Blumstein, A., and J. Cohen. 1974. *An Evaluation of a College Level Program in a Maximum-Security Prison*. Pittsburgh: Carnegie-Mellon University.

Boaz, M. E. 1976. An evaluative study of project outreach to inmates: A higher education program offered by the University of Virginia at three of Virginia's correctional institutions. *Dissertation Abstracts International* 37: 4887A

Bortz, J. M. 1981. A study of university level prison education in penal institutions served by Southern Illinois University at Carbondale from 1956 to 1975. *Dissertation Abstracts International* 42: 4214A.

Bourdieu, P. 1984. *Distinctions: A Social Critique of the Judgement of Taste*. Translated by Richard Nice. Cambridge: Harvard University Press.

Brewster, Lawrence G. 1983. An evaluation of the Arts-In-Corrections Program of the California Department of Corrections. William James Association.

Brockway, Zebulon R. 1912. *Fifty Years of Prison Service*. New York: Charities Publication.

Brodt, S., and J. Hewitt. 1984. Teaching cons about crime and justice: Experiment with non-traditional students in a non-traditional setting. *Journal of Correctional Education* 35.

The Bush Anticrime Plan that Meowed. *U.S. News & World Report*. 106:20 (May 20, 1989).

California Department of Corrections/Arts-In-Correction's (A-I-C). n.d. Research synopsis on parole outcomes for A-I-C participants paroled December 1980–February 1987. California Department of Corrections.

Calisti, Kathryn McEwen. 1986. A post-G.E.D. writing curriculum for incarcerated women planning for college. *Journal of Correctional Education* 37 (1).

Camp, G. M., and C. G. Camp. 1991. *The Corrections Yearbook 1991*. South Salem, NY: Criminal Justice Institute.

Carlson, James. 1989. *Catalogue for Light. Another Country Exhibit*. Sacramento: California Department of Corrections.

Carp, Scarlette V., and Linda S. Schade. 1992. Tailoring facility programming to suit female offenders. *Corrections Today* (August).

Catillaz, Michael J., and Joseph A. Russo. 1976. The funding of prison education programs: An approach. *Journal of Student Financial Aid* 6 (3).

Chaneles, S. 1983. Current trends in correctional education theory and practices and practice. *Journal of Offender Counseling, Services and Rehabilitation* 7 (2/4).

Chapman, Jane Roberts. 1980. *Economic Realities and the Female Offender*. Lexington, MA: Lexington Books.

Chase, Lawrence J., and Robert Dickover. 1983. University education at Folsom Prison: An evaluation. *Journal of Correctional Education* 9 (3).

Chesney-Lind, Meda. 1986. Women and crime: The female offender. *Signs* 12 (1).

Chesney-Lind, Meda, and Noelie Rodriguez. 1983. Women under lock and key: A view from the inside. *The Prison Journal* 63 (2).

Chickering, Arthur, and Zelda F. Gamson, eds. 1991. *Applying the Seven Principles for Good Practice in Undergraduate Education*. San Francisco: Jossey-Bass.

Chronicle of Higher Education Almanac. 1992. 34 (1): 3-4.

Cioffi, F. 1980. *Unlocking Shackled Minds—A Handbook for the College Prison Classroom*. Bloomington: Indiana University.

———. 1981. Teaching college humanities courses in prison. *Alternative Higher Education* 6 (1): 49-59.

Coffey, Osa. 1982. The use of Pell Grants in corrections. Unpublished report. Washington, DC: U.S. Department of Education.

Cohen, R. 1991. *Prisoners in 1990*. Washington, DC: U.S. Department of Justice.

Collins, M. 1988. Prison education—A substantial metaphor for adult education practice. *Adult Education Quarterly* 38 (2): 101-10.

Corcoran, F. 1985. Pedagogy in prison. *Communications Education* 34 (1): 49-58.

Cosman, J. W. 1981. Penitentiary education in Canada. In *On Prison Education*, edited by Lucien Morin. Ottawa, ON: Canadian Government Publishing Office.

Cox, William B., and F. Lovell Bixby. 1938. *Handbook of American Prisons and Reformatories*. New York: The Osborne Association, Inc.

Crites, Laura, ed. 1976. *The Female Offender*. Lexington, MA: Lexington Books.

Curry, W. J. 1974. Academic and motivational characteristics of prison inmates enrolled in the community college program at North Carolina correctional institutions. *Dissertation Abstracts International* 35: 7593A.

Dansie, G. S. 1988. Attitudes of correctional adult educators toward inmate learners in Ohio's prisons. Ph.D. diss., Ohio State University.

de Beaumont, Gustave, and Alexis de Tocqueville. 1833. *On the Penitentiary System in the United States and Its Application in France*. Philadelphia: Carey, Lee and Blanchard.

De Joie, Carolyn M. 1979. The university and social education for prisoners. *Negro Educational Review* 30 (4): 242-52.

Deming, A. L. 1983. Career choices of male college students in prison. *Journal of Offender Counseling* 4 (1): 21-27.

Department Administrative Manual. 1987. California Department of Corrections.

Devor, H. 1988. Teaching women's studies to male inmates. *Women's Studies International Forum* 11 (3): 235-44.

Dobash, Russell P., R. Emerson Dobash, and Sue Gutteridge. 1986. *The Imprisonment of Women*. Cambridge, MA: Basil Blackwell.

Doyle, Kenneth O. 1983. *Evaluating Teaching*. Lexington, MA: Lexington Books.

Dufour, M. M. 1989. Retention rate for inmates in higher education programs. *Journal of Correctional Education* 40 (1): 28-33.

Duguid, Stephen. 1980. Postsecondary education in a prison: Theory and praxis. *The Canadian Journal of Higher Education* 10: 31-34.

———. 1980. Three components of prison education. *Crime and Social Justice* 15: 30-38.

———. 1981. Prison education and criminal choice: The context of decision-making. In *On Prison Education*, edited by Lucien Morin. Ottawa, ON: Canadian Government Publishing Office.

———. 1984. *Ameliorating Savage Man: Humanities in Prison*. Vancouver: University of British Columbia.

———. 1987. Prison education: A case for the liberal arts. *Journal of Correctional Education* 38: 108-12.

———. 1990. Sitting on the cutting edge: Creative tension in prison education. *Adult Learning* 1 (6): 17-19.

Duguid, S., and H. Hoekema. 1985. *Simon Fraser University Prison Education Program*. Burnaby, BC: S. Duguid and H. Hoekema.

Eble, Kenneth E. 1988. *The Craft of Teaching: A Guide to Mastering the Professor's Art*. 2nd ed., San Francisco: Jossey-Bass.

Feinman, Clarice. 1983. An historic overview of the treatment of incarcerated women: Myths and realities of rehabilitation. *The Prison Journal* 63 (2): 12-26.

Flowers, Ronald Barri. 1987. *Women and Criminality: The Woman as Victim, Offender, and Practitioner*. New York: Greenwood Press.

Fontana, L., and A. Beckerman. 1989. Professional education in a maximum security prison: A comparative study. *Journal of Correctional Education* 40 (4): 174-81.

Fourcault, M. 1977. *Discipline and Punish: The Birth of the Prison*. New York: Pantheon.

Franklin, H. Bruce. 1979. Rehabilitating prison education. *Change* 11 (8): 18-21.

Fyfe, J. 1991. Why crime won't stop. *Miami Herald*, March 31: lc.

Garrett, Paul W., and Austin H. MacCormick. 1929. *Handbook of American Prisons and Reformatories*. New York: National Society of Penal Information.

Garrison, D. R. 1989. *Understanding Distance Education*. New York: Routledge.

Geertz, Clifford. 1973. *The Interpretation of Cultures: Selected Essays*. New York: Basic Books.

Gendron, D., and J. Cavan. 1990. Managing a successful inmate-education program: Why and how? *Community College Review* (Summer): 31-38.

George, P. S., C. Ramsey, and G. Krist. 1980. College program in the Georgia State Prison. *Community College Frontiers* 8 (2): 21-24.

Gibson, Helen E. 1976. Women's prisons: Laboratories for penal reform. In *The Female Offender*, edited by Laura Crites. Lexington, MA: Lexington Books, 93-119.

Glick, Ruth M., and Virginia V. Neto. 1977. *National Study of Women's Correctional Programs*. Washington, DC: U.S. Government Printing Office.

Glover, John W., and Eric W. Lotze. 1989. Prison schooling: Who gets educated? *Journal of Correctional Education* 40 (3): 108-14.

Glueck, Sheldon, and Elenor Glueck. 1930. *500 Criminal Careers*. New York: Alfred A. Knopf.

Goldin, C. 1984. Adult education in correctional settings—symbol or substance. *Adult Education Quarterly* 34 (3): 123-34.

Haber, Gilda Moss. 1983. The realization of potential by Lorton, DC inmates with college education compared to those without UDC (University of the District of Columbia) education. *College Journal of Offender Counseling, Services, & Rehabilitation* 7 (3-4): 37-55.

Hall, Frank, Commissioner; Director of Public Safety of Maryland Corrections, 1972–74. Conversations with Walter Silva.

Hardie, James. 1824. *The History of the Treadmill*. New York: Putnam.

Harris, Jean. 1992. Finding the gift in it. *Parabola* (17): 22-27.

Harvey, Linda. 1989. Testimony presented to the California Task Force to Promote Self-esteem and Personal and Social Responsibility.

Haviland, J. 1982. A study of the differences between prison college graduates and the total released inmate population on recidivism by risk category. *Dissertation Abstracts International* 43: 1304A.

Herron, R., and J. Muir. 1974. *History and Development of Project Newgate—A Program of Post-secondary Education for Incarcerated Offenders—Final Report*. Washington, DC: U.S. Office of Economic Opportunity.

Herron, Rex H., et al. 1973. *National Survey of Postsecondary Education Programs for Incarcerated Offenders*. Washington, DC: Office of Economic Opportunity.

Hinck, J. 1975. Differences in selected variables of prison inmates who are completers and non-completers of a three year college program. *Dissertation Abstracts International* 13: 1836A.

Holbert, R. 1976. The technical community college system and community based corrections in Nebraska: A collaborative program and service model. *Dissertation Abstracts International* 37: 72A.

Holmberg, B. 1990. *Theory and Practice of Distance Education*. New York: Routledge.

Homant, R. 1984. On the role of values in correctional education. *Journal of Correctional Education* 5: 8-12.

Hutchinson, R. 1978. Attitudes of selected college administrators and correctional facility personnel toward the development of post-secondary prisoner education programs in New York state. *Dissertation Abstracts International* 39: 5873A.

Jengeleski, J. 1984. Reintegrating the ex-offender: A critique of education and employment programs. *Journal of Correctional Education* (September): 90-95.

Johnston, William B., and Arnold H. Packer. 1987. *Workforce 2000: Work and Workers for the Twenty-first Century*. Indianapolis: Hudson Institute.

Jones, Ann. 1980. *Women Who Kill*. New York: Holt, Rinehart & Winston.

Jones, E. 1988. The moral impact of teaching literature behind bars. *The Chronicle of Higher Education* (March 30): A48.

Jones, Raymond L. 1991. *Mass Education and the Legitimation of Prison Higher Education*. Corrections & Higher Education Monograph. Richmond: Eastern Kentucky University.

———. 1992a. A coincidence of interests: Prison higher education in Massachusetts. *Journal of Prisoners on Prisons* 4 (1): 3-20.

———. 1992b. Massachusetts prison higher education: An exploratory cultural analysis. Ed.D. diss., University of Massachusetts, Amherst.

Jones, W. 1982. Attitudes of corrections educators and residents towards post-secondary programming for the incarcerated. *Journal of Correctional Education* 33: 4-6.

Kamens, D. H. 1977. Legitimating myths and educational organization: The relationship between organizational ideology and formal structure. *American Sociological Review*. 42.

King, J. 1978. An assessment of the effectiveness of post-secondary vocational education in the Texas Department of Corrections. *Dissertation Abstracts International* 50: 337A.

Kiser, G. C. 1987a. Disciplinary problems among college students. *Federal Probation* 51 (1): 42-48.

———. 1987b. Teaching colleges courses to inmates. *Journal of Correctional Education* 38 (3): 102-06.

Klinger, George, and Paul Cromwell. 1973. *Penology: The Evolution of Corrections in America*. St. Paul, MN: West Publishers.

Laird, C. A. 1971. A study of the college-level educational program of the Texas Department of Corrections. *Dissertation Abstracts International* 32: 4376A.

Langenbach, M., M. Y. North, L. Aagaard, and W. Chown. 1990. Televised instruction in Oklahoma prisons: A study of recidivism and disciplinary actions. *Journal of Correctional Education* 41: 87-94.

Lawrence, D. W. 1991. An exploratory study of the perceived role of the student-teacher relationship within correctional education. Ed.D. diss., University of Oklahoma.

Lerer, Albert. 1939. A study of the education program at the Massachusetts Reformatory. Master's thesis, Boston University.

Leventhan, Gloria. 1977. Female criminality: Is "Women's Lib" to blame?*Psychological Reports* 41: 1179-82.

Lewis, M., and B. Fritz. 1975. Prison education and rehabilitation—illusion or reality? *Crime and Delinquency* 21: 291-322.

Lewis, Oswald F. 1922. *Development of American Prisons and Prison Customs*. Albany, NY: Prison Association of New York.

Lewis, W. David. 1965. *From Newgate to Dannemara: The Rise of the Penitentiary in New York, 1796–1848*. Ithaca, NY: Cornell University Press.

Lind, C. 1985. Comparison of prison inmate college students with campus students: Emphasis on self-concept. *Dissertation Abstracts International* 46: 2584A.

Linden, Rick, and Linda Perry. 1982. The effectiveness of prison education programs. *Journal of Offender Counseling, Services and Rehabilitation* 6 (4): 43-57.

Littlefield, John F. 1989. Post-secondary correctional education survey: Preliminary report. Correctional Education Association.

Littlefield, John F., and B. I. Wolford. 1982. Survey of higher education in U.S. correctional institutions. *Journal of Correctional Education* 33 (4): 14-18.

Long, D. 1973. College education for youth in correctional institutions. *Dissertation Abstracts International* 34: 1738A.

M. 1990. Student Essay. Stanton, VA: Mary Baldwil College.

MacCormick, Austin H. 1931. *The Education of Adult Prisoners*. New York: National Society of Penal Information.

———. 1936. Prisoners' progress. *Journal of Adult Education* (June 8): 254-58.

Maclean, Brian D. 1992. Post-secondary education in the prison: Cognitive and moral development or social control? *Journal of Prisoners on Prisons* 4 (1): 21-28.

Maguire, Kathleen. 1992. Academic programs in state and federal prisons: Results of a national survey. Paper presented at the meeting of the Academy of Criminal Justice Sciences, Pittsburgh, Pennsylvania, March 10-14.

Malott, K. 1982. Higher education in the Illinois correctional system. *Dissertation Abstracts International* 43: 1689.

Manual of Correctional Standards. 1954. New York: The American Correctional Association.

———. 1959. New York: The American Correctional Association.

Marsh, J. 1973. Higher education in American prisons. *Crime and Delinquency Literature*. (October).

McCarthy, Bernard J., and Belinda Rodgers McCarthy. 1984. Are study release programs making the grade? *Journal of Correctional Education* 35 (2): 42-46.

McGee, Richard A. 1959. *Manual of Suggested Standards for a State Correctional System*. New York: The American Correctional Institution.

McKelvey, Blake. 1936. *American Prisons*. Chicago: University of Chicago Press.

Minahan, J. 1990. Mapping the world: Some thoughts on teaching the humanities in prison. *Journal of Correctional Education* 41 (1): 14-19.

Mogilnicki, Robert L. 1972. Continuing education in prison. *Journal of Continuing Education and Training* 1 (4): 251-57.

Moran, L. 1981. *On Prison Education*. Ottawa, ON: Canadian Government Publishing Office.

Morris, Roger. 1968. State programs in college education for inmates. *American Journal of Corrections* 30: 2.

Morrison, D. 1984. Letter to the executive assistant to the director of criminal justice. Proceedings from the Inmate Higher Education Conference of 1984. Available from the National Institute of Corrections—Information Center, Longmont, CO.

Naffine, Ngaire. 1987. *Female Crime: The Construction of Women in Criminology.* Boston: Allen & Unwin.

National Council on Crime and Delinquency. 1966. *Corrections in Oklahoma: A Survey.* New York: National Council on Crime and Delinquency.

Norton, L., and B. Simms. 1988. *The Status of Correctional Education in the United States: A Report of the 1987 Annual Survey of State Directors of Correctional Education.* Columbus: The Ohio State University.

Ohare, Kate R. 1923. *In Prison.* New York: Alfred A. Knopf.

Oklahoma Department of Corrections. 1992. Monthly report for September and October. Oklahoma City: Oklahoma Department of Corrections.

O'Neil, M. 1988. A study of correctional post-secondary education and its possible impact on recidivism. *Dissertation Abstracts International* 49: 3166A.

Oppenheimer, Heinrich. 1913. *The Rationale of Punishment.* London: University of London Press.

Osborne, Thomas M. 1924. *Prison and Common Sense.* Philadelphia: J.B. Lippincott Co.

———. 1925. *Handbook of American Prisons.* New York: G.P. Putnam's Sons.

Palmer, Ted. 1992. *The Re-Emergence of Correctional Intervention.* Newbury Park, CA: Sage Publications.

Parker, E. A. 1990. Social-psychological impact of a college education on the prison inmate. *Journal of Correctional Education* 41 (3): 140-46.

Parsons, M. H. 1982. *Hagerstown Junior College Prison Program Operations Manual.* Hagerstown, MD: Hagerstown Junior College and Maryland Correctional Training Center.

Pendleton, E. 1988. Student-centered instruction: A prison college model for building self-esteem. *Journal of Correctional Education* 39: 82-84.

Pisciotta, A. W. 1983. Scientific reform: The "New Penology" at Elmira, 1876-1900. *Crime and Delinquency:* (October) 613-68.

Pittman, Von V., and Eileen M. Whipple. 1982. The inmate as college student. *Lifelong Learning: The Adult Years* 5 (7): 4-5.

Pollock-Byrne, Joycelyn. 1990. *Women, Prison and Crime.* Pacific Grove, CA: Brooks/Cole Publishing Co.

Price, Barbara Raffel, and Natalie Sokoloff, eds. 1982. *The Criminal Justice System and Women.* New York: Clark Boardman Co., Ltd.

Proposal for the development of the Vacaville Prison Arts Project (submitted to the California Arts Council).

Reagan, Michael V., and Donald Stoughton, eds. 1976. *School Behind Bars: A Descriptive Overview of Correctional Education in the American Prison System.* Metuchen, NJ: The Scarecrow Press.

Research and Evaluation Division. n.d. *Research Synopsis on Parole Outcomes for Arts-In-Corrections Participants Paroled December 1980-February 1987*. Sacramento: California Department of Corrections.

Riggs, D., and J. True. 1981. *Kentucky's Inmate College Program—The Program and the Participants*. Study conducted by the Kentucky Department of Justice Bureau of Corrections Research and Evaluation Section, Frankfurt, KY.

Roberts, Albert R. 1971. *Sourcebook on Prison Education: Past, Present and Future*. Springfield, IL: Charles C. Thomas.

Robinson, Louis N. 1921. *Penology in the United States*. Philadelphia: John C. Winston Co.

Robinson, T. 1977. The invisible student. *New Society* 41: 66-67.

Ross, R., and E . Fabiano. 1981. *Time to Think: Cognition and Crime: Link and Remediation*. Ottawa, ON: University of Ottawa.

Rossman, P. 1992. The emerging worldwide electronic university. *Information Age Global Higher Education*. Westport, CT: Greenwood.

Ryan, T. A., 1984. *Adult Female Offenders and Institutional Programs: A State of the Art Analysis*. Washington, DC: U.S. Government Printing Office.

Ryan, T. A., and J. C. Woodard. 1984. Linkages between higher education and corrections. Paper presented at the American Correctional Association Congress of Corrections, Houston, TX.

————. 1987. *Correctional Education: A State of the Art Analysis*. Washington, DC: U.S. Department of Justice.

Schell, J. F. 1981. Designing an English curriculum for prisons. Paper presented at the 12th annual meeting of the College English Association, Cherry Hill, NJ.

Schulman, M. D. 1975. Teaching sociology in prison: A personal note. *The Insurgent Sociologist* 5 (4): 86-88.

Schwartz, Sheila. 1975. Teaching at Walkill Prison (Oops, I mean correctional facility). *English Education* 6 (2): 101-08.

Seashore, M., et al. 1976. *Prisoner Education: Project Newgate and Other College Programs*. New York: Praeger.

Siano, J. N. 1985. An analysis of the attitude of correctional officers toward inmate educational programs in Oklahoma's minimum, medium, and maximum security institutions. Ph.D. diss., University of Oklahoma.

Silva, Walter. 1993. Unpublished survey of state departments of correction and the Federal Bureau of Correction, May 24-June 4.

Simon, Rita J. 1975. *Women and Crime*. Lexington, MA: Lexington Books.

Smetzer, J. E. 1989. Physics with a new approach. *Journal of Correctional Education* 40 (4): 182-84.

Smith, Alexander F. 1930. The history and present status of prison education in the United States. Master's thesis, Boston University.

Sommer, Robert. 1976. *The End of Imprisonment*. New York: Oxford University Press.

Sorenson, Virginia. 1981. Educational and vocational needs of women in prison. *Corrections Today* 43 (3): 61-69.

Sourcebook of Criminal Justice Statistics. 1982. Washington, DC: United States Government Printing Office.

Stein, M. 1989. Teaching deviance to deviants: the prison classroom experience. *Free Inquiry in Creative Sociology* 17 (2): 185-91.

Sykes, Gresham. 1958. *The Society of a Maximum Security Prison*. Princeton, NJ: Princeton University Press.

Taylor, Andress. 1974. Beyond rehabilitation: The Federal City College Lorton Project—A model prison higher education program. *Journal of Negro Education* 43 (2): 172-78.

Taylor, J. M. 1992. Post-secondary correctional education: An evaluation of effectiveness and efficiency. *Journal of Correctional Education* 43: 132-41.

Teeters, Negley K. 1955. *The Cradle of the Penitentiary: The Walnut Street Jail at Philadelphia*. Philadelphia: The Pennsylvania Prison Society.

Theall, Michael, and Jennifer Franklin. 1991. *Effective Practices for Improving Teaching*. San Francisco: Jossey-Boss.

Thorpe, T., et al. 1984. Follow-up study of offenders who earn college degrees while incarcerated in New York State. *Journal of Correctional Education* (September) 35: 86-88.

Tiller, G. L. 1974. A study of the dual administration of a penal education program: The case of Lee College and the Texas Department of Corrections. Ph.D. diss., University of Houston.

Toch, H. 1987. Regenerating prisoners through education. *Federal Probation* 51 (3).

Tulardilok, A. 1977. Assessment of college level educational program at the state prison of southern Michigan. *Dissertation Abstracts International* 39: 159A.

Unger, C. A., and R. A. Buchanan. 1985. Managing long-term inmates: A guide for the correctional administrator. National Institute of Corrections Report. Washington, DC: U.S. Department of Justice.

Unkovic, C. M., and R. A. Maimon. 1988. Penal education: A background and assessment. *International Review of History and Political Science* 25 (2): 42-46.

U.S. Department of Justice, Bureau of Statistics. 1982. *Sourcebook of Criminal Justice Statistics. 1982*. Washington, DC: U.S. Government Printing Office.

————. 1989. *Sourcebook of Criminal Justice Statistics. 1988*. Washington, DC: U.S. Government Printing Office.

————. 1991. *Women in Prison: Executive Summary*. Washington, DC: U.S. Government Printing Office.

Weis, Lois. 1985. *Between Two Worlds: Black Students in an Urban Community College*. Boston: Routledge & Kegan Paul.

Werner, D. 1990. *Correctional Education: Theory and Practice*. Danville, IL: Interstate Publishers.

Whetstone, Keith. 1981. How the Prisoner Sees Education. Paper, Proceedings of the National Conference on Prison Education, edited by J. D. Ayer. Victoria, BC, University of Victoria.

William James Association. 1977. Proposal to San Francisco Foundation to Fund Prison Arts Pilot Project Program at the California Medical Facility. Santa Cruz, CA.

Wolford, B., and J. Littlefield. 1983. Post-secondary education programs in U.S. Prisons: A report of the findings from a national survey. Paper presented at the

Correctional Education Association's 38th International Conference, Houston, TX.

———. 1985. Correctional post-secondary education: The expanding role of the community colleges. *Community/Junior College Quarterly of Research and Practice* 9: 258-72.

Wooldridge, Susan. 1976. College for prisoners: Ohio's open door college for prisoners. *Change* 8 (9): 17-20.

Wright, Richard. 1987. Are 'Sisters in Crime' finally being booked? The coverage of women in journals and textbooks. *Teaching Sociology* 15.

Yarborough, T. 1980. Motivational, demographic, and academic characteristics of prison inmates enrolled in community colleges in the state of Maryland. *Dissertation Abstracts International* 41: 3409A.

———. 1989. Analysis of why inmates drop out of higher education programs. *Journal of Correctional Education* 40.

Young, C. 1987. Deconstructing prison education: An ethnographic study of the contexts of prison schools. *Dissertation Abstracts International* 47: 3879A.

Zimring, F., and G. Hawkins. 1988. *Special Report: Recidivism of Prisoners Released in 1983*. Washington, DC: U.S. Department of Justice.

Index

by Linda Webster